How to Get a Job in a Museum or Art Gallery

How to Get a Job in a Museum or Art Gallery

Alison Baverstock

A & C BLACK • LONDON

First published in Great Britain 2010
A & C Black Publishers Ltd
36 Soho Square, London W1D 3QY
www.acblack.com

A CIP record for this book is available from the British Library.

ISBN: 9–781–4081–0934–2

Design by Fiona Pike, Pike Design, Winchester
Typeset by Saxon Graphics, Derby
Printed in the United Kingdom by Cox & Wyman, Reading RG1 8EX

Contents

Foreword

Museums and galleries are a microcosm of the world: places of pleasure and learning. And working in them is an exciting way to be involved with the big questions of where we have come from and who we are. What used to be slow-paced and sometimes backward-looking organisations have, by and large, become lively and audience-centred, concerned with how issues of current public interest can be understood through collections of art and objects – and also be engaging. The key element of a good museum is making someone's visit wonderful and memorable.

One of the many changes over the past 20 years has been a new focus on training and professional development. Museum directors and managers have realised that however much energy is devoted to collecting and understanding objects, the people who work in the institutions matter just as much. The many skills of the staff are needed so that objects and works of art can be carefully conserved, beautifully presented, properly recorded, researched and understood and then communicated to a broader public. The range of museum skills has now been extended to include fields such as digital programming, educational outreach work, specialist marketing and fundraising.

Those working in museums, both small and large, will therefore have a mix of talents and experience, and increasingly come from diverse backgrounds and educational routes. What they will probably share is an inquisitive nature combined with considerable creativity, self-reflection and a passion for teamwork. Objects matter, but enjoying the processes of learning from other people is crucially important.

If you think you might be interested in working in a museum or gallery, go and visit one, examine it critically, and consider whether this is a place to which you would like to contribute. I hope that reading this book will help you on your way.

Sandy Nairne, Director, National Portrait Gallery
October 2009

Part 1:
The world of museums and galleries

Chapter 1

Why work in a museum or art gallery?

Working in a museum or gallery is an appealing career prospect for many; it often attracts those who visited them during their childhood, found them places of solace in their teenage years – or rather liked the look of what Ross in *Friends* did for a living. Visits as part of a university course may strengthen that desire – and students of history or history of art may find themselves particularly drawn to such a career (although experts are needed in many fields of speciality, as broad as a museum's range of content, from palaeontology to machine tools).

But while it's easy to dream of working in such an institution, the practical details of what's involved are less easily come by. This book provides guidance on how to discover if the world of museums and galleries is really for you, and how to find a job if you decide this is indeed your chosen path.

A word of warning before we start. Entry is highly competitive and there are many more people seeking jobs than there are positions available. But then if you don't try, you stand no chance at all.

What working in a museum or gallery is really like

'I did work experience in The Courtauld Gallery during the summer before my final year at university, and found the real privilege was in seeing the pictures in different lights each day – from the harsh light of the early morning to the balmier light of the afternoons. I really felt I got to know the pictures and this was hugely satisfying.' ALISON BAVERSTOCK

If you cherish the notion that working in an art gallery or museum is a peaceful escape from the hurly-burly of modern life, or that it offers a haven away from more commercial choices, then think again. These days, galleries and museums not only have to compete for funds but also raise a substantial portion of their own revenue. Loving the items under your care is not enough, and your employers will want more from you than simply the knowledge that you are enjoying your surroundings.

What's so satisfying about working in this world?
1. Close proximity to things of significance

Working in a museum or gallery offers you the chance to get close to items that have witnessed, or played a part in history, over both the long and short term.

People who work in galleries and museums feel that what they do matters; that they are looking after the cultural capital of the world and preserving it for future generations, and that by explaining the significance of items to a wider audience they are enhancing life.

'Many of the skills needed by those working in museums and galleries are needed in other working environments too, such as website development, accurate record keeping and an appreciation of wider access. What museums give you is the added interest of applying these skills to something that matters, and the opportunity to engage other people in an area that is so fascinating – and one perhaps they had not thought about before.

'I would say that the one thing that unites all who work in this world is a respect for the original object; the frisson gained from holding the actual item that has played a part in history. And this is true whether the object is frequently found and of little or no commercial value or a unique and highly valuable specific item, with a charted pedigree; it is the connection to the past that matters. For example, it can be just as fascinating to look at an early example of the sticks used in the millennia-old method of creating fire by rubbing one stick in the hollowed-out centre of another, as a

Similarly, selling items of historical pedigree or works of art can be a commercial venture, but those handling the sale must feel that what they are offering has a long-term validity and will reflect well on their role as seller in the future. Commercial galleries and specialist retailers want to build long-term relationships with their customers, who view their purchases as ongoing sources of pleasure and investment.

2. The satisfaction of putting on a show

Most galleries and museums have a permanent collection on display and a series of special shows that highlight particular aspects of what they hold (some of which may be from a collection that is not always on view); they may also put on special stagings to celebrate specific anniversaries and national and local events. Many will also receive and house the temporary installation of a touring exhibition as part of a national or international schedule – a bit like theatrical repertory – although in the case of museums and galleries, the collection usually tours the provinces *after* its main exhibition in a city rather than the other way round. Smaller organisations may have no permanent collection but a rather a series of temporary exhibitions.

There is a lot of creative freedom within museums and galleries in deciding what to feature:

'This is a non-prescriptive world in which the contribution of the individual is key – the opposite of corporate slavery! There is the opportunity to think

People who work in museums and galleries are likely to enjoy the coming together of an event; the teamwork involved in ensuring the show is ready for opening on the date announced, with the final stages in preparation – catalogue, posters, publicity, local and national PR and related merchandise in the shop – and all the while aware of what might be coming next. This aspect of the work, which can be compared with that of theatre managers leading up to a production or restaurants preparing for their opening, is important because, whether the funding is public or private, the institution will usually be having to justify its budget. Engaging visitors' interest in the fascination of what is on offer as well as conveying a sufficient sense of urgency so they feel motivated to come along to see it while it's available, is very much part of this mission.

If you can relate to this sense of putting on a show, drawing your colleagues into the demonstration of something that's fascinating and that you can all be proud of, then this world may be for you.

3. Educating the public

Museums and galleries share information and often provide understanding to people who have no previous knowledge of a specific subject or area. There is much discussion about how groups who are not used to visiting such institutions can be made to feel more welcome, and being part of this can be very satisfying.

'One afternoon, when we were quiet, someone asked me why in pictures of the Nativity the Madonna's cloak is always blue. I explained about symbolism and went on to talk about the other elements that are often there – lilies, crosses of straw on the ground, and how the figures in the picture

If you don't like sharing observations and feel that the world of selective treasures, in any area of interest, is your private passion rather than one you want to talk about or share more widely, then this world may not be for you.

4. Connectedness

Museums and galleries are connected internationally and share their findings. Most special shows depend on the loan of key items from one institution to another, with long-term reciprocity. It's not uncommon for junior members of gallery staff to accompany items on their passage to temporary locations, and to get correspondence or emails from colleagues asking for help on specific queries.

This connectedness has become greater with online access – scholars, and people who are just interested, worldwide can obtain information on a particular gallery or a museum's collection and download images before setting off on their travels.

'One of the best things about this world is its connectedness or rather, the culture of reciprocity which exists amongst museums and museum staff. We live in a permanent state of insecurity – funding may be cut, staff may be lost or not replaced, and at worst, we may be axed all together – but I feel connected to and supported by colleagues who are often geographically distant.'   PETA COOK, CURATOR, KINGSTON MUSEUM

5. A very varied workload

Some people prefer a sedentary job where the scope of their endeavours is predictable and under their control. Very large museums and galleries may have a formal departmental structure, but in the early stages of a career, and later on too if you work in a local museum or gallery, life can be anything but predictable.

In addition to looking after the collection you might find yourself answering queries from the public, dealing with the press, working with insurers and those responsible for security, organising plumbers and electricians, writing copy for marketing materials and installing exhibitions. The workload is varied and stimulating but if this sounds like an over-diversification of your talents, then think carefully before seeking a career in this field. Museums and galleries need staff who are happy to multi-task and not too grand to attend to the most basic of functions.

6. The chance to meet interesting people

Working in a museum or gallery offers you the chance to rub shoulders with, or just observe, a range of interesting people, from international scholars who travel the world to comment on new finds and possible acquisitions, to members of the public who bring items into their local museum for possible identification. If you work in a commercial gallery, meeting an artist whose work you admire can be a fascinating (and sometimes disappointing) experience; many artists communicate through their work and sometimes aren't comfortable – or even able – to talk about why they developed a piece in the way they did or communicate with the general public (particularly those who do not see a value in what they do).

7. Working in a pleasant place

Even if you work in the bowels of a national building, you probably still have the chance to walk in and out of its famous portals. Or perhaps using the staff entrance at the side of the building, in the hour before it's open to the general public, gives you a thrill. Many museums were built long before modern regulations about ease of access and bathroom facilities were introduced, and programmes of refurbishment and restoration are slow and expensive, but the sight of the building when it is closed along with the thought that 'I work there', can give you a real sense of pleasure.

8. A job that other people find fascinating

Mention at a party that you are a dentist or an accountant and people tend to look away. Mention that you work in a museum or gallery and their reaction is likely to be quite different. People may not be interested in your actual job status but simply have an image of you ambling round the gallery having fine thoughts in the presence of masterpieces. It's a job with a high level of kudos.

'I was responsible for the day-to-day running of the books section in the huge Level 1 shop at Tate Modern. The fundamentals of bookselling are the same in any venue. What was different was how other people responded when I said I worked there. Tate Modern was recently identified as one of the 10 coolest brands in the UK, and friends with teenagers would tell me it was the one cultural venue they would willingly enter. I must admit I enjoyed the associated cachet.'

JANE CHOLMELEY

Why *not* to work in a museum or gallery

It's a good idea too to think about the frustrations of working in a gallery or museum. If any of the following strike a chord with you, you may find this a less than satisfactory choice of career.

1. Reciprocity may not appeal

At university, did you enjoy group work? Or did you find it aggravating to hear your ideas developed and even purloined by others? At school, were you able to work with a group of people you did not particularly like, in order to achieve a pre-determined goal, or did you prefer just to get on with it and do it on your own?

Working in a gallery or museum requires collaboration and teamwork. Frankly, if you do not enjoy this, or find yourself anxious to hang on to your specific contribution and have it fully acknowledged as such, then think carefully about choosing a such a career.

2. Is it your role in life to educate others?

'During a work experience placement our whole company, which only consisted of 15 people, was taken out to lunch in a local Italian restaurant. I was asked to go too. When we arrived there was a lot of giggling about a wall painting, and how you could see "all the man's bits". When I went over to have a look at what they were talking about, it turned out that the image was the world famous image from the Sistine ceiling, of God touching Adam.'

PUBLISHER

The sheer scale of the public's lack of awareness can be daunting – their lack of knowledge about things you think you have always known (although you must have acquired the information at some stage too). Being honest, if this makes you wonder at their level of ignorance rather than feel motivated to try and make the case for their involvement, or at least tolerate what they are deriding, then think carefully about a career in museums and galleries. You will be confronted by ignorance all the time, and rather than trumping them with your knowledge and seeing their impressed reaction, it's far more likely that you will be met with a bemused stare and confusion about why on earth you care.

This can become a particularly sensitive issue when you discover this lack of knowledge is located in those you cannot ignore. Working in a gallery or museum will require you to deal with bureaucrats who *don't* esteem what you do, but who *do* control access to funding. You need to make links with them, patiently explore areas of common ground (perhaps your desire to put on an exhibition, theirs to see the local borough featured as a place of innovation and prestige) and tactfully maintain the relationship. You will need to become an effective communicator to defend the value of your work, making a bridge between it and those who think it is a complete waste of money, time and effort.

If you have never been exposed to this, here are two short exercises for you to experiment with:

- try explaining the value of modern art to a sceptical relative – using the example of the most recent winner of the Turner Prize is usually sufficient challenge;
- justify why museum staff should be funded by the public purse when they are so isolated from the real world.

3. Being distracted from your main work

On a daily basis you will be interrupted constantly. You will have to juggle lots of priorities, rather than just getting on with the cataloguing you had imagined would be your role for that day. And many of the people who distract you with questions will be dissatisfied with the response you are able to give them – members of the public might want to know the value of something they have had in the attic for ages, but have no interest in its date or provenance (and you are not allowed to tell them how much it is worth).

Similarly, if you like high levels of support and/or infrastructure in your working life, or particularly appreciate the comforts of a benefits package (free canteen and sports facilities, company car), then this may not be the career for you. You will have to stuff your own envelopes, mend your own PC, create your own labels and manage your own career development.

4. Income levels

The financial remuneration for working in galleries and museums is poor, and anyone who wants to work in this world needs to understand this. Even for a starter job, an essential element on any CV is an internship or work experience, but in most cases these are unpaid roles, so you will have to seek support or part-time work to fund any volunteer work, and all in the hope of a job in the future. The Museums Association will only advertise posts on its website over a certain salary level, but there are other places to advertise – and employers know that the advertised salary level tends not to diminish the number of applicants. There are always people who want to work in this world.

Why the low pay? Firstly because it's evidently a buyer's market – there are more people seeking jobs in this sector than positions available. But this understanding also seems to be fuelled by an expectation of low pay. Jobs that have a civilising effect on society – working for a publishing company, a charity or a theatre company, purveying fine wine, and working in a museum or gallery – tend to pay badly. There is a close link between measurable profit and commensurate rewards, and the roles described are often hard to quantify in terms of financial success.

Such jobs can be depicted as pleasurable, self-indulgent, isolated from stresses felt by the rest of the population and perhaps elitist, and are therefore not ones that the public tend to rally behind, unlike nursing or certain other public sector work. Comparisons are invidious but interesting. When I started in my first job in publishing, editors who had excellent honours degrees and several years' experience were earning the same amount as a retail assistant with just a few O-Levels working in a national chain of department stores: working in a museum or gallery is unlikely to make you rich.

As to what can be done about it, the longer-term issue is how to teach society to value its national museums and collections more. Certainly, whenever a museum is threatened with closure, locals are usually ready to protest at the loss of a resource they say they value, but when closely questioned will often freely admit that they seldom, if ever, visit. They want it there for their children or grandchildren, but do not realise it houses material that would interest them too. Currently, unlike schools, museums and galleries are not an essential service that local authorities *have* to provide. There are many more cultural alternatives (sport, theatre, music), and those with more popular appeal may be more highly valued by the general public. There are wider issues too. Does *not charging* for entry to an exhibition have an impact on how the collections are valued – do people assume that something is only worth doing if it has to be paid for? The value structure expressed by the respective costs of entry to a national exhibition and a round of drinks in a pub has not been effectively made.

In the meantime, rewards from working in a museum or gallery have to be more internally felt: privileged access to a world most people know little about; enhanced status when you tell people where you work; access to the latest thought about artistic, scientific or technological discoveries – but none of these pays the bills.

5. The pace at which this world moves

It's possible to love galleries and museums but feel frustrated by the pace at which they operate. This world is not fast-moving; rather it is considered and ponderous; consultative and collaborative. Compromise will be needed, after weighing up very different, even contradictory, requirements. If you are the sort of person who just likes to get on and do things, preferably on your own, you may find this frustrating.

The same goes for the style of language used. Traditionally scholarly and academic in origin, it has become suffused with a more modern marketing speak – full of 'customer facing' initiatives which promote wider participation and engagement. If you want your voice to be heard, you will have to appreciate and adopt this language too and if this is going to be a major irritation or a struggle for you, think carefully before going any further.

6. Museums as a lifelong habit rather than a working environment

You may decide you want to continue to enjoy museums and galleries as a member of the (sometimes paying) public, rather than being actively involved in the preparation and staging of what you eventually see. Consider the following comment:

> 'Having always thought I would do English at university I had a last-minute change of heart. I found I was no longer able to read for pleasure, but rather compelled to hunt for significant quotations, deconstruct the plot and analyse rather than simply enjoy. It is not a choice I have ever regretted. I remain a voracious reader but am happy to enjoy all sorts of books as an enthusiastic amateur.'   PUBLISHER

Likewise, working in the field of curating may interfere with your enjoyment of exhibitions:

> 'I do go to exhibitions in my spare time but confess I am distracted by looking at their curatorial mechanisms. I can't seem to concentrate on the object in the box, but rather my attention is drawn to the device indicating the prevailing level of humidity. Working in this world has certainly blocked my enjoyment of objects for their own sake.'   CONSERVATOR

Visiting galleries and museums can certainly provide lifelong enrichment, and you may decide that you want to keep it that way rather than be part of the effort, just as you may enjoy food, but opt to be cooked for rather than be hands on in the kitchen yourself. And as a supporter of museums and galleries, there are many valuable roles you can play: as sponsor, visitor, collector and enthusiast. You don't have to be part of the management team to enjoy what they have to offer.

'There is in the British Museum an enormous mind. Consider that Plato is there cheek by jowl with Aristotle; and Shakespeare with Marlowe. This great mind is hoarded beyond the power of any single mind to possess it.'

VIRGINIA WOOLF, *JACOB'S ROOM* (1922)

Whether or not you decide you want to be part of its organisation, the world of museums and galleries still belongs to you.

Chapter 2
Important issues you must be prepared to grapple with

If you are attracted by the idea of a career in museums and galleries, your motivation probably starts with your own feelings and interests – how it might feel to work within such an environment; the personal inclinations that drive the idea. Your potential employers, however, will be far more interested in your engagement with the world as a whole.

Securing work experience in a relevant location can help you decide if this type of environment is where you want to belong, but the following delineation of key issues may also be helpful. It's important that you care about these issues, and preferably have an opinion on them – or if not yet an opinion, at least an understanding that they matter. And, of course, this is useful preparation for interviews.

1. Poor funding

Most museums and galleries work within a constant state of financial instability, not knowing whether or not they will be here next year. Funding them is not a statutory obligation – unlike the library or education service – and it's up to local funding bodies to decide whether or not the local museum is worth supporting in future. And as a manager within this environment you will have to motivate others through periods of instability and seek the support of those you know not to be entirely sympathetic to your cause but who are nevertheless influential, when all the while you may be feeling far from confident about your own job prospects.

Things to be aware of

- The name of the current Culture Secretary (and their most up-to-date job title); their interests and inclinations as demonstrated by what events and institutions they attend, support and mention in official speeches and pronouncements.
- The latest names for government departments that hold the purse strings.
- Government (national and local) spending priorities.
- Useful platforms for lobbying and possible partnerships.
- Sources of expertise housed within the museum or gallery that might prove useful to others, and draw in related consultancy/loan fees. For example, period dramas set in certain professional fields may require the expertise of relevant museum staff and the loan of specific objects.

'The arts is a non-statutory service – local government doesn't have to fund or support the arts or employ arts officers and, when times are tough, politicians look closely at non-statutory services, so it's important to build a high profile, maintain that profile and always be ready to argue the case for the arts. We do this by lobbying cabinet members with a cultural portfolio, by inviting politicians to open and launch events, by creating steering groups chaired by senior colleagues, by making sure we are included in all key strategy documents, by appearing in staff and council magazines, by doing a good job and by making the time to do it.'

JAYNE KNIGHT, ARTS DEVELOPMENT MANAGER, SUFFOLK COUNTY COUNCIL

2. The fragmented nature of work in museums and galleries

Staff in museums and galleries are required to multi-task, and this obligation does not lessen as your career progresses. Your job title may say 'curator' but you will find yourself responsible for a wide variety of other roles: collection development; recruitment and management of staff, including volunteers (unpaid should never mean unconsidered); publicity and PR; exhibition planning; security; cleaning; retail; catering; IT management and much more.

Things to be aware of

- examples in your life so far that demonstrate you can think about several things at the same time, and emerge feeling confident rather than crushed;
- similarly, any instances in your past that demonstrate teamwork or using your initiative.

Examples might include:

- achieving a Duke of Edinburgh's Award;
- responsibilities at school (as a prefect or a year co-ordinator);
- evidence of playing an active role within societies at university – or even better, starting up a new society or club;
- the planning of group holidays, which required negotiation and attention to detail, and effective use of a gap year;
- family responsibilities: planning parties or shared events and dealing with the inevitable politics; organising holidays; regular responsibilities where others were relying on you and you had to motivate the group as a whole.

3. Understanding and implementing accessibility within museums and galleries

By 'accessibility' I don't mean ramps for wheelchairs and suchlike; in the world of museums and galleries the term has a much wider implication.

Museums and galleries store stuff, but the way in which they make it accessible to the public is changing: no longer is putting on a display of items for people who choose to visit the sole issue. Today, museum and gallery staff need to be aware of the possibilities for online access, and see their adoption as an increasing part of what they do. Online searches of the gallery's collection may precede physical visits and increase the extent of an organisation's outreach – and in turn prove that the community relying on the organisation is much larger than those who cross the portals (useful ammunition for point 1 above).

Things to think about and try to have an opinion on

- How actively is the organisation reaching out online to new and existing audiences? Is the best, or indeed any, use being made of social networking sites such as Facebook, MySpace, LinkedIn and Twitter?
- Which is the most appropriate department or individual to have responsibility for the website of a gallery or museum? For example, it could be the curator, retail manager, front of house or marketing manager – bearing in mind that these roles may be split between a very small team.
- How many people in the organisation know how to work and update the website? Have you avoided the scenario of the key person being struck down and no one else knowing how to access it – requiring a new and expensive start from scratch?
- What share of attention and funding should the website receive? What percentage of the overall budget should be allocated to it? How do you decide on this figure – through the number of people accessing it; the potential number who could access it; or a comparison with the number of people who visit the organisation in person?
- Have you considered the costs of updating the system (renewal of hardware and software, licences for display, training costs for operators)?
- How is the overall image of the organisation represented through the website, and is this appropriate? Marketing theoreticians like to talk about the 'positioning' of an organisation – the emotional response drawn by the image presented: an impression is gained from a website in the same way as from a brochure or flyer. Theoreticians also like marketing to be joined up, so that the various

platforms used are conveying a similar message. So is the most appropriate image being presented?

- Who can update the website and how quickly? Is there a system in place so that only certain people are allowed to access the system to make changes? Sometimes a website can be altered *too* quickly, leading to inappropriate or contradictory messages which remain there until someone thinks to check.

4. The cultural capital offered by museums and galleries

Not everyone sees the point of museums and galleries, and many regard them as repositories of scholarship that are there 'just for the sake of it' and which are visited by relatively small numbers of the population (but by lots of overseas visitors, who get in for nothing while having to pay back home).

This is the era of 'dumbing down'; reality television and the resulting fame that is based on simply being in the public eye rather than for being good at anything. Programmers look for popular entertainment that can reach truly mass audiences, with voting mechanisms to prove it, and often promote presenters who are inarticulate yet camera-genic. Some schools are replacing their libraries (and librarians) with 'learning resource centres' – which seems to be a code word for more and more computers without a staff presence to help effective searching or teach an understanding of bias.

Things to be aware of

You need to be convinced by, and able to express yourself articulately and at unexpected times about:

- the value offered by museums and galleries on an individual, local, national and international basis;
- the value they deliver over a longer time frame, in the minds and memories of those who visit, and be willing to justify this to wider and unconvinced audiences.

It may help you to have the following at your disposal:

- Examples of gallery and museum events that have had a big impact on society and are long remembered. For example, the Treasures of Tutankhamun exhibition was first shown in London at the British Museum in 1972. More than 1.6 million visitors came to see it, some queuing for up to eight hours, and it was the most popular exhibition ever held in the museum. The exhibition moved on to other countries including the US (where it was visited by more than eight million people in 1976–9), the USSR, Japan, France, Canada and West Germany. And in 2007 the Royal Academy of Arts put on an exhibition of the pastels and drawings of the impressionist artist Claude Monet and it proved so popular that they ended the run with 24-hour opening.
- Some thoughts about how we value such experiences in the longer term, and what they contribute to society are helpful. How many of those who attended the 1972 Egyptian exhibition took their own children to see the 2007 exhibition in The Millennium Dome? Have those who attended the 2007 exhibition at the Academy since made the trip to Monet's home at Giverny in France to see the successors of the water lilies he painted?

5. Juggling the commercial with the intellectually significant – and achieving consensus

All museums and galleries have to juggle the commercial with the intellectually significant. You may feel a particular subject area has been overworked, to the neglect of other significant fields that are important to a wider understanding of culture or representation, but which, at the same time, are difficult to sell to the general public. While you should never underestimate the impact of personal passion and how engaging it can be to listen to someone talk about something they really care about – and be convinced the rest of the world should know too – if a more 'popular' subject matter is likely to attract a bigger audience of the paying public, and get the institution a higher profile, you may have to compromise your ideals, perhaps keeping your particular interests on the back burner.

Compromise may be needed for now, but an understanding that you have specific passions and a willingness to fight for what you believe in, provided it is tempered with realism about how long this might take, is a healthy trait in an employee in this field. In any case, big 'box office' successes may fund expositions of particular hobbyhorses in future.

Things to be aware of

- The major interests of the general public (e.g. the most popular programmes on television, cinema box office successes).
- Opportunities that overlap your collection with popular culture. A perfect example is the 2008 film about Georgiana, Duchess of Devonshire, which was launched using the famous remark of the late Princess of Wales that there were 'three people in this marriage'.

In the meantime you should:

- develop some specific passions you can talk about – trends, individual creators and movements you would like to feature in detail and why;
- build an awareness of public champions who might help you make your case.

It's worth looking to the world of politics where individuals can be persuaded to promote a specific cause on your behalf if they are convinced that the cause is a good one (and don't forget the value your project may offer them for being seen in a good light through association).

Celebrities, too, can be encouraged to champion what you hold dear, and can be hugely helpful in raising the associated profile. As an example, see the interview with Gyles Brandreth (page 28), who promoted British children's writers in an initiative at the National Portrait Gallery. Also, consider John Paul Getty II's huge donations to Lord's Cricket Ground, or Joanna Lumley's championing of the cause of the Gurkha soldiers who fought for Britain but did not receive an automatic right to stay in this country (if they retired before 1997). The actress has done a remarkable job in raising their profile. Her interest was personal – she was herself born in India, the daughter of an army officer who served in the 6th Gurkha Rifles (a regiment of the British Indian army).

As a guide to whom to approach, a copy of *Who's Who*, which helpfully lists background, affiliations and particular interests is useful, as well as just keeping your eyes and ears open.

A very important asset for staff working in museums and galleries is to be well connected – not by birth, but simply being aware of the interests of others (through reading the papers) – and then being able to make appropriate synaptic connections and a clear case for why a particular celebrity should be interested in what you are doing, while carrying your colleagues in the museum or gallery with you.

Disposal of items

Most museums and galleries have more material than they can possibly display. Items in their care have been gifted by people who thought they would be interesting to others, although their motives may not have been entirely altruistic (they may want to avoid death duties or storage costs), and the museum may no longer find the items of interest or worth preserving – if they ever did.

But gifts are gifts, and the donors may conclude that what was given should be looked after if not cherished.

Things to think about

● What should happen to items that the museum holds but does not have the room, or the future inclination, to make public?

Should the cost of their careful storage mean less funding is available for storage and acquisition of new items?

- Should you have a policy of accepting donations but ask donors to contribute to the costs of their care in future? (The National Trust accepts far fewer properties than it is offered.)
- How could you tactfully broach the subject of selling items to the relatives of those who donated them? Should you have a standard form that all donors sign saying that the item passed on then belongs to the recipient and that therefore no notification of disposal is required?
- How could you explain to a surprised donor that their chattel has indeed been disposed of, in words that make them feel they have contributed to the general good (by creating funds to help keep the museum open) rather than been deceived?

Tact, in print and in person, is a very useful asset. Compare the following two examples.

Example 1

'We have sold the item given by your grandfather.'

Example 2

'All museums have to see items they are given in the context of the collection as a whole. Of the various items given by your grandfather, one was something we already had within the collection and so rather than not be able to display it, we decided to use the money it could raise to further increase what we can display. So the kind donation of your family, while not being specifically on display, has contributed very significantly to the collection as a whole.'

Bear in mind that the second example, which some may see as 'spin', is in fact copywriting – thinking about the recipient's point of view before presenting information they may find unwelcome or unpalatable. And spin does not necessarily mean it is untrue, only that it becomes a message that is easier to absorb.

6. Sticking to the original conditions of a bequest

Mrs Ronald Greville, former owner of the National Trust property Polesden Lacey, was the illegitimate daughter but sole heir of the brewery owner William McEwan. She was a fascinating woman and it's easy to interpret her love of hosting house parties attended by a range of celebrities (e.g. King George VI and his mistress Alice Keppel, President Roosevelt) as demonstrating her final arrival in polite society. She left her house and its contents to the National Trust, on the condition that her correspondence be destroyed – and this was done.

But what does 'destroyed' mean in this context? Could it mean putting the material in an inaccessible vault until those involved and their immediate families were long dead? Or does it have to mean physically reduced, by burning or shredding? Given that she was proud to have her home and its contents made accessible to future generations, might not a similar impression of her connectedness now be maintained by publishing her diaries and letters and cross-referencing these with the allocation of rooms and the visitors' books? Unfortunately most of the material is long gone.

The Deed of Gift for Glasgow's Burrell Collection (signed in 1944 but with many documents added between then and Sir William Burrell's death in 1958) stated that:

> 'the collection shall be housed in a suitable building...within four miles of Killearn and not less than 16 miles from Glasgow Royal Exchange...the collection shall be retained there as a complete collection, and shall be called the Burrell Collection.'

This is generally assumed to relate to concerns about pollution, which was severe within industrial cities at the time, and possibly undertones of Burrell's preference for a more domestic setting for the collection. But trying to marry the founder's wishes with the practicalities of display, brought enormous problems for the housing of the donation, until the Clean Air Acts of 1956 and 1968 and the gift of the Pollok Estate, (now Glasgow's largest country park) in the 1960s.

Burrell was also very keen to preserve the integrity of his collection. His will stated that:

> 'the building shall contain only the pictures and works of art etc. bequeathed or gifted by me...or as may be purchased...and no other works of art... shall at any time be housed in said building. And it is my wish that the collection should contain works of the highest merit only...the Corporation shall not on any pretext whatever be entitled to sell or donate or exchange or part with any item of the Burrell Collection...but this stipulation is not intended to prohibit... lending temporarily to responsible Bodies.....for exhibition in any Public Gallery in Great Britain.'

So, should the original conditions be stuck to, or adapted? In the case of Burrell a compromise was worked out:

> 'The conditions of the gift laid a geographic limit on where the museum could be, and this was eventually set aside sticking to the spirit rather than the letter of the law – by finding a site that provided the clean atmosphere Burrell had sought. The museum was originally to house only the Burrell Collection (though now loaned material can be displayed in our main temporary exhibition gallery), and everything was to be stored as well as displayed within the museum building. Loans are permitted, but not overseas. Additions can be made to the collection by purchase with the funds being managed by a testamentary trust which still exists and oversees the residual monies and the city's adherence to the Deed of Gift. That income is applied only to the purchase of items for the Collection.'
>
> MURIEL KING, CULTURE AND SPORT GLASGOW, ON BEHALF OF
> THE BURRELL COLLECTION

Something to think about

How do you frame the conditions under which material is accepted, and be sensitive to loose wording that preserves the spirit rather than providing future generations with truncated options?

7. Widening participation

Given that funding decisions in the public sector are often based on footfall – taken as a crude measure of local value – it is vital to consider the participation of the community in the amenity. How can you increase visitor numbers, particularly among the specific sectors whose engagement (or not) is seen as the current political objective?

All galleries and museums have to think about new experiences and services that can be offered in an attempt to woo wider participation. The commercial sector, too, has to think about how to widen access to customers and encourage them to become regulars rather than one-offs.

Museums often run holiday schemes for children, which may interrupt the peace of the surroundings for regular visitors, but draw new generations into involvement with an organisation they may not previously have noticed.

Things to think about

- Introducing a new 'experience' to attract specific local groups, such as schools or teenagers, who might not have thought it relevant to them.
- How would you sell the local history museum to schools in the area as a possible day trip? What special programme could you lay on? How could teenagers be encouraged to come in?

8. Measuring your efficiency

Whether or not you consider it an appropriate response to the cultural heritage on offer, all publicly funded organisations need to be able to measure their effectiveness and impact in order to promote their efficient management of public resources and sustain future funding. Private institutions will need to satisfy their boards of trustees – or their bank manager. As spending gets tighter, this becomes more of a priority.

The world of marketing has done this for a long time, thus a magazine's circulation (the number of copies sold) may instead be expressed as its readership (the number of people who read it, which may be many more than just the original person who passed over the money). I even saw a marketing campaign expressed in terms of eyes that saw the poster, and if we consider that most people have two eyes, the number quoted must signal half the quantity of individuals who walked past. This kind of commercial sleight of hand, or on occasion duplicity, is often difficult for those involved with the care and preservation of objects for future generations, but is increasingly important.

Things to think about

How you can prove that the public value and support your organisation in order to secure its future access to funding? How can you prove that you are efficient stewards of the public purse?

If you have to monitor the number of visitors to a gallery, what time of day would you make your recording? How can you express the value denoted by those who attend but do not pay? You could consider:

- providing an experiences book which you ask visitors to write in – this might produce a useful series of quotes that you can use for wider promotion;
- sending a form to schools who visit that asks them how the visit went (but is not so long that they delay returning it);
- giving visitors a short introduction to your collection and its history – this can increase their satisfaction in attending and encourage them to communicate the positive experience to their friends.

Case Study

Interview with Gyles Brandreth, joint curator of the exhibition 'Beatrix Potter to Harry Potter: Portraits of Children's Writers', National Portrait Gallery, 2003

Like most professions, the world of galleries and museums can seem relatively closed to those who are not part of it, so the experience of someone entering from the outside is illuminating – hence this interview.

How did he come to get involved?

This was not a completely new departure – Gyles Brandreth has been involved in the business of putting on exhibitions and shows for a long time. When he was in his early 20s he ran several 'son et lumières', bringing history to life, and has also run free enterprise exhibitions. For example, in 1988 he opened the Teddy Bear Museum in Stratford-upon-Avon, which exhibited the first Paddington Bear, Winnie the Pooh, Pudsey and Sooty. The Teddy Bear Museum ran in a Tudor house for nearly 20 years after which it was necessary to secure its long-term future and to find a permanent home and it is now housed at the Polka Children's Theatre in Wimbledon. So the world of museums – putting items on display and their wider exposition – was not new to Brandreth.

The National Portrait Gallery initiative came out of another meeting – Brandreth had been interviewing the then director, Charles Saumarez Smith, at the gallery and as they walked through the building afterwards Brandreth commented that the view of British culture displayed on the walls was very much that of high art and Establishment taste. So, cinema since the Second World War was represented by John Schlesinger, with no mention of the 'Carry On' films enjoyed by a far wider slice of the population; and Victorian theatre was represented by Ellen Terry and Henry Irving, with no mention of the hugely popular music hall performers Dan Leno or Marie Lloyd.

Warming to his theme, Brandreth mentioned the example of British writing for children, through which Britain exercises an international influence way above what might be expected from its geographical size or population – but whose chief protagonists were scantily represented within the gallery.

The founders of the National Portrait Gallery saw the collection as 'about history not about art'[1], and this philosophy still applies; the works included were there for their public and long-lasting significance, not their popularity. But the director listened to what

---

1   Interview by Gyles Brandreth with Charles Saumarez Smith, *The Sunday Telegraph*, 2001.

Brandreth was saying about children's writers, absorbed the message – and the result was the Portraits of Children's Writers exhibition.

Of course it did not happen overnight. The basic idea had to be run past the trustees, and various committees, but eventually Brandreth and his wife were given a budget, a schedule and a member of the gallery's in-house team to work with them, and the project came to pass.

How things progressed

Gyles Brandreth and his wife Michèle Brown became joint curators. As a publisher, Michèle has a range of skills that complemented what Gyles brought to the party. He cited himself as the impatient catalyst, full of good ideas and wanting to get on with it, whereas she was the reality check, with the vital skill of understanding what was possible. He came up with a series of exciting ideas – a tunnel which only children could access, leading to a hidden room; a series of high-swung ropes on which they could climb; a tree next to which they could stand and listen to recordings of the featured writers reading from their own work. She then took a more reasoned look at whether this was possible within the context of the gallery's facilities and the requirements of health and safety. But his abiding view was that art often takes place in unlikely places – such as Jean-Louis Barrault's theatre in a wrestling ring – and it is the show that counts. Some of his ideas had to be scaled down (the concept of flying Quidditch players culminated in a display of J. K. Rowling's work in progress), others were dropped completely – but they did manage to have a tree in the centre of the exhibition where you could stand and listen to writers reading; the sound came out of knots in the wood.

Gyles claims they were a strong partnership. As a team you need someone wanting to drive things forward but also someone else able to handle colleagues, negotiate in meetings and offer a more consensual way of working. The gallery staff certainly found his wife easier to understand and get along with, but he was happy with that – and, given that he had her careful negotiating skills to fall back on, he was liberated to drive the project, to have wacky ideas and encourage everyone involved to have big ambitions and take it all seriously.

How did his world and that of the gallery get on?

Overall pretty well. Of course there were creative tensions over what went in. He was delighted that he got Frank Richards, the creator of Billy Bunter, included – pretty politically incorrect today but essential in considering the history of children's writing, for without his Greyfriars there would have been no Hogwarts. Gyles came up with the title for the exhibition.

There were also cultural differences. The culture of museums and galleries in general is one of a hushed voice, a slightly furrowed brow, a ponderous slowness – Brandreth just wanted to get on with the project. Galleries and museums often display a rather old-fashioned and frankly snobbish view of culture but popular writing and entertainment is just as much part of our inheritance and wider impact on the world.

The museum world uses quite an esoteric vocabulary – accessible if you are a habitué, but otherwise quite dry and not particularly empathetic. But having operated in a number of other worlds (the church, politics and the theatre), Brandreth was used to being a chameleon, so he learned to use the language too. He had little real involvement in all the practicalities of the exhibition – the health and safety and other bureaucratic procedures required – but was in the happy position of being able to leave this sort of thing to the full-time gallery staff.

He would have loved to write the accompanying book, but time and resources did not permit – and a very good author was found instead (Julia Eccleshare[2]).

---

2   An expert on children's literature.

What came out of it long term?

As an exhibition it was widely visited (it toured after its London manifestation), brought pleasure and recognition to the writers included and spread both an increased awareness of the pleasure of reading and the impact Britain has had internationally through our exceptionally good writing for children. Gyles remains proud of this.

From a personal point of view, it was an interesting project to be involved with – and Gyles likes to do interesting things (it was he who pointed out that the fourth plinth in Trafalgar Square should have something on it and helped promote national momentum for it to be used).

His challenge to those wanting to work in this world is that they should remain committed to putting on exhibitions to satisfy and extend the passions and curiosities of those who visit, rather than those who are part of the administration; that exposure to large spaces, high ceilings and wooden floors should never stop them seeing that museums and galleries are there to be enjoyed. And they should strive to see that the spirit of the places that people tend to appreciate most – notably the shop and cafe – should percolate the rest of the organisation.

And for the rest of us, he feels that we all ought to care what goes into our museums and galleries and how we are representing ourselves to the world. We have a choice: either to absorb the pervading atmosphere of hush, and accept it as part of the status quo – or encourage a wider sense of ownership; marvelling at all that is contained within their walls. What is on display (and in the vaults) is just as much ours as those who have the privilege of sitting with it all day.

Ultimately, Brandreth is in favour of multi-tasking. Most of us can drive and it's apparently possible for most of us to fly an aeroplane, so more brains contributing to a general pool of ideas in discussion, more people talking about their passions and with the determination to see things through will in the long run lead to a wider and more stimulating appreciation of culture and heritage for us all.

Part 2: *Employment options*

Chapter 3
Current options for employment

Working in a museum or gallery may be appealing and if this is your aim then a number of locations you might like to work in probably quickly springs to mind. However, it's important to spend some time thinking about the different sorts of organisations available and being clear about their history, constitution, current role and future plans.

The first thing to understand is that there are so many different types of institutions – from individual artists' studios, commercial galleries and dealerships, to small regional institutions, big national collections and charitable foundations. Moving from one type of institution to another is possible – but in the process you will have to explain and cross-sell your experience. So, before you start, it's a good idea to think carefully about where you want to end up; not necessarily what department you'd like to be head of (although there are always people with big long-term ambitions) but in what kind of organisation you see yourself thriving in the future.

This may not seem an obvious thing to think about right now. It's commonplace for journalists, in the early stages of their career, to work for a regional paper or TV station before moving on to one of the nationals, but in the museum world it's more likely that if you want to end up in one of the big nationals, you will start out there too, albeit in a lowly role. The same goes for a career in local museums, which in the long term can lead to a job in one of the bigger provincials; where you could eventually become the voice of a specialist subject area or particular community or region and enjoy an associated elevated position in the local community (what was once 'bank manager status').

You can become clearer about your own motivation and ambitions by wandering around the various types of organisations, picking up the vibe and seeing if it attracts you. Work experience can help provide this too (see Chapter 12).

Consider, too, what kind of role you would like to have. There are certain functions that every organisation must try to cover, so think about which ones appeal to you.

The functions that every museum or gallery must fulfil:

- collection identity – what is being held and what should be added or borrowed to supplement it; further research into the holding to improve understanding;
- collection care and management – ensuring the collection remains in good condition;
- financial management and fundraising – ensuring that agreed funding arrangements are complied with; negotiating to find new sources of money; fundraising through a variety of different mechanisms;
- education and learning – teaching people of all ages (education is not confined to the young) who visit the collection, whether in person or online, about what is held;
- marketing and audience development – ensuring information on the collection reaches new audiences as well as established ones, and that they use the information or visit the collection (this may be a condition of certain types of funding); establishing methods of counting traffic and thus demonstrating effective management of resources;
- general management and human resources (HR) – all the tasks that are common in any organisation: hiring and ensuring good working practice; keeping the building in good condition; people and health management; pay and pensions.

How these roles are allocated will obviously depend on the size and budget of the organisation. When recruiting, a large organisation will seek staff who have the relevant qualifications and/or experience for each role – so someone applying for a retail position will need selling experience, marketers a marketing background, and those responsible for building maintenance will have the appropriate professional qualifications. Within a smaller organisation, these functions will usually be amalgamated (so the person who orders stock for the shop may also be responsible for marketing). As each role will have to be covered by somebody, staff must be flexible and not inclined to stick to strict demarcation zones of involvement, which means attitude can be as important as experience.

Next, consider whether you would like to be a generalist, utilising a broad range of knowledge and skills, or if you would prefer your career to progress in a linear fashion, along a specific path of expertise. Having said that, if you plan to progress in this world you will need a working knowledge of all aspects of running a museum or gallery.

General staffing issues in museums and galleries

- There is a general shortage of staff with science or technology qualifications for related collections. It is possible to do an MA in curatorship and technical preservation, and for this a science background would be required, with a strong interest in chemistry.

- Museums and galleries are inundated with applications from people who want to work in curating or interpreting a collection, but have much greater difficulty attracting staff with a broader range of skills, such as experience of IT and finance – in part at least because rates of pay tend to be low. So if you are seeking work experience and a first job, any provable experience of being good at managing money and doing accounts, database care and having an understanding of data protection would help improve your chances of success.

- The competition for entry at starter job level may be intense, but this puts a ceiling on the number of future colleagues you'll have, so competition for the second job or midlife role can be much less stringent (which is why senior staff are sometimes recruited from allied professions with relevant expertise, such as academia or specialist publishing).

As you explore the various roles and accompanying issues you will begin to appreciate that there are both conflicting and equally valid priorities within museums and galleries. For example, if an organisation has a shop (which may trade as a separate company for tax reasons), then its mission will be to enrich and develop the brand, but at the same time make money – because most, if not all, of its profits will go back to the host organisation. The retail staff will be looking to charge for special items and services that enhance the experience of visiting and probably do this through a shop, restaurant or cafe, merchandise specific to particular exhibitions, such as catalogues and posters, and other selling opportunities. In some cases this may be helped by their initial charter (for example, the V&A, as a museum of commercial design, has a brief to improve industrial practice and so sells things closely linked to this), but in other organisations the space allocated to a visitor restaurant or sales racks may be resented by staff mounting exhibitions for taking up too much space, while staff on the reception desk who are trying to give visitors instructions on how to find what they need may find it difficult to keep an eye on the stock of pencils and postcards at the same time.

While retail staff try to make money, their colleagues in Learning and Interpretation promote *free* access at as many levels as possible and try to encourage footfall through the institution, in particular to new groups and individuals who have not previously visited. The curatorial team, meanwhile, have specific knowledge about particular parts of the collection and may find both the money-making and the learning activities a distraction and a risk to the environment they seek to protect.

The logistics team, responsible for maintenance of the building, installing bathrooms, dealing with visitor movements, and so on, may want to improve signage or flow of movement around the building and find themselves thwarted by regulations and patterns of usage that seem illogical. It can be really hard to explain the rationale of why things are (or more commonly are not) possible, and this can lead to frustration. Hence, what the in-house team considers obvious, and takes for granted, is often overlooked or insufficiently explained to outside contractors, until late in the process. For them, it may seem obvious that signage must fit the style of the building rather than being 'airport style' and visible from 100 metres; their external partners, without the background or explanation, may find this surprising (and odd that they were not warned earlier).

There may be similar restrictions arising from the conditions under which donations were made, and there needs to be discussion about whether these can be lifted or worked around. Planning takes a long time; you can't just *do* things. And you need to think clearly about whether you are a good fit for this environment; whether you are struck by its charm or just its frustrations.

In general, you will find that museums and galleries are poorly resourced and funded, the work is seldom well paid – and is not (as is often imagined) particularly relaxing. People who want to work in this world often imagine it's a gentle place where you can do the job you are accustomed to, but at 75 per cent of your capacity – so 'marketing light'[1] – but this is not true.

There are of course many compensations. Working in a museum or gallery is pleasant because you tend to be surrounded by interesting people and objects. Museums and galleries tend to attract an engaging and eclectic mix of people, all sharing a common purpose of supporting something that matters. At an annual party of a large institution you might find yourself talking to a variety of people – an expert on something highly specific, one of the guards and the person who runs the shop. This is a civilised place to work in the true meaning of the term. You are part of an environment that is bigger than you are, with a lovely ambience, doing something for the good of society and leaving a lasting legacy. It is the antithesis to corporate, where the need to remunerate the shareholders can seem rather hollow by comparison.

---

1   Jo Prosser, Managing Director, V&A Enterprises. See her chapter 'Commercial opportunities in museums and galleries' on page 131.

What is the difference between museums and galleries?

It's difficult to come up with a precise definition of the current role of each institution that highlights the differences between the two as, in practice, there are many working departures from the original stated principles. To complicate matters further, the terms 'museum' and 'gallery' are regionally specific, so in the US most art galleries are called museums.

The Chambers Dictionary describes a **museum** as 'a place of study; a resort of the learned; an institution or repository for the collection, exhibition and study of objects of artistic, scientific, historic or educational interest; a collection of curiosity.' The International Council of Museums (ICOM) defines a museum as a 'non profit-making, permanent institution in the service of society and its development, and open to the public, which acquires, conserves, researches, communicates and exhibits, for purposes of study, education and enjoyment, material evidence of people and their environment.'[2]

Generally, museums are involved in equipping visitors with information. The type of information can vary immensely – it could be anything from social history to machine making – but the emphasis is on the 'how' and 'why' of what is displayed in the museum.

The word **gallery** comes from the Italian *galleria*, and originally meant a covered walk, long balcony, upper or long, covered room and from this came the meaning of a room or building for the exhibition of works of art.

In the main, galleries are more concerned with the whole experience of what is displayed and how items relate to each other within the space. Although information on what is on display and how it came to be there may be available (either in printed form, on wall panels, or through guides standing by) an important part of the gallery experience is allowing people to make up their own minds about what they have seen and in the process to grasp their own appreciation of how items relate to each other. This general impres-

---

2   ICOM Statutes art.2 para 1.

sion was rather neatly summed up by a 13-year-old boy, who recently visited a 20th century arts centre/gallery:

> 'When I arrived, the entrance hall was quite dull and I was not sure where to go. There wasn't much on the walls to tell you what to do. Once we got into the gallery the explanations next to the pictures did not really explain what we were looking at, for example tell us the story. It only told us the size and the media used.'   ELLIOT LAMBLE

In a more contemporary context, 'museum' is often associated with a permanent collection and the identity and care of the same, whereas 'gallery' is more usually a venue focusing on temporary exhibitions, where the items exhibited may be for sale. The lines between the two types of institution are increasingly blurred. Today, many museums also house a gallery with a changing exhibition and items for sale, and galleries describe themselves as museums in order to attract a more serious engagement – e.g. the Design Museum in London (www.designmusuem.org), which hosts a collection of temporary exhibitions. And both types of organisations are on the lookout for unusual or innovative events that might attract a new kind of attendee (and their families and friends).

The different types of institution

There are many different organisations that fall under the umbrella of museums and galleries, but what follows is a general guide. In reality the situation is more of a Venn diagram, with lots of different organisations and roles overlapping. Trying to stick to an original donor's wishes or the original founding ethos of an institution in the light of new technological solutions or changed patterns of access can cause specific problems, which have to be reinterpreted as time goes on.

1. Big national collections

Examples include the British Museum in London (www.britishmuseum.org) and the National Gallery of Scotland in Edinburgh (www.

nationalgalleries.org). These tend to have a wide variety of patrons and, although they receive some state funding from the Department for Culture, Media and Sport (DCMS), they are required to raise funds to bridge the gap between what they are given and what they need to keep going, and seek big sponsors to cover this, such as (at the time of writing) BP and UPS[3]. Many items have been given, either outright or to avoid death duties and if you wander around these collections you will see just how varied the source of gifts is (they are usually listed on the accompanying panel or in the showcase).

2. Private collections

There are collections that are the result of substantial donations, but which also rely on endowments and other private sources of finance. Some may come about through the gift of just one patron, as in the case of Glasgow's Burrell Collection (www.glasgowmusems.com), and there may be associated conditions of display. Similarly, Dulwich Picture Gallery (www.dulwichpicturegallery.org), England's first public art gallery, was founded by the terms of the will of Sir Francis Bourgeois who died in 1811. The collection was first put together by Bourgeois and his fellow art dealer Noël Desenfans from 1790–95, and was originally intended to form the core of a national collection for Poland. But the collection receives no public funding and must raise its own resources.

The Museum of Brands, Packaging and Advertising in London (www.museumofbrands.com), which depicts the history of consumer culture, displays a small percentage of the fascinating range of product packaging and advertising memorabilia from the personal collection of Robert Opie, author of books on British consumerism.

Gyles Brandreth amassed a unique collection of teddy bears – such as Paddington Bear and bears donated by celebrities – in the Teddy Bear Museum, which was open to the public in Stratford-upon-Avon for many years and has now relocated to the Polka Theatre in Wimbledon, south London (www.polkatheatre.com).

---

3   United Parcel Service, www.ups.com

Glover House in Aberdeen was the former home of Thomas Blake Glover, 'The Scottish Samurai', who was one of the founders of Mitsubishi Heavy Industries Ltd in Nagasaki, Japan in the 1880s. The house was gifted by Mitsubishi to the Grampian Japan Trust in 1997.

3. Regionally funded museums

Most cities and many towns have their own museum, sometimes with a gallery attached. Kingston upon Thames has the Kingston Museum (www.kingston.gov.uk); Stoke-on-Trent has The Potteries Museum and Art Gallery (www.stoke.gov.uk/ccm/navigation/leisure/museums/potteries-museum—art-gallery) and Aberdeen has a range of institutions, which include the Aberdeen Art Gallery, the Maritime Museum and Provost Skene's House (see www.aagm.co.uk for further information).

These are largely funded by local authorities, but as there is no statutory duty to provide museums and galleries, they are often first in the line of fire when cuts are contemplated, which can lead to funding problems. On the positive side, the staff are slightly better paid than their counterparts elsewhere because their wages are tied to fixed employment status bands, although when financial difficulties arise, staff who leave tend not to be replaced and roles are amalgamated.

4. Galleries that sell work

Again, the variety here is enormous. There are big commercial galleries, such those in London's Cork Street, which is famous in the British art world, and others with a reputation for specialising in contemporary art such as Albion (www.albion-gallery.com), Victoria Miro (www.victoria-miro.com) and Haunch of Venison (www.haunchofvenison.com). Some specialise in regional art – such as the Eakin Gallery in Belfast (www.eakingallery.co.uk), which sells only Irish art, and the Torrance Gallery in Dundas Street, Edinburgh (www.torrancegallery.co.uk), which sells Scottish contemporary art. As well as having a physical presence, most galleries now sell through their websites, and there is a small band of galleries that only sell work online (see www.newbloodart.com) and through temporary exhibitions and venues that are available over the short term.

You may think of these organisations as purely commercial ventures, but in addition to cultivating a list of clients who visit and make purchases at regular intervals, many have education programmes and see their role very much in terms of nurturing artists.

5. University museums

In general, these are government funded but the funding comes via a different route from local authority and national museums. University museums also tend to have a slightly different culture from other organisations, with a strong cultural affinity to the university they are part of and incorporating the intentions of the principal founder (and often bearing their name). They were usually the brainchild of an enthusiastic member of staff, who obtained basic funding and then developed something which they persuaded the university they could not manage without. For example, the university museum at St Andrews (www.st-andrews.ac.uk/museum) charts the history of Scotland's oldest university and is closely linked both to the courses taught within the art history department and the more recent MA in Curating.

The University of Oxford Botanic Garden (www.botanic-garden.ox.ac.uk) has museum status[4] and its 'Horti Praefectus' (the title given to the head gardener), Timothy Walker, runs tutorials for university students of botany as well as a wider range of educational initiatives (for anyone from age 4 to 104). Multi-tasking within smaller museums is obligatory and Timothy Walker listed his recent achievements as acting as on-site photographer (no problem because he is a keen amateur photographer) and installing a new pump in the

---

4   Within the university the garden is classified as a 'collection' along with the four museums (Ashmolean, Natural History, History of Science and Pitt Rivers). But while the four museums have Museums and Library Association (MLA) accreditation, the botanic garden has not.

---

garden's fountain (having taken a crash course in plumbing by consulting various reference books).

6. Artist-run galleries

This is a growing area of initiative as artists find it increasingly difficult to get their work accepted by galleries. Some artist-run galleries feature a range of work, for example, The Embassy Gallery in Edinburgh (www.embassygallery.org) encourages artists to pay an annual subscription which entitles them to use the space to display artworks. The gallery works closely with the Edinburgh College of Art.

The Devon Guild of Craftsmen (www.devonguildofcraftsmen.co. uk) offers membership to local craftspeople, who then have the opportunity to display and sell their work in its crafts shop and online shop.

Recently, artists have become much more proactive in setting up displays in empty shops, buildings and other space that is temporarily available. For example, The Centre of Attention, curated by Pierre Coinde and Gary O'Dwyer, offers an experimental approach stemming from an ongoing enquiry into the phenomenon of art production, presentation, consumption and heritage-isation (see www.thecentreofattention.org). See also Dan Thompson's description of 'pop up' galleries (www.a-n.co.uk/artists_talking/projects/single/516692).

7. Studios

Some artists allow visitors into their place of work, and artists working in a collective environment may employ someone to do occasional escorted walks around their premises and explain what is going on. Some studio space is available at preferential rates to artists at an early stage in their careers, and open weekends and open days may be a useful way of promoting their work directly to potential customers.

For example, Cockpit Arts (www.cockpitarts.com) is described as a 'creative-business incubator' for designer-makers, where 165 resident designer-makers can grow their businesses, and hundreds more benefit from a programme of associated professional development through courses and workshops.

Ceramicist and potter Tim Andrews (www.timandrewsceramics. co.uk) is a member of the Devon Guild of Craftsmen and he also runs open days at his studio which offer an opportunity to both explain and display his work and to build longer-term relationships with clients.

8. Charitable foundations

Many properties and institutions have been bequeathed to heritage associations such as the National Trust and English Heritage, some-times to avoid death duties and sometimes to ensure a building or piece of land remains intact. Heritage associations are offered far more properties and institutions than they accept, and it is often a condition that money is also given to support the maintenance. In some cases these organisations preserve an expertise or specific skill that might otherwise be lost, as in the case of Patterson's Spade Mill, Templepatrick, County Antrim and The Dolaucothi Gold Mines in Camarthenshire, both of which are owned by the National Trust.

9. Places of study

There is growing interest in professionally run courses, on everything from practical skills such as pottery and watercolours to art history and conservation, and organisations that run them may hold regular exhibitions to display what is produced in the process. For example, West Dean, The Edward James Foundation near Chichester (www. westdean.org.uk) runs a wide variety of courses and offers both temporary displays of students' work and a permanent display of the benefactor's rich art collection. Dartington College (www.dartington. org) also runs a range of courses, in particular a summer school offering a very wide variety of activities, and this has an associated exhibition.

Related employment options

1. Providing relevant support services for museums and galleries

There is a range of support services that museums and galleries will need to use from time to time and some may ultimately become a permanent requirement. So, supplying a relevant service on an ad hoc basis could eventually lead to a full-time role that becomes an integral part of the institution. An obvious example of this is museum website creation, which began as an after-hours freelance activity funded on a very fragmentary basis and is now a full-time function at the very core of how such organisations deliver their mission. Other examples of support services might include the digital photography of objects (for online dissemination), copywriters who can prepare effective messages (and experience in writing bids for funding or proposals for collaboration would be particularly useful) and designers who understand the organisational brand and can produce appropriate promotional materials.

2. Working in 'heritage'

'Heritage' is a growing sector offering a number of (mostly) publicly funded jobs that are designed to promote engagement with different audiences and encourage wider participation amongst the public. This may be through conservation and preservation of historic buildings and parks, but the scope for involvement is much wider. There may be the opportunity to create awareness of more modern or unorthodox examples of buildings, landscape and activities which need to be cherished, recorded and maintained – or else forever lost. Some of these roles are in the public sector, but there are also a lot of self employed options: as interpretation/heritage consultants, interpretative designers and script writers as well as a body of design agencies that focus on heritage interpretation, and public bodies that buy in these skills and services when needed.

Along similar lines, working for a heritage charity can be an attractive option, offering a variety of roles such as administrative, fundraising, publicity and so on. Possible outlets include The Art Fund, The National Trust, English Heritage or NADFAS (National Association of Decorative & Fine Arts Societies). See Appendix for contact details.

3. Academic involvement in your specific subject area

This is a common route for people considering a curatorial role in the longer term. For more details, see Chapter 4 on 'Curating'.

4. Working in heritage or art publishing

If you enjoy books, this can be a rewarding option, particularly if you are producing works about artists you admire. It requires close liaison with museums and galleries, the exhibitions they put on and an awareness of the retail opportunities for selling merchandise. You can gain particular satisfaction from selling a product that represents an organisation or artist, but at a fraction of the price of the artwork on sale and therefore accessible to a wider market. (See the interview with Andrew Hansen, Managing Director of Prestel Publishing Ltd, on page 141.)

5. Working for an interpretation consultancy

Museums and organisations who want to display their archives, but don't know how to go about it, may use an interpretation consultancy to design and put together a display or exhibition. The interview with Dr Lorna Ewan, Head of Interpretation for Historic Scotland, on page 51, gives an insight into what might be involved in such a role.

6. Becoming a live-in warden at a historic house

You may see advertisements in the local press or on the websites of relevant heritage/management organisations; duties will probably include upkeep, maintenance and cleaning as well as researching and maintaining the collection.

7. In-house heritage manager for an organisation

In this role you can become the (sometimes unofficial) custodian of interesting information about a collection and the organisation it belongs to. An unusual example of this is the librarian on board the liner Queen Mary 2 who has, largely through her own interest and initiative, become the on-board repository of information about the history of liners and their heritage. Other such roles often start off within libraries and resource centres and grow from there – and there is much discussion now about how to capture the information that individuals hold and ensure it is recorded for the organisation to use in future.[5]

8. Working in associated professional associations

Examples include the Museums Association, the Museums, Libraries and Archives (MLA) or any other organisation listed in the Appendix. Most now offer training and consultancy to their members.

The perfect employee

We have already discussed the issues that must excite you in order to pursue a career in museums and galleries. Here is an ideal person specification for someone who wants to work in this world. Obviously, some of these skills and personal qualities will be more relevant than others, depending on the job you are applying for.

About you personally. Are you:

- Intellectually and emotionally satisfied by close proximity to objects?
- Determined and resilient? You will need to take yourself sufficiently seriously to keep going in your search for a job. And, when you find it, you will have to defend both your specialist area of work and your profession in general to others who are less convinced of its value.
- Satisfied by creative, often open-ended processes? This requires a combination of patience with systems that must be worked

---

5   The Museums Live project, Kingston University.

through (the associated bureaucracy can be agonisingly slow) and long-term determination to get there in the end.

- Curious? It's essential to be able to get involved both emotionally and intellectually with the contents of the collection/exhibition/ project you are working on, whatever it might be, and to be well informed about its relevance to the local region and population as well as to wider trends in society
- Enthusiastic about passing this information on? Interpretation and communication are becoming increasingly linked to public funding.
- A good communicator? You will need to be able to translate your understanding, or that of your colleagues, to other markets and maintain their attention as you do so. For example you may be called on to explain 'Hoch Kunst'[6] to those who haven't a clue, and be a mediator for all levels of interpretation in between. And it helps enormously if you can find satisfaction in enabling these disparate groups to communicate with each other rather than seeing it as a necessary chore.

Your method of working and organising yourself. Do you have:

- A logical mind – for data collation, review and synopsis?
- An ability to express yourself clearly, on paper and in meetings?
- Good organisational skills? Co-operation, teamwork and effective time management are essential. It helps if you are a lateral thinker – it's a valuable asset for problem-solving.
- Flexibility, resourcefulness and a willingness to muck in? There is no team of worker bees to help out behind the scenes.
- An ability to be multi-focal? You will need to be able to keep your eye on the long-term goal (e.g. staging and funding a new exhibition on a much-neglected artist) as well as manage the minutiae of detail (e.g. what effect will closing the museum shop on a Sunday to allow for the press call have on overall profitability?).

---

6   Or high art; serious work executed to a high specification.

Specific skills to acquire and demonstrate. Can you become:

- Aware of opportunities for publicity – and hence able to turn areas of your organisation's involvement into stories the media will like?

- Well informed about the local area in which your organisation is located – so you can spot useful opportunities for networking and bringing new audiences in-house (e.g. by making links with a local festival or society that could hold meetings in your museum and thus widen understanding of where you are and what you do)?

- Patient with a long fuse so you can deal with all the irritating questions you will be asked, from people who insult the exhibition you have devoted the last two years of your life to installing, to those who assume that because they need the loo, you have to provide one?

- An effective communicator on behalf of your profession – to stick up for it and be clear about what you can and can't do? You can advise on the provenance of the pot just brought in for examination, but, no, you can't say what the local antiques dealer should reasonably pay them for it.

Where can you go for more information?

See Appendix for a list of useful addresses.

Case Studies: Two non-linear careers

Interview with Dr Lorna Ewan, Head of Interpretation, Historic Scotland

'I am neither an art historian nor a curator. Nor am I a conservator, arts administrator or museologist. In truth I have never found it easy to label myself professionally and there is never an appropriate entry on those dreadful drop-down menus supplied by insurance companies and the like. In my current guise my title is Head of Interpretation for Historic Scotland (HS) which, for most people working in the arts, is probably of little value in explaining what I do or how I might have got here. For some, the role won't even recognisably fall into that broad "arts" category even although the in-house Interpretation Unit at HS produces over 500 perform-ance days a year; works with our own Collections Team and other museum curators and conservators to display and interpret our objects and commissions 3D and graphic design, illustrations and, of course, the written word on a daily basis. I do think of myself as an interpreter, although I have been working in the sector since almost before the term was invented and certainly since before it had any common currency.

'How did I get here? As a teenager I had a summer job in a visitor centre at the Loch of the Lowes in Perthshire. Even then I was producing interpretative material, though I certainly would not have recognised the term. I was managing the volunteer rota, serving in the shop and talking to visitors. Though wholly unaware, I was already laying the groundwork for the wide range of skills I would need in the future. A few years later I wrote a PhD thesis. Having the degree is not the point, having done it is. It gave me the research and thinking skills which have supported my professional career since. Whilst finishing the thesis, I had to support myself, which led to a small historical research consultancy that included writing and producing audiovisual programmes for museums. Then came the day that I sprained my ankle playing squash, so was back home early. In consequence I answered a phone call from one of Scotland's first, commercially successful interpreters. He had seen one of my audiovisuals and, to cut a very long story short, over 150 projects on and ten years later I had gained the remarkable experience of helping build up and manage an interpretative design agency for which accuracy, quality and commerciality were bywords. The team designed and built museums, many visitor centres and even interpreted and displayed Scotland's crown jewels and I knew more about design for exhibitions, budget and project management, scenic joinery and display lighting than I could ever have anticipated. Bolting that knowledge and those skills on to the research and content development experience, which ran through every project, gave me the quite unintentional, and certainly unplanned, skillbase to move on to a slightly different platform based in York.

'Working, at first, as a freelance project manager for interpretation-led permanent (a minimum of ten-year lifespan) exhibitions I was now involved in projects in Malta, Austria, and the Middle East as well as across England and Wales. The learning curve – working with multiple currencies and appreciating the differing expectations of other cultures in an interpretative context – was steep. Dealing with construction project managers who had neither awareness of nor interest in the "interpretative content" was challenging; but there are now a few out there who build in the content development time at the beginning of their projects *before* the design work commences – a quiet triumph for those of us who believe function should inspire form. Fairly soon I was running the design and build team of the agency and latterly also the multimedia group.

'And then an opportunity presented itself to come back to working on Scotland's built heritage. The subject matter is "home" for me but, after a quarter of a century in the private sector, moving to the Civil Service was a slightly daunting prospect. But, in truth, although there are more acronyms there is no less commitment or passion and the drivers are largely the same – accuracy, quality and commerciality with another layer comprising community, partnership and value for money and, I am thoroughly enjoying myself.

'Looking back, my career has been moulded around me by myself and others. My skillset is broad but not deep and not one which could emerge directly from any tertiary education or management course on offer either then or even now. Where can you set out to develop skills in interpretative messaging, design awareness and palaeography alongside budget management and construction site certification? Like so many people, my personal amalgam of knowledge, experience and, one hopes, some ability has brought me to where I am now. And the fantastic part is next week I might be helping guide the interpretation of cutting-edge research, critiquing our signage strategy, drafting material which may make its way into government thinking or advising on the colour of claws for a lion costume. Is any of it art? I have no idea, but if it encourages people to appreciate, value and enjoy the built heritage I think it is something of worth.

'Throughout my career I have taken many complex subjects – from aluminium smelting to the history of belief in Ireland – and found ways of drawing out the essence for portrayal in exhibitions, in museums, visitor centres, historical properties and more. Most people use interpretation fairly regularly but few could tell you what it means. For those still wondering, interpretation in my current role can be defined as "the public explanation or discussion of a cultural heritage site, encompassing its full significance, multiple meanings and values" while what we produce, the interpretative infrastructure, comprises "all physical installations, publications (guidebooks, digital applications, etc.) and communications media devised for the purposes of interpretation, as well as the personnel assigned to the task (costumed interpreters and stewards)".'

Interview with Jayne Knight, Arts Development Manager, Suffolk County Council

'I was brought up just outside London and we went to the theatre as a family for treats. I remember Willy Russell's *John, Paul Ringo and Bert*, *Godspell*, Danny la Rue and *A Chorus Line* and wondering why my sister and I were often the only children in the audience. And then came art – my mediocre comprehensive school took us to the Tate (now Tate Britain) and Simon Williams took us on a tour. It was a light bulb moment for me. Living close to London, I regularly took myself into town and cruised the galleries and museums – mostly alone. By my mid teens I loved the arts, but chose to study a science degree. No one pushed me or advised me, it was my decision and I learnt some useful skills. I learnt that I could argue (often better than anyone else), that I could present ideas and that I was good at maths. Naturally my next love became politics! So when the Greater London Council (GLC), led by "Red Ken" in Thatcher's 80s, advertised for graduate recruits I realised that my two loves could work together and I got a job.

'I was a graduate trainee at the GLC. I learnt about arts funding and about local government and I loved every mad minute of it.

'I worked at the GLC until it was abolished and then I became a freelance arts administrator. I did the books, I worked on Amstrad computers, I dabbled with film production and learnt the ropes. I worked with Four Corners film Workshop, Circles Film Distribution and Cockpit Arts. I saw the front line of arts delivery and knew that the arts were important to lots of people – these were my evangelist years.

'During this time the Arts Council realised it needed more advocates in local government and it successfully persuaded local authorities to create specialist arts officers, people who knew about the arts, with responsibility for the arts. These were great jobs. They were new; and most officers wrote their own job descriptions, worked with limited funds but had a lot of freedom. I worked my way through these jobs, and a career path emerged.

'I quickly realised that there was more to arts funding than meets the eye and was hungry for some analytical thinking, so I did an MA in Arts Management at City University. This was excellent, relevant, inspiring learning; it taught me that loving my job wasn't enough. I needed to be strategic, to be critical and to deliver change.

What gives you particular satisfaction?
'I dragged my regional arts council into funding professional development for artists – before it was a national priority – this led to *Making art work*, a county-based project focused on the needs of visual artists striving to make a living. We persuaded our regional

government office that artists were valuable small businesses and that they deserved support.

'We got the investment we needed and used it to support artists with training, equipment, mentoring, commissioning, exhibitions and networking. We built an excellent team including Susan Jones, Michael Pinsky, Eddie Chambers and Isabella Oulton – and we supported over 300 artists. This project had a profound impact on individuals and on the network of artists in the county [Suffolk] – this continues to resonate today.

'One of the pleasures of working in the arts in local government is the range of responsibilities – we work across art forms and across audiences, so there are always new challenges and issues.

'One of the issues we needed to address was young people – how could we get more young people involved in the arts. It's a constant question and the more we talked about it, the more we realised that young people were passionately involved in the arts – they were involved in rock and pop music – not because their parents encouraged it and paid for it – but because they loved it.

'We decided to look at how young people, in a big rural county, get to explore and develop their passion for rock and pop and we built a project. We battled for funding. We recruited tutors who were gigging "rock and poppers" with a desire to support young people. We skilled them up to teach and mentor, we identified spaces for people to meet and make a noise, we bought loads of decks, drum kits and guitars and we launched *Amplifer*[7].

'Now in its fifth year, *Amplifier* has produced numerous CDs, held hundreds of gigs and launched some fantastic bands. It is delivered by four community interest companies – run by those same tutors, who have given up the "day job" and now work full time on music.

'*Amplifier* has added to the experience of growing up in Suffolk for a lot of young people and has created work for musicians. That's the great thing about working in the arts in local government – we

7   A music project working with young people.

get to do things for people, we get to plug into the creativity of individuals and communities – great work if you can get it!

'And then there's the paperwork, the funding applications, the committee reports, the policies and activity plans. It doesn't have to be boring and badly written – that is up to you. There is a template for everything but if you enjoy writing, the paperwork isn't a burden – it's an opportunity to tell a story, to campaign for investment and to assert the value of the arts. Data collection and evaluation is also really important. If we don't collect data and evaluate, we don't have the evidence and we will lose the argument – so statistics are an important part of my day!

'I love working with creative people, being the interface between local politics and investment in the arts, shaping an argument, playing a role in social change, knowing that politics is important and does make a difference, being involved in projects that play a part in transforming individuals' lives, going into battle and sometimes winning!

And the frustrations?
'Politics, endless meetings, telling good people with good projects that their funding has been reduced or cut – and knowing it was you that lost the argument.

'Looking further ahead, social change is long term; projects like *Amplifier* and *Making art work* don't happen overnight and they definitely have their bad days! So it's critical for local government arts managers to be able to assert what is needed for the arts sector and not to get sidetracked by the latest government or arts council "fashion".

'Some people working in the arts in local government feel isolated and marginalised, so it's important to keep your own networks lively and fresh. There's a National Association of Local Government Arts Officers (Nalgao) – a terrific professional network – and there are plenty of arts organisations that want good board members, so no need to feel alone.

'All local authority arts services are managed in different ways, with different resources, but the nuts and bolts of what we do is generally the same – we all invest in the arts sector by awarding grants and we all develop and deliver projects and activities. Some authorities also directly manage arts venues.

There are plenty of opportunities for personal development. I could go up the local government ladder if I was prepared to get more involved in local government and less involved in the arts. I could work for a bigger authority with a bigger budget. I could run an arts organisation that was involved in broad arts development. I could teach on one of the many arts management courses. I could work in the voluntary and community sector and other things too. With a range of transferable skills – mostly suited to public sector work – there are lots of opportunities.'

Chapter 4
Curating

The role of the curator is at the heart of the museum or gallery, so let's look at this role in some detail and what it involves.

What does 'curating' mean?

The Chambers Dictionary defines 'curator' as 'the person who has the charge of anything; a superintendent, especially of a museum; a person appointed by law as a guardian of something'.

The word curator comes from the Latin '*curare*', meaning 'to care for', 'have charge of' or 'to cure', and the term *curate*, which has a similar derivation, means 'a member of the clergy in the Church of England who assists a rector or vicar and has the "cure of souls"'.

The term 'cure' in this context is interesting: an archaic word that means 'healing'; a means of improving a situation; a course or method of preserving or arresting decomposition; a treatment by which a product is finished or made ready for use' and, of course, the term's extension to include 'the preservation of food, by drying, salting or finishing by means of chemical change', which is relevant to our purposes here.

So, from this, it would seem that a curator is someone who:

- is appointed and given authority to look after something;
- then preserves it to the best of their ability to prevent further decay;
- can interpret, explain and permit appropriate access to whatever they are looking after in future.

Within the world of museums and galleries today, the responsibilities of curatorship fall into two main areas:

- The care and research of a specific collection: understanding the collection and keeping up to date with new developments that might alter that understanding; writing about the collection; locating the whereabouts of new material that would augment the collection (or relate to its wider understanding); adding to the collection; preserving it for a new generation.
- Its display and interpretation.

Both these responsibilities are fuelled by a strong understanding of the context – the organisation being represented, its authority and reputation.

How this works in practice

A curator forms the intellectual heart of a museum or gallery. In the 1970s there was much discussion about whether these institutions should be run by professional administrators. The diaries of Sir. Roy Strong, former Director of the V&A, of that period hold this out as a long-term governmental ambition (and fear on his part), but today museums and galleries are still mostly run by curators. However, while management power tends to reside with those who can explain and interpret a collection, in the same way that pilots exercise power in the RAF, academics within universities and doctors within medicine, changes are afoot, more quickly in some organisations than others, and several examples can be highlighted where people who have followed a non-curatorial route are already part of the organisation's senior management team. There is a widening appreciation that the curatorial role is not all it used to be, and in the longer term, is not the only route to seniority.

In small organisations such as town museums, the curator may have sole responsibility for the acquisition and care of objects. It will be the curator who decides what to collect, looks after what is held, researches and writes about it and implements the policy about whether to lend it more widely. If the organisation is particularly small – such as a local history society – the curator may be the only paid member of staff, with one of their duties being the co-ordination of volunteer help.

Here is a job description for a curator's role within a smaller organisation, in this case a historic house.

The Museum and Heritage Service is looking for a committed and enthusiastic curator to lead on the day-to-day management and running of one of its historic houses. The post will be responsible for all aspects of service delivery including exhibitions, a wide range of activities and events working with partners and volunteers along with the active Friends group. You will also be part of the Museum and Heritage Team, helping to shape and develop services across the Borough.

Required skills: You will have the ability to work as part of a team and to communicate well with the whole community, particularly young people. You will have experience of running activities including class visits. You will be required to work late nights, weekends and public holidays on a regular basis.

In larger organisations, the curator's role tends to evolve into that of subject specialist, who conducts research into what is held and provides guidance on what should be acquired or shared in future. Larger organisations have many curators, each specialising in a particular area, under the overall direction of a head curator. In such organisations, the actual physical care of the collection may be handled by conservators, while documentation and administration is looked after by other specialists.

Here is a job advertisement for a curator within a major national art museum:

As an experienced curator of modern international art, with particular experience in the period 1900–1965, you will contribute intellectual, art historical and curatorial expertise to the museum's programme. You will be responsible for researching, developing and curating large and medium scale exhibitions and projects, seeing them through from idea to realisation. This will encompass the entire process from initial concept and research for exhibitions and collection displays to managing substantial budgets, leading organisation-wide project teams, overseeing installation designs and acting as an advocate for the organisation. You will also contribute texts and editorial supervision to a range of publications in conjunction with the programme. You will have proven excellent research, scholarly and curatorial planning and project-management skills. While the emphasis is on curatorial work on the programme, you will also contribute your expertise to our acquisitions process.

The term curating originally meant the care of tangible things such as paintings, archaeological findings and machinery, but more recently new kinds of curating are evolving, such as the care of digital data objects, or biocurators (the accurate and comprehensive representation of biological knowledge). There is also a significant trend in that a curator may not necessarily look after a collection or objects at all, but rather engage with its cultural meaning – and become an advocate for professional practice and the role of the creator

Also under consideration is the value of the curator's objectivity. Traditionally, curators had specific expertise which enabled them to take discerning decisions; to use the funds at their disposal to preserve the best and then explain it on to visitors; they were people of enhanced judgement who had an eye on both history and the future.

'Curators must serve the past and the future as well as the present. And they must attempt to be fair to all comers and not succumb to prejudice or *parti pris*. They may wish to lead public taste but can only do so by selecting those artists who seem to bear the creative flame. Curators cannot simultaneously work in the public domain and collect privately, or work as artists: these roles could be fatal to the requirement that the curator

aspires, like an independent critic, to objectivity, impartiality, and, in the
end, justice.'

MARK HAWORTH-BOOTH, VICTORIA & ALBERT MUSEUM (V&A), LONDON[1]

Today there is discussion of the selection of objects as being in itself
an art form with a 'curator-artist' at its centre.

'While the traditional curator maintains a collection of art, artifacts or
curios by preserving, exhibiting and studying the objects therein, the
contemporary curator need not work with a collection or objects at all, and
instead engages with cultural meaning and production, often from a position of development that is shared with the artist.'

MELANIE O'BRIAN, ART SPEAKING: TOWARDS AN UNDERSTANDING OF THE
LANGUAGE OF CURATING, BANFF, JULY 2005[2]

'The role of curator has come to occupy a deliberately less academic stance,
often embodying a more participatory or hands-on function. As such, curators are no longer limited to being critical observers but increasingly are
understood as instigators, subjective participants actively defining (or
redefining) art and culture as-it-happens. ... The 'job' of curating becomes
a sophisticated form of intellectual gameplay, which posits the curator in a
position sometimes parallel to that of conceptual artist. The challenge is to
continually negotiate a balance between the desire for critical and creative

---

1 'Remarks toward an Ideal Museum of Photography', in V. D. Coke (ed.), *One
Hundred Years of Photographic History: Essays in Honor of Beaumont Newhall* (1975).
Haworth-Booth, M., *Photography: An Independent Art. Photographs from the Victoria
and Albert Museum 1839-1996*. London: V&A Publications, 1997.

2 *Unspoken Assumptions: Visual Art Curators in Context*, curatorial mentoring round-
tables in Banff (July 15-17, 2005) and Toronto (December 1-4, 2005). See: http://
curatorsincontext.ca/en

There is also the issue of representing the completeness of the collection by displaying different selections in turn, or pandering to the public appetite by concentrating on the items that have popular appeal. In the process, the integrity of the whole may be compromised by the public's misunderstanding of an artist or work of art – but that misunderstanding may be the key to getting people in. For example, do you include Van Gogh in an exhibition on the Impressionists, simply because so many of the public think he was part of this movement? Or do you include him because of this understanding and then seek to correct it – perhaps by including a panel on 'Antecedents' or 'Why Van Gogh is not an Impressionist?'

In any case, today's consumer wants to interact and take part in decisions about purchasing and display – rather than simply admire what has been selected for them to view. Stores such as IKEA and home makeover shows on television have raised the issue among the public of what to put on their walls at home and offer cheap solutions, so the public can vote with their feet, buying the images they prefer through posters and greetings cards rather than relying on gallery shops to sell them what scholarly opinion has decided is worth hanging on their walls. Along similar lines, should decisions on what should be bought for or displayed in public institutions be made solely by those with public money to spend, or by those who want to come and see it? This is aptly illustrated by the fact that there is still not a single painting by Jack Vettriano in a public collection in the UK, despite the huge popularity of his images (as shown through the sale of reproductions and related merchandise).

---

3   *ibid.*

Becoming a curator

If curating is your long-term career goal, you'll need academic pedigree (a really good university, an excellent degree), and for a post in a national museum or gallery, probably a PhD supervised by someone well connected and a track record of publication in academic journals. Your first job would usually be that of curatorial assistant.

People with such a profile are often scholarly and self-effacing, but if they are going to progress to running the institution they are part of, they will need to have good communication and diplomatic skills, persuasiveness and to be well connected. The role of curator involves negotiating for funds, building links with those who control the purse strings and making a case for funding in competition with other organisations, all the while keeping a weather eye on prevailing public opinion (which may not be on your side). Currently, for example, most funding in Britain is directed towards the 2012 Olympics, so cultural institutions need to state the case for their own funding pragmatically, by emphasising the long-term benefits to the current population and the wider interests of society in future.

National museums and galleries in England are currently funded by the DCMS, so curators must know the government minister[4], their priorities, build relationships with them and have a sound grasp of finance. There are many different financial models for the running of institutions and, increasingly, any public funding has to be matched by self-funding initiatives such as membership schemes and income from exhibitions. For example, the Metropolitan Museum of Art (The Met) in New York is privately funded with a strong tradition of endowment and donations. The Royal Academy and Historic Royal Palaces in the UK receives no DCMS funding and therefore must raise revenue through events and entrance money – and without the benefit of the prevailing US culture of donating to public collections. Curators with responsibility for these major institutions may be

---

4 Currently The Secretary of State for Culture, Media and Sport – although watch out for reorganisations of responsibility.

experts in specific areas of their own interest, but must also become masters of more general management techniques.

At all times, curators have to look out for the collection's interests. They must work with the trustees and think carefully about whom to appoint in these roles (how well connected are they, do they bring any added value in terms of expertise or the support of particular groups?) and how to train them to best serve the organisation's interests. Once appointed, trustees have a term to serve, and spotting those who have a private agenda can be difficult – as the MP Barbara Follett allegedly once commented: 'The more radical your ideas, the more conservatively you need to dress.'[5]

If you are running a local collection, you should be well grounded in local issues, with a knowledge of local history, and understand how what you have to preserve fits the wider environment – how it can be promoted further afield to draw significance to it. There will be local partners who can work with you on this – such as regional development boards, estate agents and business community, all of whom benefit – but maintaining the collection's integrity and ensuring that its support survives changes of government, can be a difficult tightrope to walk.

Where to start your curatorial career – in a gallery or museum or in a university?

If you are serious about wanting a major curatorial role within a significant collection, there are two principal routes: either by entering the museum and gallery world after acquiring an honours degree (perhaps having taken a course in museum studies first) or by taking the next stage in academic qualification, usually a PhD. Both routes would be considerably eased by taking unpaid work experience in appropriate organisations.

---

5 See *Board matters, a review of charity trusteeship in the UK* produced by New Philanthropy Capital: www.philanthropycapital.org

The advantages – and disadvantages – of going straight into the world of museums and galleries

Advantages

- You show initial commitment to your chosen world and gain relevant experience that can go straight on to your CV. This arguably makes you more marketable in future.
- You gain an appreciation of whether or not this world really is for you.
- You acquire a representative role in the institution you work for and, if you do your job well, you have the chance to exercise this at professional and training fora internationally.
- You have the opportunity to build up patronage from those in charge of your own institution, and to listen to – and possibly meet – people who are significant within this world as a whole.
- You are well placed to hear about vacancies that arise within museums and galleries.
- You can cultivate your expertise in a particular area, as jobs come up. Your skills as a generalist, as you emerge directly from an undergraduate or MA university course, are more malleable for presentation in support of a range of job applications and, ultimately, this can lead to a decision on what to make your special area of study.

Disadvantages

- You may be seeking closer proximity to objects, but not to people who decide on the allocation of the arts and leisure budget (and who do not think museums and galleries are a priority).
- If you are serious about a career in curating, you will need to build up a publications profile – through scholarly articles published and contributions to academic books – and these publications will have to be produced largely in your own time. Many people have no idea how much time is taken up maintaining the public face of an institution: answering queries from members of the public; giving talks to societies who ask for one; delivering

lunchtime lectures and other contributions to the (increasingly monitored) 'outreach' of the organisation, and this means that you may have little time to concentrate on research and publication during the working day. Similarly, sustained time off to concentrate on this – along the lines of the academic sabbatical – is difficult. If you are the expert in a particular field, your institution needs you to be available to answer questions and maintain its public position amid a swathe of political initiatives, funding opportunities and working parties that require participation. A junior member of staff, even if well informed, would not have the same clout.

The advantages – and disadvantages – of studying for a PhD first

Advantages

- Time. As an academic you will have more free time to work on your own research interests; your contract will be divided between teaching, research and administration. All academics complain about the increasing administrative burden, although it is not as great as that in galleries and museums and much more predictable (limited to your student body and wider professional contacts), whereas in a public institution, you have to answer questions from anyone who may roll in off the street. You get long summer vacations and, once you are established, you may get the chance to take research leave through a sabbatical (it's relatively straightforward to get someone else to do your teaching and marking). As your institution will benefit from the prestige of your publications, they will be actively supportive.
- Remuneration. You may struggle financially when studying for a PhD although you can usually supplement your income with some teaching or part-time work. The pay for a starter academic position is generally better than for an ordinary starter job in a museum or gallery.

- You may be able to form part of a university bidding for AHRC[6] funding, and thus be able to earn money for your institution by sharing information at the same time as doing your PhD. These days, universities place a high priority on the transfer of knowledge and there are substantial funding opportunities. A track record in such initiatives will also impress managers of galleries and museums – they too are increasingly required to seek wider public funding rather than rely on central or local government support alone.

Disadvantages
- You commit yourself to your specialist subject. If a job comes up in applied arts and crafts and you are just finishing off a PhD on the work of Vermeer, it will be hard to explain your real drive for the job.
- You are not building up hands-on experience in museum management, which is becoming an increasing priority for publicly funded institutions that have to justify their share of the public purse through widening engagement and increasing access. Although you can take a stance on all these things, you will lack first-hand experience of managing them.

Ultimately, whichever route you choose, the number of applicants for jobs in this world far outstrips the number of positions available and often it's a question of being in the right place at the right time; of having the right bit of experience that convinces the interviewing

6   Arts and Humanities Research Council. There are seven UK Research Councils, established under Royal Charter. The Department for Business, Innovation and Skills has statutory control of the Councils, supported by the Director General for Science and Research. Council members are appointed by the Secretary of State for Business, Innovation and Skills, who is answerable to Parliament for the Councils' activities. The UK Research Councils are: Arts and Humanities Research Council (AHRC); Biotechnology and Biological Sciences Research Council (BBSRC); Engineering & Physical Sciences Research Council (EPSRC); Economic & Social Research Council (ESRC); Medical Research Council (MRC); Natural Environment Research Council (NERC); Science and Technology Facilities Council (STFC).

panel on the right day. And of course there are so many variables. You cannot predict who will be on the panel, the chemistry (and tensions) between the different members, their unstated objectives, and what they will have just heard on the grapevine that shapes their understanding or appreciation of what you offer in comparison with other candidates.

Grasping the language and culture of curating

Whether you opt for the museum or the academic route, one thing you will have to grasp quickly is the appropriate language and tone of voice, in order to be heard. Most professions have a particular way of talking to each other, and an accompanying set of initials and acronyms, and curating is no exception. As a generalisation, curators (as perhaps do academics in general) tend to talk in quiet and respectful tones, using long words, lots of clauses, and extended sentences. Art historians speak in a language that is uniquely complicated. My own theory (based on a degree that was half history, half history of art) is that as a relatively new subject, art history had to establish a complicated vocabulary in order to both distinguish itself and fully inhabit the new field it was staking out, and this has stuck; older disciplines such as history and English use a vocabulary that is far easier to understand. It is significant that the famous art historian Ernst Gombrich, who, in addition to his scholarly output of books and monographs, opened up this world by writing an accessible book on the subject, *The Story of Art* (16 editions during his lifetime, translated into 30 languages and millions sold) was viewed within art history circles as having rather let the side down by widening access. There was a similar feeling towards historian A. J. P. Taylor, whose television lectures in the 1960s reached vast numbers of people in their living rooms, but attracted unremitting negativity from his academic peers. Writer Alain de Botton wrote recently of the:

'...hostility to anyone attempting to communicate ideas to a broader public is a staple of academic life. You can either fight for academic status or you

---

can address the world at large. But in the current British climate it's very difficult to succeed in both fields.'[7]

Perhaps this is changing. The elevation of Carol Ann Duffy to the role of Poet Laureate in May 2009 was accompanied by an appreciation that her work has both academic approval and popular appeal – her inclusion on the GCSE syllabus has given many pupils the important experience of realising that they both like and can understand poetry; a tremendous endowment for their future.

It's an undeniable trend too that the world today is less influenced by scholarly detachment than by ready-made opinion, preferably expressed in everyday language. There is a search for the interpreter, the opinion-holder – so we tune into chat show hosts who earn a fortune because they serve up an interesting cross section of current experience and ask the right questions on behalf of us all – and think of the right retort straight away, rather than several hours later. Over his career, Richard Littlejohn has scuttled back and forth between the *Sun* and the *Daily Mail*, and is one of the highest paid journalists, because the owners of the papers he writes for know that his opinion-packed columns are the only things some readers look at. Arts festivals have guest directors whose tastes match that of the audience (e.g. the Cheltenham Literature Festival has author and philosopher A. C. Grayling, and the Edinburgh International Festival Richard Holloway, former Bishop of the city), and in bookshops, we like to see the individual selections of authors put forward (at the time of writing, Nick Hornby's favourite books are laid out as a special section within Waterstone's). As a society, we look for strong opinions to adopt to save the trouble of thinking of our own.

So what is the role of the museum and, by default, its curatorial team in this new development? Should an institution be reaching out into the local community and, in the same way as theatre companies, put on performances in shopping centres and parks? Should content

---

7   *The Times Magazine*, 26 August 2006.

be dictated by what people are familiar with or what they ought to know about? Should an institution housing treasures that belong to all of us try to draw us in to understand the collection in more detail, using the familiar as an enticement, or should it just be the repository of all that is valuable, the collective spare room of the nation, with the long-term aim of keeping stuff safe to sell on in future – because each time material is displayed it is further dilapidated?

In part, the answer is being given by politicians: institutions in receipt of public funds must demonstrate that they are offering value and widening participation. Today's government culture requires constant measurement of targets, proving that what has been set up is an effective use of resources. Journalists are fond of comparing the costs of a museum or gallery purchase with that of a new hospital or school.

As public institutions, museums and galleries certainly need to demonstrate the value they are delivering, but rather than just responding to the criteria set by politicians, arguably they must play a part in trying to establish the measures by which their aspirations and effectiveness will be judged. This will involve communicating a vision, using language that others relate to, spreading enthusiasm, justifying it to popular opinion and hence influencing how it is perceived. For example, the local press was resoundingly negative about the installation of Antony Gormley's 'Angel of the North' sculpture, but the local council (Gateshead) and artist were undeterred. The aims of the various groups involved will have been different (artistic values/example of public art/civic pride) but they united to support and maintain a shared ambition and there is now a strong sense of regional satisfaction, with those who were initially hostile referring to the pride their children and grandchildren take in 'our angel'.

In any case, who are 'the public' that need to be considered – and counted? Is the organisation appealing to those who walk past and appreciate the posters but never go in; those who use the cafe, shop or bathrooms, but seldom visit the accompanying exhibition; those who find it a romantic place to walk around but don't notice what they are seeing; those who drop in occasionally to find out if they have treasure in *their* attics or those whose children go there on school trips which cost less than trips further afield because there is no entrance price to pay? The role of the cultural repository in breaking down class and educational barriers is also significant, and curators will have to discuss how much of their attention should be directed at existing audiences, and how much at potential new ones – and how much funding/fund-raising should follow these decisions.

'I view curating as something I do with and for others. It is in this spirit that I aim to create exhibitions and public programs that investigate the social aspects of cultural production in ways that encourage alternative modes of thinking, foster new relationships, and inspire increased owner-ship in the development and articulation of culture. I believe strongly in the capacity for the arts to affect positive change by expanding percep-tions of day-to-day experience, and I am enthusiastic about the role artists play in the building of sustainable and equitable communities.'

MILENA PLACENTILE, CURATOR[8]

All these are questions that the new generation of curators will have to deal with – perhaps you will be one of them?

Case Studies: Curating as a Career

Interview with Desmond Shawe-Taylor, Surveyor of The Queen's Pictures, The Royal Collection

'I read English at Oxford and then embarked on an MA in Fine Art at The Courtauld. I had no particular career plan in mind and while I was still doing my MA one of my lecturers suggested I apply to teach art history at Nottingham University, where they were recruiting. It would (quite properly) be impossible nowadays to

---

8 ibid. *By the time I decide what to call this paper, the world will be different*, July 2005, Banff.

secure a post like this without doing a PhD first, but I applied and was appointed.

'After many years teaching there I began to wonder about a change. I suppose if you have always been determined on a single career option you would probably decide to stay within the security of what you had striven to be part of, but given that my becoming an academic had been largely circumstantial, I decided to think where else my passion for art might be useful.

'Neil MacGregor [then director of the National Gallery] has always been interested in people and their aptitudes rather than their specific labels or experience. He suggested that I apply for the position of Head of Education at the National Gallery. This has always been an art historian's job, rather than an educator's one. Other museums and galleries employ educators in order to involve younger children. The National Gallery does this as well but has always waved the flag for art history in general; seeing its mission to inform all ages and create wider enthusiasm for art.

'Having been an academic (and thus teaching adults) I was qualified in the technical sense but, although a frequent visitor to museums and galleries, knew little about how they worked from the inside. So in preparation for my interview I embarked on extensive research, which included talking to those working there, observing what was going on and finding out more about the National Gallery in particular. The more I found out, the more I became engrossed. I did not get the job – it went to the very able Kathy Adler, who has done it extremely well – but on the interviewing panel was a trustee of Dulwich Picture Gallery. It just so happened that the then director of Dulwich, Giles Waterfield, was about to retire, and was active in the search for his successor. Having staked out my claim for wanting a job in this world, I was invited to apply and this time secured the role – and spent nine very happy years there.

'Working with a really dedicated team, we oversaw the building of an extension, put on new exhibitions, grew the education programme, increased the number of the gallery's Friends[9] and tried to reach out into our local and national communities. But Dulwich Picture Gallery receives no state funding, and so maintaining its income is a constant struggle. You would announce exhibitions with definite start dates, uncertain of whether you would have the funds to put them on, and were continually mindful of the opportunities to raise cash to support what you had begun. After nine years I was proud of what we had achieved together, but confess also exhausted by the process of constantly seeking funding, and began to think about one more job before I retired.

'The role of surveyor of the Queen's pictures became available and I applied. The job is to be chief curator of paintings in the Royal Collection, and there are colleagues with a similar role handling 'works of art' (our term for furniture, decorative arts and sculpture), and works on paper (drawings, prints and books). We all work under the director, who is also Surveyor of Works of Art. We manage the artwork in Buckingham Palace, Windsor Castle, Holyrood Palace and the Royal Collection (a gallery open to the public within Buckingham Palace) and this involves both putting on exhibitions and taking care of artworks that need restoration and further research. The funds from the opening of these buildings come back to The Royal Collection Trust, which is run as a business, with a board of trustees. This is a business that has grown steadily in recent years – the summer season openings of Buckingham Palace (to help pay for Windsor's restoration after it was damaged by fire) began in 1993 and Windsor Castle was only reopened again in 1997. In financial terms our size is comparable to that of a national museum.

'We are curatorially led, without compromise. We look after the treasures in our care, learn more about them and ensure they are

---

9 Supporters who agree to pay a regular subscription (often at different levels of commitment) and in return receive privileges such as invitations to the opening of new installations and a discount in the shop. As they commit for a period of time ahead, they are a particularly valuable source of reliable income.

kept in excellent condition. I am passionate about presentation and want to ensure all looks beautiful, taking particular care with hanging, lighting, visibility and access. High values in display and presentation matter hugely – we are, after all, putting the work on show in royal palaces. We mount special exhibitions and encourage a climate of research and scholarship. We are very fortunate to work with a collection of such extraordinary range and depth as The Royal Collection.

'I work with a range of committed art historians and we encourage students to come in and get involved in research and administrative projects (if you would like to be considered, the best way is to write a letter of application requesting work experience, telling us of your particular research interests). We oversee and recommend applications for loans from the Royal Collection for other exhibitions and organisations – all are approved by the Queen, who is the final decision-maker, and she is generous in making provision.

'It's true that many of those visiting the palaces often choose to visit as part of a tourist itinerary rather than as an art history fest, but once inside visitors are often struck by the excellent quality of the paintings, and how exciting it can be to see an image you are familiar with – maybe from a book illustration or the media – "in the flesh". An oil painting seen at first hand can be so much more compelling than any reproduction. I like to think that if we encourage more people to look at the artwork on display, we enrich their understanding of art in general, and that they go forth with more than they had bargained for.

'Above all, this job is a huge privilege. We look after a rich endowment of work that was begun by Charles I, added to by subsequent monarchs (George III was a great collector of drawings) and is now the private collection of their ancestor, the Queen, held in trust for the nation. My job is to increase public awareness of the treasures held, add to the sum of knowledge we have about them, and to put on exhibitions and loans that spread wider understanding – both of what is in the Royal Collection and the value of art history in general.'

Interview with Peta Cook, Curator at Kingston Museum

Peta and I were due to have lunch the day of this interview, but as a member of her staff had phoned in sick that morning, she was unable to leave the building. Writing up our discussions later that day, this became a useful metaphor; firstly for the significant responsibility she carries and secondly for her total commitment to her job. Her job title is officially curator, but in reality her work is much more varied. That same day she was due to attend an important meeting at 4 p.m. and in between would have to organise the volunteers, put out the chairs and ensure the facilities were clean in preparation for the lecture she was giving that evening to the Friends of the Museum.

'My undergraduate degree was in archaeology, at Liverpool University. Whereas I had started out with the intention of becoming an archaeologist, I had always loved museums and in my last year I began investigating this as a career option. I sought advice from those already involved and did some work experience in Liverpool Museum (classifying lithics – or stone age tools). What followed was more work experience, two years in Liverpool and then a year in Newcastle, in order to qualify for the hugely competitive (just 24 places) MA in Museum Studies at Newcastle University. Work experience did not yield an income and had to be subsidised with part-time paid work – in my case cleaning the students' union, working for Boots and in a call centre for BT. After graduating from my MA I did more volunteering in the hope that a paid position would eventually turn up, which is the most usual route; those who are working for nothing are first in line when paid opportunities occur. I eventually got some paid work as a museum interpreter for Norfolk Museums and Archaeological Service, which looked after a network of 11 regional museums and was funded by the local authority. All posts seem to be developmental in that the individual occupying them brings specific talents and interests and will develop the role in the way they are best able to serve the museum. The funding always arrives later, if at all.

'After working for a year as a museum interpreter for Norfolk Museums and Archaeological Service, I worked as curator of human history (social history and archaeology) at Peterborough (a job share role I held for three years), during which time I worked at Ipswich Museum as a volunteer on my days off, as well as a flower seller at the weekends. My next job was working full time for East of England Museums Libraries and Archives Council, as regional standards advisor for museums in the east of England. This role saw me training and advising museums on a range of issues but with particular responsibility for managing the accreditation scheme in this museum-packed region. After three years in the post, I decided to put my advice into practice and return to curatorial work at Kingston Museum, and I have now been here for three years.

'While I love what I do, and find it very satisfying, the role is also frustrating in that so many different job functions are fulfilled by me with insufficient time and resources to do any of them properly. For example, in addition to being curator, I have half the job of head of heritage services (when the previous incumbent left she was not replaced and her role was divided between me and another colleague). I am also manager of front of house, collections manager and exhibitions officer. This means that my job stretches from planning the different temporary exhibitions and overseeing their installation to ensuring that the electrical equipment has had its safety checks and that health and safety procedures get adhered to. Managing the volunteers takes a lot of time – we have over 40, from a range of backgrounds (not everyone is seeking a career here). Some are provided by volunteering agencies, who are not looking for museum-specific work experience but rather experience of a workplace for the volunteers they send; others are looking to spend time in a museum, perhaps because they live locally and want to be more involved in their community; others want a job like mine.

'Funding is a headache. As provision of museum services is non-statutory, we are afforded no security, and always seem to be first in line when cuts loom. We are not seen as an essential service. We have to be political and both understand and connect with the agenda, strategy papers and higher (and sometimes unstated) objectives that are established, and which determine the allocation of resources. We are now part of the Library and Heritage Service but it concerns me that "museums" are no longer specifically mentioned in the organisational title.

'Keeping our connectedness to the wider agenda is easier at some times than at others. It is important to measure who has been here and what use they have made of us, both in person and via our website, and this is fairly straightforward. Just recently, however, we put on an exhibition of sculpture for the blind where we displayed materials that visitors were invited to touch and hold. This had a substantial effect on all who got involved, from those preparing the exhibition and the facilities needed to support visitors, to the visually impaired who attended, their carers and companions. Once the exhibition is over it has to be explained and presented in a manner that enables us to meet the targets we have been set. We face a wider misunderstanding from society that museums deal with the past – rather we feel we are working in the present to inform the future and change lives; we often have an immediate and lasting effect on those who visit. But the economic climate is particularly difficult at the moment, money is in short supply and there are major projects on the horizon needing substantial income – most notably the 2012 Olympics – which draw resources that could really benefit local initiatives such as our museum.

'At the same time as putting on displays and looking after our collection, we have to keep an eye out for collaborative ventures and funding opportunities. We are involved in a major international exhibition, which is in essence a retrospective of the work of pioneering moving image photographer Eadweard Muybridge. This means working with the museum developing the exhibition – The Corcoran Gallery in Washington – as well as one of the UK host museums, in this case Tate Britain. In order for us to put on something in Kingston that maximises the massive potential offered to us via these partnerships and which links us to these major initiatives, we will need to apply for external funding from bodies such as the Heritage Lottery Fund or the Arts Council. These major initiatives aside, we find ourselves applying for funding or support for projects on an almost constant basis, be it for conservation, learning, advocacy, audience development or simply to fund our next exhibition, the sources for which are varied, but might be local, national or international grant-giving bodies, local individuals, sponsorship from local firms or through collaborative developments with Kingston University. Each application takes considerable time and effort to prepare, and the projects themselves take time to plan. The amounts we seek may be very small scale but vital to our delivery and, therefore, while the accompanying bureaucracy is always extensive, it is vital that we keep doing this.

'One of the best things about this world is its connectedness, or rather the culture of reciprocity that exists among museums and museum staff. For example, when we were threatened with closure, the MLA (Museums, Libraries and Archives Association) or regional agencies could offer support. There are also many colleagues in the West London Museums Group or the London Museums Group, all of whom I am in touch with via regional meetings or e-mail. Then there are various networks to which I can submit queries for almost instant and engaged help, such as GEM, or to give it its full title, Group for Education in Museums, or MANN (the Museums Advisor Network). Networks like these prove invaluable as museums are often breaking new ground and involved in areas of work for which they require the advice of those who have trod that path before or who know of people in other sectors who can share their skills. Owing to the multifaceted nature of museum roles today, staff themselves are facing new challenges every day, for which advice is often appreciated and, with everyone under massive time/resource pressures, the more we can avoid reinventing the wheel the better! I am on the committees of the Society of Museum Archaeologists and the London Museums Group, and am curatorial adviser to both the Wimbledon Windmill Museum and the British Airways Museum (private museums receiving no state funding).'

Interview with David Falkner, Director of the Stanley Picker Gallery, Kingston University

'My start in this world was not unusual as people tend to arrive via a variety of different paths. I trained as an artist, did my BA in Fine Arts at the Chelsea School of Art and then was determined to be a practising artist. I faced the dilemma common to many artists of how to support my practice while meeting the costs of living, and moved to Spain where life was cheaper – although I always had to subsidise my practice with additional work – mostly teaching and doing odd jobs. I wasn't selling much work, although by this point I had exhibited across Spain and Belgium. While in Spain I started organising exhibitions on an artist-led basis, sometimes promoting my own work, but always in combination with other artists, and sometimes for them alone. An artist friend pointed out that for an artist (usually necessarily more fixated on their own work than that of others) I was unusually good at engaging with and promoting the work of others, and I began to realise that I enjoyed all the other aspects of setting up these shows – finding suitable locations, arranging the hanging/presentation, being in touch with people and asking them to attend.

'I started teaching art through a visiting lectureship at Winchester School of Art, which at the time had a base in Barcelona, and in this way became involved with university teaching. Looking back, I was also always drawn to the world of public rather than private galleries. I wanted to work on artist-projects, helping artists make their own work happen, and the shows I put on were never publicly or privately financed. I have often been told that my own training as an artist is a real help here, and that I tend to look at projects from the artist's point of view rather than as an administrator or theorist.

'Through teaching art I had to engage with the other aspects of being an artist, such as how the art world works, and how to work with the commercial sector. This made me realise that there was a gap in my grasp of the commercial and technical realities of arts management – much of what I had been doing up to that point had been based on instinct.

'About this time, Arts Council England announced a pilot-project offering an administrative traineeship at Bury St Edmunds Art Gallery, with time off to do a postgraduate diploma in arts management. I got the traineeship and spent four days a week working in the gallery – and a fifth studying all the practicalities of arts management that were missing from my CV. This was a marvellous opportunity and I spent four years there, rising to be assistant director. From there I moved on to the Pumphouse Gallery in Battersea Park, which is run by the local authority but gets additional project funding from Arts Council England.

'From my first experience I had always enjoyed working within a university and when I saw the new position of director of the Stanley Picker Gallery in Kingston I was immediately attracted. University galleries tend to have a slightly different culture from other institutions and from each other. Each one is an individual model, often set up with funding from a specific bequest, thereby blending the founder's ethos with the university's wider aims: so places like the Margaret Harvey Gallery at the University of Hertfordshire, the Reg Vardy Gallery at Sunderland University and the Norwich Gallery all have a slightly different feel and ethos.

'Stanley Picker was a Kingston businessman, collector and benefactor who died in 1982 having set up a trust in his name to support young arts practitioners. The university had been running since the 1970s, allowing nascent artists, and now also designers, to make new work and when the Kingston local planning authority approved the development of a light industrial site into student housing on condition that the site included a building offering access to the public, it was a logical move to make that building a public art gallery, something Stanley Picker had longed for in his lifetime. The then Head of Fine Arts, Professor Bruce Russell, set it up, with the Stanley Picker Trust paying for the building and a long-term commitment from the university to staff, run and develop it. We now administer two fellowships a year, which usually run for about 18 months each. We put on a wide range of different shows and try to engage with the local community as much as possible – our outreach programme with local primary schools is a particularly important part of this. We have a full-time staff of two (me and my assistant Jackie) and a team of students who offer to be involved during their time at Kingston, plus others who get in touch to make themselves available. A contemporary art gallery in the heart of Kingston, the vision of Stanley Picker, is becoming an increasingly valued reality.

'Our other main representational value is as part of the university. Universities are being encouraged to reach out into the community and play their part in widening participation and I feel we fulfil an important role here. All communication to schools goes out under the name of the university. In addition to our involvement with schools, we run an art club on Saturdays and set up other events to celebrate what has been achieved and give the participants' families, friends and carers a taste of our activities. We make considerable efforts to send formal invitations to both the children and their families and when these events take place I am always impressed by the commitment shown – parents take time off work, want to try things themselves and there is a real spirit of engagement. The parents and carers go away having had an experiential visit, and one they will remember, and the young people will grow up having had the experience of taking part in art and seeing a gallery as somewhere they enjoy going – and so in turn will hopefully take their own children. All this is an important part of making our presence felt within the community and building a relationship with our audience, both actual and potential. Building a constituency for art in the future is something that takes commitment and time – but will reap long-term rewards.

'Looking back, I am in the satisfying position of loving what I do and feeling that my initial desire to help artists make their work a reality is something that is at the very core of what we do here in Kingston. The fellowships are a particular satisfaction, and watching artists grow while feeling supported by a base – both now and in the future – is a source of pride. Having started out as an artist myself, I have always felt that having a supportive base matters very much. I am delighted to have one here myself, and to see Kingston foster the careers of other artists and potential art lovers.'

Chapter 5
Collections and collections management

'Collections' is a blanket term for thinking about what an organisation holds and what it is responsible for looking after. This includes many functions, such as keeping what is held in order so that things can be found, preventing further decay through conservation, adding to it in a planned way, loaning it and receiving loans to supplement understanding, and learning more about it.

Developing a collections policy

Developing an associated collections policy means deciding what should be in the collection and what are the gaps, and looking to fill them within the budget available or by encouraging donations. It also means deciding what *not* to collect and how to dispose of items that are no longer needed. Under MLA Accreditation Standard, all museums must have an acquisition and disposal policy.

But collections management is not just about managing the items in the collection, or what you might add or decide to release, it is also about managing people, budgets, projects and so on. Helen Ward, collections manager for Kingston University Library commented:

'Collections management in libraries is very similar to that in museums and galleries. While the types of item we handle may be different, the skills required are much the same, and many of them are managerial rather than specific to the collection you are looking after. For example, it is essential that the Collections Manager can offer:

● team leadership and supervision;

- project management;
- negotiation, for example with potential donors and suppliers;
- budget management.

'Thinking about my specific responsibilities as collections manager of a large university library, I am responsible for the acquisition and maintenance of our printed books and journals, audiovisual material, archival papers, electronic books and databases. This includes accessioning new items (e.g. dealing with the paperwork involved in legal transfer of ownership), creating and maintaining location records (cataloguing) and, of course, conservation. We need to be constantly aware of our own collections policy and of the university's teaching and research profile, to ensure that we are buying material that will get used. We also need to be alert to national initiatives which may present funding opportunities for new projects. The "digital revolution" has presented all sorts of interesting challenges to us in giving access to our collections in different ways – downloading, streaming video, making digital copies of fragile material.

'This specific application to the library, with my wider managerial responsibilities, and involvement within the politics and development plans of the university as a whole, make it a far more varied and interesting role than may at first be apparent to those from outside.'

Case Study: Collections as a Career

Interview with Malcolm Chapman, Head of Collections at the Manchester Museum

'The Manchester Museum is divided into three areas: Collections Development; Access, Learning and Interpretation; and Operations.

'To deal with the last two areas first, Access, Learning and Interpretation puts on exhibitions, encourages people to come and see them and tries to widen the profile of those who do so. Operations handles all the day-to-day administrative functions that any organisation needs (although HR and some other functions are handled by the university we are part of), as well as those specifically involved in seeking to engage the general public (e.g. front of house, security and fundraising). So that leaves Collections Development.

'The collections policy of the Manchester Museum is based on three key criteria:

- Can the material be used in research (within the museum and the university)?
- Can it be used in teaching (for all ages, from schoolchildren and university students to the retired)?
- What is its role in audience development (will it broaden the range of visitors and what they get out of the experience)?

'We review our holdings according to strengths and general interest, changes in funding and the overall direction of the museum, so whereas we used to have keepers responsible for Vertebrate Zoology, Invertebrate Zoology and Entomology (insects), we now have just Zoology and Entomology. Conversely, the museum has two departments of Classical Archaeology and General Archaeology and Ethnology, and we now have three curators of Archaeology, Egyptology and Living Cultures.

'Sometimes the issues involved in collections management lead to conflicting requirements. For example, rather than having a 'handling collection' of copied, second-rate or spare items that visiting schoolchildren are allowed to touch, we now make real objects available to them. Obviously the mechanisms have had to be adapted – so, for some Greek vases, special Perspex packaging has been developed that allows the children to have really close access (without touch), but each time an item is exposed to close public view some element of physical decline is likely. It is a question of assessing and balancing the risk with the desire to get the object out and used. At other times we have to make compromises, perhaps trading a wider spread of information with reduced access to the original item. An example here is the very rare 'Manchester Moth' of which only two other examples are in existence (one in

London and one in Australia). We can't put this item of key local interest and pride on display because it is now too fragile, but we can make it accessible via video and film; in this case by filming the curator and conservator in discussion, and their conversation is now on show in the gallery and downloadable on YouTube. In this way we are able to explore issues such as provenance (how did the moth get here?), habitat (in what conditions did it survive and why?), social history (how does this tie in with trade routes and exporting patterns from the time when it was found?) and contemporary relevance (what is arriving with our bananas from distant places today, and is this affecting the indigenous wildlife?).

'Working in a regional partnership, we are also involved in a variety of representational activities to do with good practice in museums and grant-awarding. We try to award money on the basis of both need and access; so establishing what is needed for conservation, restoration and display in return for the provision of public access. A good example is the stone xylophone from Kendal Museum that we helped preserve, and which is now being taken out of the museum and played in various locations – which was of course its original function. In the process new audiences are engaged and more people come to appreciate what is held in public collections on behalf of us all.'

Acquisitions

'Deciding what to add to a collection needs similar detailed thought. Some organisations just collect everything offered, so as to supplement strengths of what is already held and fill in the weaknesses, but ultimately the availability of storage is an issue, as well as whether what you are collecting will ever get either found or used again – holding things 'in perpetuity' is a long-term and expensive option. There was a prevailing view a few years ago that a collection which does not get added to is a dead collection, but some collections cannot be added to, either through the provisions of the gift (e.g. The Wallace Collection) or because they chart the changing taste of the original collector, which is itself interesting. A more satisfying definition of a dead collection is one in which no research or public activity is taking place.

'In general, an acquisitions policy is likely to be based on the content of the proposed addition, and how it is likely to be used. It may also be based on the collections of other related organisations, particularly within a specific region, so that centres of specific expertise and ownership are built up. For example, the Manchester Museum does not collect fine or decorative arts, or social and industrial history (as these are the preserve of other local museums) and they have a self-imposed boundary of no archaeological findings after 1650.

'The acquisitions budget may be small – and a casualty when public expenditure cuts loom – but the collection can still be increased by encouraging donations, or long-term loans (which may eventually turn into donations), launching a fundraising campaign to purchase a particular item, and competing for items funded by art charities [see examples of job advertisements by Aberdeen Art Gallery and Museums in Chapter 14]. Donations are not the one-way street you might imagine, as having an item preserved and admired in future may offer the current owner both enhanced prestige and reduced worry, especially if the item in question is valuable and different family members are making a strong case for future ownership. For an artist or maker, being asked to donate an item to a local collection can be a source of pride, particularly if the item is then displayed alongside key items by better known protagonists of a specific form.

Case Study: Collection and acquisition for a botanic garden

Interview with Dr David Rae, Director of Horticulture, Royal Botanic Garden Edinburgh

'There about 2,500 botanic gardens in the world and, perhaps contrary to popular belief, they are far from being Victorian relics, with more botanic gardens being created now than in any other time in history. They each have their own history and reason for existence but most have an underlying scientific basis for their plant collections and include one or more of the following activities in their policy statements: research, education, amenity, plant display, conservation and horticulture.

'They range in size and complexity hugely with the smallest having just a small plot of land on which to cultivate plants, tended by one or two staff, while the largest have hundreds of staff and an array of facilities in addition to their gardens, including glasshouses, laboratories, herbaria, libraries, cafes, shops, galleries, exhibition halls and museums. Ownership and funding is also diverse and includes governments, municipalities, universities, foundations and societies.

'Galleries, museums and exhibition halls vary enormously too but most botanic gardens, however small, generally have at least some space to display exhibitions on environmental issues or the work of local artists. The bigger gardens have a range of facilities run by full-time professional staff. At the Royal Botanic Garden Edinburgh, for instance, there are two main spaces for exhibiting art and exhibitions plus smaller facilities at each of its three Regional Gardens. Inverleith House has a full-time curator and stages a series of world class contemporary art exhibitions plus a smaller number of outstanding exhibitions on botanic art or the garden's archives. The recently opened John Hope Gateway has two exhibition spaces: one of which is an area for a permanent exhibition on the Garden, its work and current environmental issues such as climate change; and the other a smaller area for temporary exhibitions on a variety of themes such as nature-inspired sculpture, contemporary botanic art, environmental topics or ethnobotanical themes such as chocolate, coffee or natural medicines.

'In the 19th century it was quite common for botanic gardens to have museums that displayed all sorts of information about plants, but these are less common now. Those gardens that still have museums, such as Kew, frequently use them to house exhibitions on plant uses such as dyes, fibres, poisons, food, fragrances and spices.

'Few botanic gardens are large enough to employ full-time exhibition and gallery staff and most exhibitions are mounted by education staff. The work undertaken by those that do employ full-time staff ranges from arranging, designing and mounting exhibitions to liaising with professional designers, undertaking research and actually fabricating the exhibition. Many gardens contract out design work or arrange for exhibitions designed by others to be displayed at their gardens.'

Case Study: Collections as part of a long-term career
Interview with Malcolm Chapman, Head of Collections Development at the Manchester Museum

'I was always fascinated by history as a child and was probably rather annoying in the process (or so my brothers have assured me). During guided tours around castles I would be standing at the front of the group, asking questions; I remember one such around Edinburgh Castle when by the end of the tour there was only me and the guide left, in animated conversation.

'I did a degree in history and social sciences at Exeter and was considering being either a history teacher or working more widely in education, although I had little idea of what that meant. I got the chance to test this out with some voluntary work at the National Maritime Museum in Exeter. The role was basic and unpaid – I was sweeping the boats and reorganising the library – but I got totally hooked on museums and started thinking about how best to present information and try to engage visitors in the experience.

'To earn some money (my partner was in the final year of her education degree at Exeter) I spent six months working for BT, cataloguing in their technical library. This was in the infancy of computers and database compilation, but I took to the role and found it absorbing.

'After six months we moved to London and I got a job in the British Museum, working on database management and cataloguing the collection – using the very same skills I had garnered at BT. I worked in the Mediaeval and Later Antiquities Department, and this included work on the Sutton Hoo collection. We had to catalogue all the department's record cards, publications catalogues and so on, print out and check them against the accession registers, and then check all the documentation against the actual objects to ensure they had the correct accession numbers on them. Some of the work was very long (e.g. counting rivets from the Sutton Hoo ship), but it was a revelation to find that the classification skills I had learnt at BT put me in a first-hand relationship with the objects in the museum.

'We worked in a small team of three. Six months later, the team leader left and I took over. I stayed for six years, involved in database design and management but always in the context of a museum. We worked on developing the electronic catalogues – a pale version of what is possible now (and held on much physically larger equipment) – but important in the realisation of what technology can do to make a museum's holdings more accessible. I also got involved in standardising what is held within museums, and how it is tracked and organised, both within the British Museum and in museums in general; it is important that as a publicly funded service we offer an approach that is consistent and ethical and so the public know what to expect from us. Within the British Museum there were a variety of different departments, all operating fairly independently at that time, and so ensuring a consistency of service was a prototype for the wider standardisation initiatives I have since been involved with.[1] I became the museum's training and development manager, involved

---

1   SPECTRUM is the UK and international standard for Collections Management (see www.collectionslink.org.uk/manage_information/spectrum).

with setting up systems to support the ideas we were developing. This included establishing a network of computers within the museum, moving away from standalone PCs, to make the collection as a whole more accessible to both colleagues and visitors. Along the way I learnt computer programming – I had done a basic course in Propositional Logic at Exeter, which turned out to be a very effective starting point. When you consider how important computers are now to museum holdings and the spread of information it's interesting to think how casually this began: what is now a large department of Web designers, working at the very heart of widening access, was begun with weekend voluntary support.

'I came to Manchester in 2000 as museum registrar and since then my role has expanded into head of collections development. While here, I took an MA in Museum Studies, part time over three years, and have widened my understanding. I do think being a university museum liberates us from short-term political decision-making: our main terms of reference are whether or not what we are doing creates knowledge that can be disseminated more widely; we are actively moving from exhibitions being "books on the wall" to the presentation of ideas that probe and challenge our understanding of ourselves and society in general.

'Computer access is at the heart of what I do here too – we have a long-term goal of making the entire collection accessible virtually. So far we have 250,000 records featuring 1,000,000 items – and the museum holds 4,500,000 items overall.[2] I feel this is a key part of our mission, that individuals should not only be able to access what we hold through the expert services of a curator, but also gain access independently too.

'Museums are changing. Individual collections used to be looked after by subject specialists or curators, who knew where things were,

---

2 As well as object-specific records we offer access at 'drawer level' – by species or type – so similar items in store would be on the same record, which may cover up to about 60 different objects.

owned the expertise in explaining them, and acted as gatekeepers. Today, while expertise is obviously still vital, we try to use it to engage those who visit (whether online or in person) in a wider appreciation of what they are looking at.

'For example, one of the questions we get asked most often by visitors is why we display a collection of stuffed animals – and why we were so cruel as to shoot them in the first place. But this collection can now be discussed in the context of changing social structures and habits, new technology (e.g. the invention of the camera and moving pictures), environmental sustainability and the records kept at the time. We can explain that some of our specimens were stuffed after a natural death at the local zoo, long before the camera or cheaper transportation made it possible for them to be seen in their natural habitat. Other specimens were 'commissioned' by the university from expeditions to Africa, and while it is easy to feel antipathy towards this today, in fact Lord Egerton, who shot many of them, kept meticulous records. He recorded how each animal was behaving just before it was shot, and the precise time of day, and so we have a substantial body of significant information about the patterns of a highly localised wildlife population at the time.'

Chapter 6
Conservation

Let's start by getting the name right. Some museums have their own conservation department; others rely on freelance support, either from individuals or specialist (and often family) firms. People who work in this capacity are known as *conservators*, not *conservationists* – which is the term more commonly used to refer to those working to conserve the environment, endangered species and habitats, or natural resources.

Whether or not an institution has a conservation department of its own tends to depend on its size – not just how many items are held, but also how many temporary exhibitions are put on and how many items are lent to other organisations.

So while the more common assumption is that the role of the conservator is to repair and prevent further damage, conservators play a significant part in monitoring the objects under the organisation's care and, in particular, charting how they both travel and age. It's common practice today for museums and galleries to put on special exhibitions, either from their own organisation's wider collection or to receive outside exhibitions that are touring a variety of locations; it is also relatively common to lend items. Every time a special exhibition is put on, a conservator has to make a careful assessment of the condition of each piece that is to be displayed and note any existing damage or vulnerabilities. The same is done with every exhibition the museum receives and with items that are lent. Each piece arriving comes with a report of its condition, which has to be examined in detail and disparities noted – particularly important in today's litigious culture. If an item arrives with damage that was not noted when it left its place of origin, or previous temporary home, it has to be logged and then the shipper and the previous venue have to sort out who pays. Along the same lines, it is also important that the object is monitored while it is on display or loan to ensure that display materials and conditions do not cause damage. The object should be in the same condition on its return to the lending museum.

People working in conservation tend to have a specialist qualification, usually an MA, MSc or postgraduate diploma in a relevant subject and a background in science. An understanding of chemistry is particularly important. A chemistry teacher explains why.

Why chemistry is so important

'Science, these days, usually appears on the school timetable as one subject, particularly at the lower end of the secondary school. Yet it is generally taught as a series of topics that are recognisably physics, chemistry, biology and earth science. Many schools deliver GCSE as three subjects, taught by different specialists, so it becomes appropriate to try and explain the difference between the sciences. A simplistic view might be that biology is about living things, physics is about how things work and chemistry is about materials. That is problematic as far as chemistry is concerned: 'materials' makes people think of cotton, nylon or wool. In science the word 'material' means just about anything and everything. Chemistry is about what things are made of and how they behave in different conditions – wet, hot, cold, dry, air, absence of air and so on. Chemists are concerned with trying to understand why things behave in certain ways (because they have different properties) and in using their knowledge to try and make new materials or to find alternative uses for familiar ones. A large part of the work of chemists involves analysis – trying to find out what substances are present in a mixture and how much of each one there is. All of this is relevant to the work of a conservator or to someone working with ancient objects.

'The chemistry studied at school sometimes seems far removed from real life applications. The emphasis is often on the theoretical principles that underpin the subject. However, an understanding of these principles can be hugely beneficial to the work of people in many disciplines. Learning about chemistry involves learning to think in a particular way. We can't see atoms and molecules, so much of it has to go on in your head and involves having to work with models. This is why chemistry is seen as the most important A-level when applying for courses in biochemistry, medicine and geology – and more important than more obvious subjects like biology and geology or geography: it trains students to think conceptually, which in turn has been shown to lead to success in a huge range of seemingly unconnected disciplines. For example, many chemists go on to make excellent accountants and lawyers. In many respects, chemistry provides a way of thinking about the world and as such it is learned most effectively over time. A crash course in chemistry is notoriously difficult as there is insufficient time to get used to the language and thought processes required. And it is important to have the opportunity to do the practical work that supports the theory.

'Conservation work and working with ancient artefacts involves understanding how materials deteriorate over time; understanding how they might be preserved either by active conservation treatments or more passive methods such as controlling storage conditions; being able to examine objects or analyse tiny fragments in order to determine what they are made of, how they were made and what changes have occurred as a result of their use, as opposed to those that have been caused by deterioration as a result of burial or historical storage.

'A major part of conservation is the control of storage and display conditions. For example the United States Declaration of Independence is kept in a specially designed display case and the environment around the document is maintained at a precise temperature and humidity to stop it from becoming too brittle. The case itself is filled with humidified argon, an inert gas that prevents photo-oxidation causing the writing to fade. Other objects, such as the Mary Rose Warship, may be on display while they are being conserved. In the case of the Mary Rose, this has been sprayed over a number of years with polyethylene glycol (PEG), a chemical used in a variety of cosmetics and other household substances. The PEG is used to replace the water within the cell walls of the wood and to bulk the voids in the weakened wood, thus preserving the molecular structure. This allows the warship to be dried without collapsing and distorting and thus preserving all the information about the ship from the cutting and shaping of the timber during the building of the ship to the stories it can tell of the ship's and sailors' lives and its eventual sinking.

'So, there are many practical benefits in studying chemistry beyond GCSE when it comes to working with ancient objects, but there are intellectual ones as well; the ability to think logically, to conceptualise and to understand the nature of the materials that you are working with at a molecular level.'

KRIS STUTCHBURY, SUBJECT LEADER FOR SCIENCE (OPEN UNIVERSITY, PGCE); EX HEAD OF SCIENCE AND A PASSIONATE CHEMISTRY TEACHER FOR 20 YEARS

For those for whom chemistry is less of a passion, another specialist role that is emerging within the general field of conservation is collection care and preventive conservation. A growing number of museums have collection care staff and there are specific training courses in the UK. Collection care staff look after the environment in which objects are held; they monitor heating, air conditioning and light and advise on all these for exhibitions. They also monitor pest control and carry out or commission treatments if necessary. Other duties include housekeeping, condition checking, helping with the installation of some exhibitions, contributing to policies, packing and unpacking objects to move them in and out of storage, advising on storage furniture and display materials, and carrying out training.

Within an organisation, conservators are usually based in Collections and Collections Development, alongside colleagues who handle the documentation and registration of holdings, and those providing other specialist services such as photography. As a group of professionals, conservators are careful, precise people. They have to be as they work with substances that are both noxious and flammable, but only in very small quantities and they do so with care, so accidents are very rare.

Case Studies

Interview with Kirsten Suenson-Taylor, archaeological conservator

'After taking arts A-levels I did an undergraduate degree in archaeology and worked for a cable television company before taking various part-time jobs in museums. I eventually decided that what I really wanted to do was work in conservation and so studied for chemistry A-level at night school and then embarked on a second undergraduate degree in archaeological conservation. Nowadays there are postgraduate courses, diplomas, MAs and MScs available, but in the early 1990s options were much more limited and, for me, the most convenient way to access the subject was by enrolling on a second undergraduate degree course. It might have been possible to do this without taking the chemistry A-level first, but I think it would have been much more difficult; chemistry is crucial to understanding material science – the raw materials from which objects are made, their manufacture and deterioration through use, burial or post-burial changes – and this is the basis of all conservation work.

'I emerged with my second degree, undertook various part-time options for English Heritage and some freelance work and then got a job with the Museum of London Archaeology Service as an archaeological conservator responsible for the conservation of objects recovered during excavations in London. One is less likely than one's curatorial colleagues to have spent a long time volunteering before finding a paid position as a conservator within the world of museums and galleries. However, there are not that many jobs in conservation, especially since many museums have chosen not to prioritise conservation work and may have outsourced their conservation services. Having said that, the role of conservators (or conservation) is clear and highly specialised, and for those with the right qualifications, opportunities for employment do exist.

'The precise meaning of the term 'archaeology' is interesting. There is a general assumption that it refers to the extraction and study of items that have been excavated, but the wider interpretation used by public bodies such as English Heritage is that it involves care and analysis of the material culture of civilisation, as opposed to their documentary evidence. So an above-ground monument, or item of clothing, may today be considered potential subjects of archaeology. Archaeological conservation is the preservation of this material culture.

'I worked for the Museum of London for several years and after leaving to have a family, today do freelance work. It is possible to offer a consultancy service in the maintenance and storage of materials of all kinds, and this I am able to do from home. I can advise on storage and display conditions and likely risks to preservation, and I tend to limit my role to that. Offering a full-blown conservation service for archaeological materials would be more difficult because of the specific equipment required for the job, the space required in which to use it, and the impact on those you are living with. While simple investigative conservation with a microscope and hand tools is possible to do from home, many objects would need further work with specialist equipment. For example, an air abrasive machine for ironwork operates on compressed air and requires complex dust extraction; in addition any chemicals needed for treatment must be bought under a special licence, stored according to current legislation, and exposure to them limited, for yourself and those who have access to the space. There is protective legislation to be observed (for example how long you can breathe certain chemicals for and how much exposure you should have to others) and a range of supporting paperwork. I am more likely to find myself advising on storage facilities, store moves, planned renovations and how to monitor or evaluate the condition of the objects within the stores.

'People offering a service like mine tend to promote themselves by word of mouth and via websites, in particular via the Conservation Register which can be found on the Institute of Conservation (ICON) website (see www.icon.org.uk and follow links to 'Find a conservator'). Sometimes museums and galleries offer conservation as a paid-for service to the public. Most people would not know how to locate a conservation expert and finding one through a museum or gallery is a useful way of accessing a service they know they need. Finders of archaeological materials, such as metal detectorists, may also find conservators through their local Finds Liaison Officer – these officers often have monthly workshops within museums as part of the Portable Antiquities Scheme.

'There are also specialist firms where several conservators, finds specialists and researchers group together to offer an independent conservation service to individuals, museums, local authorities, lawyers who need a professional and objective opinion and any other agency requiring their services (again, look on the ICON website for examples).

'Overall the role is intellectually fascinating, rewarding and satisfying – but tends not to remunerate on the same scale.'

Interview with Jane Thompson-Webb, Collections Services Manager, Birmingham Museum and Art Gallery

'My job title is Collections Services Manager, but a more accurate description might be Head of Conservation. My route to this role has been circuitous.

'After school I took a BSc in Archaeological Conservation at Cardiff University. For me, leaving university coincided with the 1990s' recession in the UK; museums and galleries were required to cut costs and conservation departments were often a casualty – the work is behind the scenes, often visible only by its absence, and sometimes considered non-essential (although obviously not by conservators). Many museums closed down their in-house conservation operation, relying instead on external services. Staff who left through this process often became self-employed and I found myself going down this route – becoming a self-employed objects conservator.

'Over the next few years I worked on a wide variety of projects, but always on short-term contracts, all the while remaining self-employed. For example, I worked on preserving silver at Birmingham Museum and Art Gallery and then on fossil specimens, including fossil fish and mammoth teeth and marine reptiles at Galway University and Whitby Museum. I prepared objects in the Birmingham Museum for exhibition as part of preparations for the G8 summit in 1998 (which was held in Birmingham and the accompanying cultural tours placed a strong emphasis on presenting the quality of the city's holdings to best advantage). I later worked on the transfer of objects from Birmingham's Museum of Science and Technology to the city's new Think Tank[1] (a three-month contract that grew into one of 18 months) and I subsequently became the conservator for the move of the remaining collections from the MST to the new Birmingham Museums Collection Centre. So ironically, my first permanent role within a museum, here in Birmingham, was as a head of department.

'I became a conservator because I wanted to be able to see what I had produced at the end of the day, rather than just generate paperwork. Although I now mainly do the latter, the privilege of working so closely with the past is one that never fails to delight me. The day-to-day work can sometimes be dull, as in any role, but on balance it's a great job.'

Interview with Gill Casson, Conservator at Birmingham Museum and Art Gallery

'After taking my A-levels, I wasn't sure what I wanted to do, so I went to see a careers adviser allied to what was then the Department of Health and Social Security. The woman interviewing me asked what I was good at and what I liked doing, and from the list I provided (art, history, repairing things, being practical) came up with the suggestion that I should consider a career in conservation in a gallery or museum. She mentioned a course on general conservation at Lincoln that I could take and gave me the details to look

---

1   Birmingham Science Museum: www.thinktank.ac

up. At the age of 18 this was all news to me – I had never thought that jobs like this were open to anyone or that you could train to become a conservator, but the fit seemed perfect and I started working towards this.

'I began with a degree in art history and design and an inclination to make work on paper my speciality, although watercolours, drawings and prints rather than documents. I chose a course at Leicester Polytechnic. There was a course in art history at Leicester University too, but the course I chose had a considerable practical element. There was a strong emphasis on experiencing studio-work and developing practical skills in a variety of different areas of art, from sculpture to print-making, under supervision. It was considered essential for an art historian to have a working knowledge of techniques and materials in order to understand the challenges or limitations of different media. I personally feel that the traditional study of art history does not place enough emphasis on this aspect and, as a result, can be too narrow in its interpretation. To be a good fine art conservator one needs to combine the historical knowledge of the art historian with the practical skills and creativity of the painter. Creativity and imagination are also important, as a conservator often has to devise solutions to practical problems.

'As part of my degree I took a course on the history of watercolours (1750–1850). One of my tutors had an impressive collection of his own and he encouraged me to consider specialising in the conservation of watercolours, prints and drawings. He also told me there were currently (1978) only two colleges in the UK offering training courses. Both courses were two-year diplomas in conservation. Gateshead (which now offers an MA in Conservation Studies at the University of Newcastle) took four students a year, and Camberwell School of Arts & Crafts (also now an MA) took eight students. Both were good courses, but when I was offered places at both, I chose Gateshead as it offered more individual tuition and supplied prints and drawings to work on, whereas at Camberwell you had to find your own and the costs of living in London were much higher. This was an issue, as I could only get a student grant to cover one year.

'The course covered art history; chemistry and physics; the history and technology of artists' materials and methods and, from the beginning, the course allowed you to specialise in either paintings or works on paper, and I already knew that I wanted the latter. I've always liked the fluidity and spontaneity of works on paper, which tend to be created more quickly. I am more interested in how a painting came about, and the early stages of its composition, than the final production; it can be fascinating to see the various sketches that precede the much more formal finished work.

'Although I completed the course, gaining a diploma with a distinction, in 1981 work in a museum or art gallery was hard to find and you had to be prepared to go anywhere. After four months I eventually found a part-time job at Bristol City Museum, working for the Area Museum Service for the South West. The service was funded by central government and covered a large geographical area, enabling smaller museums and galleries to have conservation work carried out – without this subsidy they would never have been able to afford it. My job was just two days a week and I took on a variety of private conservation work to supplement my income. The director of the museum understood the financial instability of my position and was very helpful in passing work my way. I worked on items from No.1, Royal Crescent in Bath[2] and other museums in the area. I also had the privilege, in this role, of working with an experienced paper conservator, which is really important when you first qualify.

'I had decided fairly early on that conservation work was what mattered to me, and that I did not want to run my own business; I wanted to do conservation work rather than have responsibility for finance or marketing. After three months at Bristol, a full-time job became available at the Area Museums Service for the North West,

---

2   www.ba th-preservation-trust.org.uk

based in Blackburn, Lancashire. Coincidentally, at the same time, I had been headhunted for a museum post in Sheffield, which was very good for my morale, and so I had a difficult choice to make.

'After three years of varied and challenging work for museums all over the North West of England, I decided I would like to experience work on a static collection, and began to look out for such an opportunity. I wanted to work within a big collection; one that raised a different range of conservation issues and problems. That opportunity came up in Birmingham, near my home town.

'Birmingham Museum and Art Gallery has a vast collection of works on paper – around 25,000 pieces in the Prints & Drawings collection alone, and over 22,000 in other museum collections. The Conservation Department here was set up about 1975, and at the time was the largest department outside London. I came here in 1985 – and have remained here ever since. The collection is the result of local benefactors consciously building a public collection in the 1880s. John Feeney, J. R. Holliday, William Cadbury and others were particularly generous donors in the 19th century. The gallery has one of the largest and most representative collection of Pre-Raphaelite drawings bought by subscription in 1903. There are many works by the major 19th century artist Edward Burne-Jones (1833–1898), who was born and grew up in Birmingham. The Burne-Jones collection offers a unique range and depth, with over 1200 works, 1138 of which are on paper. One of his largest watercolours on paper, *The Star of Bethlehem* (1888–1891), which measures approximately 8ft 5in x 12ft 8in, was commissioned in 1887 by the Corporation of Birmingham for the museum, and still hangs in the gallery where it was exhibited in 1891 after a brief debut in London. There are two chalk studies for this painting in the collection

'Given the size of Birmingham's collection, only a small percentage is actually regularly reviewed and exhibited, and contrary to what you might expect, exhibition and good condition tend to go hand in hand because the works are examined and conserved in order to be exhibited. It is not necessarily the case that the more frequently items are displayed the more they get damaged. The works we display or lend tend to be those in the best condition, and of course while on display they are very carefully monitored. The works are handled and installed by experienced technicians and if they are loaned elsewhere they are transported by specialist art shippers. For the past 30 years, light levels and environmental conditions in the museum galleries have been carefully monitored and controlled. Works on paper should only be exhibited for a maximum of three months in any twelve. Records of exhibition exposure are kept to determine when and how long a work on paper can be displayed, whether it is here in Birmingham, or on loan within the UK or abroad.

'Ideally, one of my responsibilities is to work through the collection as a whole to identify possible problems and spot damage or deterioration, but these days so much time is taken up on condition assessment, monitoring, administration and paperwork associated with the temporary exhibition programme and loans schedules, that there are parts of the collection that have not had condition assessment or conservation for some time, if at all. This is not necessarily a problem as storage conditions are very good, but it may be a missed opportunity. As there has only ever been one paper conservator directly employed here and no hope of more in the future, this is an unavoidable situation that is unlikely to change.

'What kind of problems are we looking for? Not damp and infestation, which most people imagine to be ongoing issues, as both gallery and storage conditions are very good. By far the most common problem is damage or deterioration of the work of art associated with inappropriate or old, acidic mounts, and damage to contemporary frames. Sometimes when you lift a deteriorated mount off an old watercolour you can see that the colours underneath the mount are brighter than in the image. This is the result of irreversible fading, but the damage will have arisen from excessive display before light levels in museums were carefully controlled; it will not be recent. The preservation of prints is less of an issue because the inks used tend to be stable in light, although the paper, being cellulose, can still be affected.

'The conservation materials we work with are of high quality and they stand the test of time – so work we carry out now should last for several decades. Detailed conservation treatment records are kept, noting all methods and materials, adhesives (which must be reversible), chemicals and solvents used, which will assist if the object is to be treated again in the future.

'The world in which I work – a local authority museum – is flexible. We are valued for our specific skills and I was able to change my contract to a job share, following maternity leave (although as there was no one to share with, I just switched to a half-time contract for four months) and a few years ago I changed from a five-day to a four-day week.

'Conservation work is highly satisfying and utterly engrossing. When I am working on a specific item I am in a studio with two other paper conservators (both of whom are freelance and mostly work on commissions from the public, rather than employed by the museum) and our environment is harmonious – our studio has been described by other staff as the museum's "oasis of calm". We play classical music, have the occasional conversation, but mostly get on with our own work. There are several other conservators working on different types of museum objects in our department. Sometimes a different perspective is needed on a conservation problem, and it is useful to discuss it with them as we all share basic principles. Sometimes we work as a team, condition checking loans in for a big exhibition, for example.

'Occasionally we act as couriers for works of art that are lent to other museums all over the world. My most adventurous trip was bringing back a large loan of our Pre-Raphaelite paintings and drawings which went on a five-venue tour of the US in 1994/95. I spent a week in Atlanta, condition checking the loans and supervising the packing for return home to Birmingham.

'The work requires a high degree of concentration and we learn to block out distractions – the risk is that we get so immersed in our rhythm that we forget to take regular breaks. Our work is also surprisingly physically demanding – repeated tiny movements require a great deal of muscle control and manual dexterity, and sometimes I am concentrating so hard that I almost forget to breathe! Bending over a table doing a backing removal for hours on end can result in all sorts of aches and pains. Equally, hours of sitting at a computer updating conservation records on a database is good for neither body nor soul – but something most conservators regard as a necessary evil. As a group of individuals we tend to be careful, organised, methodical and calm, although perhaps a little obsessive about keeping things tidy and clean, because damage can occur so easily. Most of us like to hang on to our own equipment simply because these are the tools of our trade and we rely on them. It's certainly correct that "a good workman looks after his/her tools". I can always tell if someone else has had access to my watercolour box, or hasn't cleaned the paint brushes properly. However, most of us are very colourful characters, if not to say wacky, with a great sense of fun – which is the flip-side of having to be so careful and controlled for most of the time. The subjects discussed by conservators at tea breaks can occasionally range from the sublime to the truly ridiculous – all in the space of half an hour.

'What are the frustrations? Too much administrative paperwork when I would like to be doing the hands-on conservation. There are also side effects. Having had so many years of quiet, contemplative, almost private access to all these wonderful works, whether in the studio, or in our galleries when closed to the public, I find it hard when I have to share exhibitions with others. If I go to an exhibition elsewhere, I tend to try to go when I know the gallery will not be crowded. And before I go in, I have to remind myself that I must simply enjoy the paintings as paintings and stop myself from peering at their physical condition, criticising the mount or the frame or musing about all the other many and varied mechanisms connected to storage and display – an almost impossible task after so many years as a paper conservator. Maybe when I retire...'

Interview with Sophia Plender, Senior Paintings Conservator and Senior Research Conservator (Tudor Project), National Portrait Gallery

'One of the really interesting things about working in conservation is that the role forms a bridge between the arts and sciences. Conservators of fine art start with a love of paintings but they must also be interested in the science behind their work. There is no one path to becoming a conservator; they come with a range of first degrees and include art historians, students of languages and literature, historians, art school graduates, chemists (who are interested in organic films and the how paint behaves) and engineers (who are interested in how canvases respond to tension when they are stretched and the effects of this on the painted surface). As a group we are, in general, artistic, meticulous, focused and like working with our hands, but our varied backgrounds make for interesting and useful discussions and debates. Opportunities to meet each other come through contact between the different institutions, inter-museum projects, clients we work for and through professional lectures and conferences.

'I have been freelance all of my working life, which includes working for Dulwich Picture Gallery during a very interesting and exciting time in the development of the gallery. For the past two and a half years I have had a part-time paid position at the National Portrait Gallery as senior research conservator in the Making Art in Tudor Britain project, which is examining the techniques and methods of the Tudor portraits. My impression is that it is getting harder all the time to secure work, and particularly hard to secure a permanent role within a museum. Most museums are being forced to make cuts, and the work of conservators is behind the scenes – effectively invisible. It takes a while before it is evident that a collection has not been looked after. Money is now focused on front of house functions such as widening participation and increasing accessibility.'

Interview with Alice Tate-Harte, easel paintings conservator

'It's hard to say where or when my interest in working as a conservator began, but I became aware of this role as a distinct profession when I was at school, which I think was quite unusual – sometimes it is only when studying art history that people realise they can specialise in conserving and restoring objects.

'At school I loved art but was also good at the sciences. I grew up close to Brighton and did my GCSE art project on the Brighton Pavilion – while there I saw an exhibition on how it was damaged by fire and subsequently restored. I did A-levels in both the sciences and art.

'When it came to doing work experience, our school left it largely to us to arrange. I wrote to a variety of museums and galleries asking if they could take me on and most wrote back saying that, at the age of 17, this was impossible (insurance and government indemnity schemes mean there are legal limits on the age of those who can be employed in public buildings, even in a voluntary capacity) but I did get a reply from Julian Spencer-Smith, a private conservator of oil paintings, with whom I did my placement. I also did some work experience at Worthing Museum, which was close to the school. I shadowed the curator for a week and also helped in the education department. The curator took me to visit the studio of a private restorer who at that time worked with very traditional methods and this was a useful comparison.

'I chose a degree in art history and material studies at UCL, which offered an introduction to technical art history, conservation and paint analysis, and I graduated in 2001. I wrote to the conservation department at Brighton Museum and The Royal Pavilion and did some work experience with the painting conservator during the university holidays. This was a really valuable experience and I continued to do volunteer work on various projects until 2007. It was very important to get first-hand practical experience to ensure that I really enjoyed it before embarking on a career in conservation. In 2003 I started a postgraduate diploma at the Courtauld Institute of Art, where you can specialise in the conservation of paintings. As this is a three-year course, finding adequate funding is a serious consideration. The AHRC (Arts and Humanities Research Council) fund some places and university bursaries are also available.

'Finding paid work after qualifying is difficult, particularly in the UK. There are few paid internships and often you have to be prepared to travel. Conservation work in the US was better funded at the time I graduated. Paid internships can be found, but there are also more courses producing qualified graduates, so competition for such places is greater. I found an internship at the Mauritshuis Royal Picture Gallery in Holland, which has an excellent painting collection funded by a European Union grant and by the host museum. As someone starting out in this world it is important to understand the various mechanisms and routes for seeking financial support, many of which are indirect. For example, EU funding is available for a variety of different roles (not just conservation) and there are a number of funding directories you can consult, which may provide monies to support a role that would otherwise have to be unpaid.

'Once you try seeking paid work yourself, you will find it is largely based on reputation and, hence, contacts, whether through individual clients or people you meet in the wider profession. As the conservation world is quite small, networking is perhaps easier but you have to be aware of the need to market yourself and the service you can provide. I now have a regular contract with English Heritage and do freelance work in Sophia Plender's studio, for Dulwich Picture Gallery and other museums and private clients

'I was warned when I first began that, compared with the length and depth of my training, work would be both hard to find and never likely to remunerate in line with either the extent of my qualifications or my developing expertise. This has proved to be the case and it's important to have realistic expectations. However my job is enormously rewarding. I love doing practical work and get great satisfaction from finishing a treatment. I really enjoy the technical research aspect of conservation and seeing beautiful objects so closely is always a real privilege. I also enjoy working with museum and conservation professionals and am very glad I chose this profession.'

General aptitudes that suit conservation work

- Good manual dexterity skills are essential and generally you need to be a practical person. Remember that conservation is not just the glamorous side of retouching but also involves things like framing, so woodwork skills are also required.
- Patience and dedication – I once spent three days scraping glue off the back of a lining canvas.
- Being careful and mindful of the objects around you.
- Resourcefulness and good problem-solving skills – if you are working on site you may not have the exact tools or materials you need and so have to be inventive.

The pros and cons of working this world

Disadvantages

- As with many arts fields, the job market is highly competitive.
- In comparison with other professionals, and in particular considering the amount of training required, the work is not highly paid. The private sector may be better paid than museum jobs, but will probably offer less job security.
- There are practical health and safety considerations to be borne in mind – working with solvents means constant carefulness.

Advantages

- The work is really interesting and enjoyable: you get to work on unique and beautiful objects and to study them in depth. A very privileged role.
- The work is very satisfying as you get to see a project through to completion. You can transform a painting that has been neglected for years into something people engage with again.

- You get to make new exciting discoveries. For example, during cleaning you might uncover a landscape which has been over-painted for years. Similarly an X-ray might reveal another painting underneath or infrared light might show you an under-drawing which has not been seen before.
- Each painting presents a different conservation problem, so you are constantly challenged.
- The role is very hands on – you are not usually sitting behind a computer all day.
- The profession is international – there are opportunities to transfer skills and work abroad.
- The profession is relatively young and has been developing into a more rigorous, scientifically led profession since the 1930s. This is a dynamic field, with changes in techniques and ethics.
- You become part of a close-knit professional community.

One top tip before you go any further:

Think early about type of objects you are interested in caring for, as most training courses focus on one type of object such as easel paintings, paper, sculpture, textiles, wall paintings or buildings conservation.'

Chapter 7
The funding of museums and galleries

All museums and galleries need financial support – private institutions depend on this to fund their very existence, and state-supported institutions require extra funds to bridge the gap between what is given to them by (central or local) government and their running costs. In both cases, financial support is necessary to fund new initiatives that can't be afforded out of their general maintenance budgets.

'...institutions such as the National Gallery and Tate, which until 10 years ago had 100 per cent state funding, now have only 60 per cent. Not only is the state in rapid retreat but the part played by the National Lottery, that decade-long bonanza for the arts, is also in decline, partly because of the diversion of funds to the 2012 Olympics but also because the nation's lotto-craze has abated.

'It is a sea-change in our way of thinking. Arts, wider cultural institutions, even universities – all now have to raise enormous sums to keep themselves afloat and functioning at their peak. They all have to fish in the same river of money, much of it new money, flowing through the UK's financial and business sectors.'

JAN DALLEY, WRITING IN THE *FINANCIAL TIMES* IN 2007

Few people planning a career in museums and galleries see involvement in fundraising as their long-term goal, but for a candidate with either the right set of attributes, or the potential to develop them, it can be a highly satisfying career.

Over the past 20 years, what is now generally referred to as the 'Development Department' has emerged in its own right and, during that time, it has gradually sloughed off the sense that asking for money is a tacky thing to do. Development staff are increasingly not only relied upon to raise core income, but also trusted to represent the organisation and its significance to the wider world, and their success becomes a source of pride and validation to all involved. But while there has never been a greater need for their role, there remains a dearth of real talent in this area:

> 'Since the US has a respectable culture of giving, it also has a culture of asking: something almost unknown to the awkward Brits, who are often embarrassed to talk about money. The professionalising of asking and thanking, and the skilled cultivation of donors (start 'em young; keep 'em keen) are tricky concepts here: it is no coincidence that many top fundraisers are American.'
>
> (IBID)

Development can be an attractive career option for anyone keen to play a central role in the future of museums and galleries.

What kind of support are museums and galleries seeking?

In the UK, state-owned galleries and museums currently have no entrance fee, but most (although not all) charge for entry to special and temporary exhibitions that are put on in addition to the permanent collection. Private museums may charge for entry, with a range of price brackets and concessions according to the economic status of the individual. But in most institutions you will find a box somewhere near the exit for (additional) contributions, and a message that makes a link between the experience you have hopefully just enjoyed and what it costs to keep the institution open. Not all visitors contribute and this income cannot be relied upon, so most institutions encourage their supporters to donate in a planned and sustained way, enabling them to reap maximum financial advantage.

Regular income

At the top end of the scale are sustained sponsorship schemes to support significant organisations – for instance (at the time of writing) BT sponsors Tate Online and Credit Suisse sponsors the National Gallery. It can be an important endorsement for an organisation or individual to show themselves to be both deserving of, and able to manage, sponsorship support. There is the opportunity to swap and value each other's name and/or branding, perhaps in a lasting format if a gallery or wing is named after a sponsor.

Membership schemes (often called 'Friends') ask individual patrons to commit to regular contributions for a specific period of time and, in return, they offer benefits and privileges, structured wherever possible to enable the organisation to claim gift aid from HMRC,[1] which hopefully assists both parties. Such membership schemes encourage those who participate to subscribe via bank direct debit – because individuals are much less likely to cancel a direct debit than remember to send in their yearly subscription – and in the process to see the donation as a regular, routine expenditure rather than something that requires additional consideration. There are also legacy departments that encourage people to consider remembering an organisation they favour by way of a bequest in their will.

Corporate membership schemes allow companies to donate to museums and galleries (and other charitable foundations) and again get tax benefits as well as a range of other perks such as passes for their employees, access to corporate hospitality spaces either free or at a discount.

---

1   HM Revenue & Customs.

Capital projects

Most museum directors see it as a key part of their role to lead an organisation forward, with schemes of development, renewal, renovation and perhaps extension and new building. These tend to be expensive and so need special funding. Some money may be accessible from the government, maybe via the Arts Council or the Heritage Lottery Fund, but some will almost certainly need to be raised by the organisation itself. The funding of the Sainsbury Centre for Visual Arts at the University of East Anglia and the extension (the Sainsbury Wing) to the National Gallery in London are good examples of this.

Other sources of funding

Galleries and museums are increasingly trying to entice those who visit, or who just appreciate an institution, to get more involved. Most organisations have their own shop on site and, rather than just selling postcards and copies of the items in the collection, many of these shops are now attractively designed boutiques that can become destinations in their own right. Some of the larger organisations may have several shops, perhaps one for children, a second for more general merchandise, a third selling jewellery, specialised clothing and other high-ticket items, and perhaps a bookshop too.

As well as shops, there is a variety of different establishments available for refreshment, from high-ticket restaurants to cafés and coffee shops and, for many, these venues become a 'third space' (after home and work) where individuals choose to spend leisure time or meet friends, associating themselves with the institution and the cultural capital it represents in the process, without needing to visit the collection each time. Many galleries and museums have taken out licences to organise events and hospitality and even private functions such as marriages and civil partnerships.

Other sources of income can come from developing aspects of the collection, through an in-house publishing company that produces both exhibition catalogues and a range of associated titles, some co-published with third parties who appreciate the brand. Similarly, image licensing can be profitable – this is where the right is given to include an image from a specific collection within a product produced by a third party, and the product may be anything from a television programme to a t-shirt. The trading profits from all these enterprises, which are sometimes housed within a separate company for tax reasons, come back to support the host organisation.

Case Study: Licensing in museums

Interview with Brenda Conway, Image & Brand Licensing Executive, NMSI Trading Ltd

'It is mostly only the larger museums (or groups of museums) that have their own licensing department, but where these do exist they can provide a substantial income to the organisation. Broadly speaking, their job is to market the intellectual property of the organisation, to create an income stream out of the information housed within the museum, whether this is held within objects or staff. This may mean working with third parties to create a range of merchandise that the public wants to buy, perhaps toys and gadgets, or items specific to a particular location, such as railway-related items that are produced to link with the collection in the National Railway Museum in York. Or it may mean approaching a potential supplier and asking if they can produce something on behalf of the museum, for which we have spotted a potential market.

'Most of the merchandise is sold either through our retail outlets or high street stores, and it also often sells well through "off the page" advertisements in the Sunday supplements, where the Science Museum branding can serve to reassure the customer buying at a distance of the quality of the merchandise on offer. A typical item would be a chemistry set sold through retailers, with particularly high levels of sale at Christmas. Whereas there are other sets on the market, the one licensed by us would contain information from the relevant curators within the museum on the science behind the experiments and have an added educational value; thus everyone buying it would be confident they had a superior product within its specific market, and something they could give as a present with confidence. Sometimes we arrange for merchandise to be created that will not be sold, but rather used as an incentive available only with the buying of a membership package, or as a special offer to those who have already taken one out.

'All this activity has grown since museums stopped charging for entry and were forced to look for a range of other opportunities for funding. Each year we display at the Brand Licensing Show and are active members of LIMA[2] (which has its head office in the US but also an office in the UK – see Appendix for contact details). We are a separate trading company offering licensing and also an image bank and we make a significant contribution to the museum's funding.

'As a career option, most staff working in this area come from an arts licensing, product development or a legal background. It is a sharper atmosphere than other aspects of museum work, with a huge scope for development. For the individual who finds this work interesting, and wants to be part of this development, such a role offers a lot of potential.'

Why would people give money to museums and galleries?

'The world is not ungenerous, but unimaginative and very busy.'

EGLANTYNE JEBB, FOUNDER OF THE SAVE THE CHILDREN FUND[3]

Three key points to bear in mind:

- people may not give unless first asked – or if they do give, probably never at the level they are capable of after research, cultivation and a well-managed 'ask';

---

2 International Licensing Industry Merchandisers' Association (see appendix)

3 Mulley, Claire. *The Woman Who Saved the Children: A Biography of Eglantyne Jebb.* Oxford: One World Publishers, 2009.

- in general, people do not mind being asked for money as much as many people fear and many are pleased (and often flattered) to be asked;
- asking for too little is a common mistake: you cannot insult by assuming that the potential donor you approach is either more generous or more wealthy than they really are.

People decide to support a charity for a variety of reasons. In *The Seven Faces of Philanthropy: A New Approach to Cultivating Major Donors[4]*, Russ Alan Prince and Karen Maru File describe a variety of different kinds of donor and accompanying motivations, from those who give from a sense of dynastic obligation ('my parents and grandparents supported this institution, so it behoves me to do the same'), through the altruistic (wanting to give to the community) to those who rely on business models that make financial sense (it is tax efficient and helps me promote my business or organisation). Different individuals and groups require different messages, and the key skill in securing money is often in spotting (or rather listening out for) what it is that the donor gets from association with a particular museum or gallery.

It is also important to pay attention to the criteria that will influence a decision. Most buying decisions are based on both rational and emotional grounds, and most of us assume we are rational at all times. In effect, emotional factors are hugely important although, having felt their impact, we may then justify our decisions under the 'rational' heading. The effective message of asking for support communicates both emotional and rational messages, which are mutually reinforcing.

Rational reasons for supporting an appeal from a museum or gallery:

- an effective use of resources;
- makes good use of financial planning, especially in connection with tax and inheritance liabilities;

---

4 Published by Jossey-Bass, John Wiley and Sons Inc., 2001.

- prominent display of the name and logo and hence wider visibility of the organisation/individual;
- public support for an organisation that is doing an effective or important job, and hence the resulting halo effect includes you/ your organisation;
- networking with significant others likely to be useful in future, both within the organisation asking for the money and other patrons you may meet in the process;
- a springboard for changes you want to implement too, e.g. showing that you are an organisation that values culture or building a culture of optimism and hope by being associated with a project that attracts enthusiasm and reveals dynamism.

Emotional reasons for supporting an appeal:
- a deep sense of satisfaction;
- an awareness of doing the right thing;
- learning more about something that is intrinsically interesting;
- appreciating the opportunity to meet interesting people who have chosen to do the same thing;
- being valued and validated through the process of involvement;
- belonging to a community;
- making a difference.

Explaining the proposition

Development staff need to present a message asking for support that potential donors respond to. Different people will respond to different messages, so while one potential organisational donor may be looking for a chance to project their company's name, another may be looking for the opportunity to make their brand seem more 'family friendly' and thus see a link with a cultural and educational institution as a mechanism for achieving this.

Individuals may have similar aims, whether subconscious or conscious. Some may like to use the restaurant, and appreciate that by eating there they support an organisation they are proud to be associated with; others may relate to a particular aspect of the collection, having been taken to see it as a child, or perhaps because it displays something from the area where their ancestors originated.

Marketing materials need to be written with such core messages in mind and at the same time convey an effective description of the project, the values it encapsulates and the careful husbandry of resources (materials should be tastefully but never over-expensively produced – this would imply the draining off of funds that could have gone to the core project).

In return, the organisation will offer its supporters something back, such as free entry for members to special exhibitions, or a newsletter for Friends that reinforces a sense of pride every time they step through the doors. Most organisations are particularly keen on family memberships that develop and extend the sense of belonging into the next generation, a habit of association that children grow up with and so see as part of what they do (and hence pass on the habit to the next generation).

Case Study: How does it feel from the donor's point of view?

Mary and Tom are sponsors of a major cultural venue and have been so for six years. Tom made a personal pledge to give 10 per cent of his income to charity a number of years ago and he and his wife support a wide range of charities.

They were approached about sponsorship by an organisation they now support, having progressed through various different types of privileged membership, and were not offended to be asked. Indeed Tom, a management consultant, appreciated the organisation getting straight to the point about what it wanted. The projects it asks them to sponsor tend to be specific, and targeted to their interests, which they feel it has taken the trouble to understand.

Tom says: 'In general it's a positive experience; we all feel at home when we enter the now familiar portals and it's rare that there is not someone we run into from the management team that we don't know. This feels pleasant. We have appreciated getting to know more about the organisation and in particular getting our two teenagers involved; it's somewhere we enjoy going as a family.'

As for little niggles, I eventually extracted the following from Tom:

- 'The development people have no idea how my world works and how far ahead I am committed. My diary is full 8–10 weeks ahead, and so when they ring to ask me to something the following week I always have to say no.' After this happened a couple of times, perhaps the development people should have got the message that a lot of notice is needed for Tom to attend, and to match their invitations accordingly.

- Development people obviously vary, but I have come across many who are not particularly good listeners, or who take insufficient trouble to empathise or intellectually engage with the sponsors they are looking after. Tom commented: 'Sometimes this results in the development people trying to control the sponsors too much; for example only allowing you to visit when they can personally host and insisting that all relationships inside the building are controlled and monitored by them. Sponsorship is often quite formal in that certain levels of sponsor achieve corresponding privileges – but the moment anyone tries to put me in a box, I try just as hard to get out of it.'

- Events which link the sponsors together purely because they are sponsors tend not to be particularly enjoyable. Mary commented: 'Just because you all give to the same organisation does not necessarily mean you are going to have lots in common and want to spend time with each other. On one particular evening I got rather irritated by the assumptive nature of the conversation, which was prompted by a political event that day. I was irritated by the presumption that because you had enough money to sponsor, you automatically voted Conservative. We have not been regular attendees of such events.'

How to identify potential patrons, individuals and organisations

There is no substitute for networking and being well connected. You may spot an organisation that could offer support, but it will be key individuals within it who are the means of accessing the funds, so knowing who's who is very helpful. And, once you have identified the key people, it's important to develop a personal relationship with both them and the people who influence them – often their spouses. You need to know not just names but also inclinations, key values and current giving patterns.

You might invite key individuals to the institution to meet members of staff, for a meal, a chance to see something that may specifically interest them, or to a launch event. The impact of 'intellectual hospitality' can be substantial – you don't just give them a glass of wine and a canapé, you give them interest, knowledge, the company of passionate experts and in doing so spark their curiosity and support, These are things they can't easily buy. And once they are inside the building you might try to get them further involved in what is planned, perhaps in an organisational capacity, say as a campaign chairman or committee member, in the hope that they may then recruit their contacts to join too. You are in part aiming to persuade potential supporters from an initial stance of 'How are *you* going to raise the money?' to one of 'How are *we* going to raise the money?' which means they have identified with the cause and now see it as partly theirs.

There is also a range of trust funds and charitable organisations that give away money, but can do so only under criteria that link their foundation with the project seeking funding. The skill here is to make the bridge; to establish the basis on which the foundation was set up and make the case for their supporting your specific project.[5]

---

5 This is a skill you may have developed to secure a university place or apply for a bursary to study or travel; lots of students have had to brush up on their connections to a particular part of the country in order to add emphasis to their application for support, whether for a place or funding.

Qualities needed by people interested in working in development

- A wholehearted commitment to the values of the organisation you represent and an eagerness to explain its relevance to the wider world. You cannot do this job without agreeing to this basic principle.
- Confidence, to establish that you have the right to ask for support and that the project you stand for merits that support.
- Bravery. Asking for money is not an easy thing to do. It takes guts to spot the appropriate amount and push for it. This can only be done effectively if you feel you have a right to ask, and the confidence to do so effectively.
- Excellent interpersonal skills and, in particular, to be a good listener; to make the case for what you are explaining and at the same time watch out for both potential interest in the donor and the factors that appeal to them most. The particular donor's interests or career choices can make a really good starting point for developing a relationship with them.
- A good memory – for names, faces and accompanying details.[6]
- Creativity – in preparing a proposal that the market identifies with and wants to support.
- Determination, to keep going and not be put off by setbacks, or take them personally.
- Calmness in handling negotiations.
- Diplomacy and persuasiveness.
- A team player; what you achieve will be through teamwork and it helps if you get personal gratification from this group goal rather than wanting your individual contribution to be recognised.
- Appropriate levels of self-presentation. Your style of dress and personal grooming should fit with your organisational brand.
- An ability to negotiate.

---

6 Think of the scene in *The Devil Wears Prada* where the magazine runs its annual party – and how the editor's representatives prepare for it by learning faces and names.

- Patience. Some donations take a very long time.
- On occasion, silence. Knowing when to stop talking is a huge asset.

Case Studies

Interview with Sandy Richardson, Head of Development for National Museums Scotland

'I took a degree in English literature at Aberdeen and my first job was in publishing, firstly for William Collins in Glasgow and later for HarperCollins in the sales and marketing of their titles. I subsequently took an MBA at Edinburgh and moved into Alumni Relations and fundraising for Heriot-Watt University (also in Edinburgh). This was in the early 1990s when development work was in its infancy; universities were waking up to the fact that they had large numbers of former students who wished them well and might help to sustain the organisation in future. I moved across to work for National Museums Scotland in 2004 and have been involved in development work here ever since.

'For me the best part of the job is the group of highly committed colleagues I work with; they are extremely knowledgeable, passionate, and fascinating. The development team consists of nine, but we have the staff of the entire museum as our wider team – and often it is the involvement of a specific curator or expert that makes all the difference between a prospective donor deciding to get involved or not. We are facilitators – people don't want to give money specifically to the Development Department, but they understand that we often make the discussions happen that enable them to connect philanthropically with the institution, its aims and values and its amazing collections. And when we are successful, it is important to ensure that everyone involved receives credit and that the institution as a whole sees how much we are valued by the community at large, which is motivating for us all.

'Our approach is long term and sustained: finding out about those who might like to support what we are doing; building relationships and maintaining contact. For each capital project that is considered, our involvement is from the earliest stages: in weighing up whether what is proposed can generate the required level of support; drafting materials to explain the proposal; perhaps commissioning consultants to take soundings from key potential supporters on what we have in mind and – if the project is approved – working with colleagues in all departments to see these goals realised. Having established our overall financial targets, we break them down into highly specific targets; trying to establish the interests of individual 'prospects' (i.e. individuals, trusts or companies who could give money), what they might seek from involvement (for example, the promotion of their name, the opportunity to find out more about our collection and learn from it or a benefit to society that relates to their own values and ethics) and then work directly with them or through others who know them well (such as trustees or members of a campaign board) to build the connection.

'We have a strong offering to make. We are, after all, *the* national museum. Among other things, our collections express the impact that Scotland made on the world. They show the role of Scottish pioneers, explorers, endeavour and the value we have always placed on education. This is one powerful message we can use to approach Scots, both here and those who have settled elsewhere.'

Interview with Ruth Gimlette, membership volunteer at the V&A

'I have been working at the Victoria and Albert Museum for 15 years, for the last 11 with Gwenda Constant, and before that with someone else. We form a regular partnership, every second Wednesday afternoon running the membership desk in the corner of the main entrance hall. The gallery is open to the public for free, but special exhibitions have to be paid for and our job is to encourage people to sign up for membership, which allows them instant access rather than having to pay and queue for tickets each time. Members get a range of other benefits such as discounts in the shop and restaurants, and of course also save time – they can just show their membership card at the entrance to the special exhibition – plus they have the satisfaction of helping to support something they believe in. When the queue for exhibition tickets is particularly long, the museum staff like us to walk up and down, reminding those who are waiting that if they had a membership ticket they could just walk straight in.

'Our unofficial function is to be the face of the organisation – we are reminded that ours are the first faces many people see. We sit in the corner of the impressive entrance hall and we do have a dress code (black and white). We also function as an enquiry desk, telling people where the nearest bathrooms are, the shop, the restaurants and specific exhibits. Having worked in the museum for so long, we know it very well and it pleases me to be able to direct people.

'I do like working here. Gwenda and I were already members ourselves, but we had to make a formal application and quote references, and of course being accepted was pleasing. We receive training, a regular printed newsletter telling us things we need to know and may be interested in, and at Christmas there is a special party at which the museum's director thanks us for our valuable contribution. We also have the opportunity to act as front of house staff for events organised for members, and if you turn up and help tick off names and do other administrative tasks, you can then stay and enjoy the rest of the day. There are many memorable occasions here – one of the best was when Kaffe Fassett decorated a huge Christmas tree in the entrance hall. He gave a demonstration of how to make the fans with which he was planning to decorate it, and I eventually had four on display. I was quite proud of that! My family are glad to see me busy – and I think working here means friends and relatives assume I am brighter than I am! I love to bring my grandchildren and show them around the collection.

'You also meet interesting people. It's fun to watch the arrivals and speculate about who are the fashion students and who are the visitors, and from which country. You can also spot famous people on their way in and out – last week I spotted Terence Stamp.'

What else can be given?

In addition to the development team seeking money, others within a gallery or museum may have a long-term eye on specific items that might enhance the overall collection, perhaps by filling gaps in what is on view, or just belongs to the public. Most large such organisations will have a legacy department, which considers material (both objects and archives) that the owners may want to pass on to the nation, sometimes to perpetuate a name or perhaps to assuage the impact of death duties.

For the family of an artist it can be appealing to have significant pieces become part of a national collection – and hence ensure that its reputation and significance is safeguarded. Several gallery and museum directors are known as being terrific sweet-talkers; able to explain the benefits of leaving your treasures to be enjoyed by all rather than just the few, and the well-publicised proclamations of the wealthy who determine to leave their children nothing because it cannot be helpful to them to inherit wealth[7] have further garlanded this path.

Some regional galleries with much smaller budgets for acquisitions will ask local artists and craftspeople to donate items for the collection, and if these are to be displayed beside fine examples of their particular art form, it is often pleasing to be asked. But the general feeling in the art world is that living artists should be paid.

Case Study

Interview with Cortina Butler, daughter of sculptor Reg Butler (1913–1981)

'My father won an international competition in 1953 for a monument to The Unknown Political Prisoner. It was due to be put up in Berlin, before the wall went up, but in the end proved too politically charged and was never made. The original model he made for the competition was vandalised, but he later remade it and in 1955 produced a working model of the sculpture, which is about seven

---

7   E.g. Dame Anita Roddick, founder of The Body Shop.

feet high. My father knew that Tate would like to own this as they have a collection of maquettes of the competition finalists. He eventually gave it to them in 1979 in my name and that of my brother. The model is rather large and frequently required for exhibitions, so making the donation solved certain practical problems as well as adding to a national collection. Now the original model is also on display, but as a permanent loan rather than a gift. Both were featured in a major respective of his work in Tate in 1983/4.

I am aware too that the legacy department are in touch with my mother, and would probably like to have his archive some day.'

Chapter 8
Commercial opportunities in museums and galleries

By Jo Prosser, Managing Director, V&A Enterprises

Over the past decade, one area of museum activity that has developed hugely is the field of commercial operations. Once seen as a poor relation of 'real' museum work, the importance of trading to a museum's profile is now increasingly recognised. A well-run business will generate both revenue and kudos for the institution; done poorly, it will taint the whole visitor experience. In short, it matters – and it's this sense of making a difference that's attracting many people to the sector.

Show me the money – museum trading

Whatever type of museum you choose to work in, money (or a shortage of it) is a dominating factor. Within the UK, many museums are regionally or nationally funded, while others are supported by trusts, individuals, businesses, or charities. Others are entirely self-supporting. Whatever the primary source of money, it's universally true that there's never enough to cover all the ambitions a museum wants to fulfil.

The result is that 'self-generated income' has become a vital source of additional revenue. This 'extra' money tends to derive from three main sources: charging (e.g. for temporary exhibitions and displays), fundraising (e.g. corporate sponsorship, private donations, membership) and trading.

Each of these activities is a specialisation in itself: in the world outside museums, each would of course be an industry all of its own.

The increasing sophistication with which museums have developed these fields has provided new ways into employment within the museum and gallery sector and widened the choice of job options it offers.

In large institutions, the result is high-profile, specialist divisions and departments, and highly focused job specifications which offer a variety of career options. It's easy enough to envisage the departments within Trading, for example: publishing, retail, catering, maybe licensing. Less well recognised are the specialisations within each of them: international rights management, say, or visual merchandising, or warehouse quality control. In a big place, each is a job in itself.

In a small museum, the opposite is true. The need for all these skills to be embodied in a single individual makes for a very different job indeed. Far from being specialist work, the trading activities of the museum will be looked after by a multi-tasking front of house manager, whose job it is to co-ordinate these with the wider visitor experience.

In terms of a choosing a career, it's a distinction worth thinking about. On the one hand, larger museums provide the opportunity to apply skills and experience gained outside the museum sector, and to use them in an inspiring and non-corporate environment. This is the motivation for many. On the other hand, a smaller museum gives you the chance to work laterally across the board, to be involved in a wide range of projects and to make the links between them. This variety is enjoyable too. As a result, the world of museum trading is a good mixture of specialists and generalists.

The customer is king

Money, and the need to make it, is not the only reason that museum trading activities have risen so rapidly in profile over the past few years. Tempting cafés, professionally produced guidebooks and appealing shops are now recognised as critically important elements of the visitor experience. Museum visitors are highly sophisticated consumers: consciously or otherwise, they rate their visit (and, by extension, the institution) not only on the merit of the exhibits, but on how well they were looked after. Many visitors have high generic expectations of museums; they will have enjoyed and remembered experiences elsewhere and are quick to make comparisons.

There is no longer any excuse for second-rate museum trading – if indeed there ever was. The increase in attractions and activities competing for people's time, the focus on customer satisfaction, the quality of the competition – all these mean that visitors expect trading standards every bit as high as they would find elsewhere. Museum trading has undergone something of a revolution in this respect: its restaurants (National Portrait Gallery, Tate Modern, Pompidou) and its shops (MoMA, V&A) are now often included in the top ratings lists. Many shops within regional galleries and museums are becoming destinations in their own right, providing a showcase for original, innovative and often local work that the high street has lost. Museum bookshops are cited ruefully as the only specialist bookshops left.

Museum trading has an important part to play in the growing trend for alternative ways to combine learning, enjoying and shopping. All of this makes for an emerging and exciting environment in which to work.

The structure of commercial activity

In the UK, many larger museums manage their trading activities through a separate company. If you choose to approach the trading operation of one of the big nationals, for example, you will find yourself directed to a limited 'Enterprises' company, which works on behalf of the parent institution to maximise trading revenues. The company then returns 100 per cent of its trading profits back to the museum at the end of each year.

Although the name of the company might make it sound like a separate business, the reality is that an 'Enterprises' operation works very closely indeed with the museum it supports. As a charity, the museum itself is not able to trade as a business but at the same time, it obviously wishes to maximise the benefit of the trading it attracts. The answer is to set up a trading company which can then covenant its profits back to the museum as Gift-in-Aid.

Establishing a separate trading company has other advantages too, which is why many museums choose this model. The company's primary aim is to deliver the museum a financial profit, and this clarity of purpose is a helpful way of making sure that business activities are run unambiguously. A museum has many parallel objectives, central overheads and cross-charges between departments: it is far easier to track the financial reality of trading if income and costs are managed independently. The constitution of each trading company varies, but it is customary for the director of the museum and representatives of the trustees to sit on the trading company's board. External board members are chosen for their commercial experience, in whatever fields the trading company may operate. This combination of external objectivity and internal understanding is an important feature of such boards.

Enterprise, museum style

By definition, a museum's trading operation will incorporate a number of smaller businesses; it is the nature of a museum to be involved in a wide range of activities and its trading reflects that. Whether those activities are managed by one person, or by hundreds, depends on the size of the institution.

Whatever the activity, what matters most is that it's done in the spirit of the museum or gallery it's there to reflect; that it fits with 'the brand' – the DNA of the place. The best enterprises work closely with their parent institution, articulating each and every commercial opportunity.

Publishing

Publishing is probably the longest established of a museum's enterprises. Whether as a simple printed sheet or a sumptuous 500-page catalogue, the concept of this type of publishing is well understood: museum publications can include anything and everything, from gallery guides to technical journals, children's books to major exhibition catalogues.

Researching collections and exhibitions is a central part of a curator's role, and this research forms the core of a museum's publishing output. Producing books is a specialist and potentially costly business, and so the job of the publisher is to identify the best possible format for a particular project, exhibition or display, and to work closely with the author to deliver this. The publishing team for a larger institution will cover all the functions that go into making a book: commissioning, editorial, production, sales and marketing. All are specialised roles, and more senior positions tend to be recruited from the wider publishing industry; experience of illustrated books is important for positions in editorial and production, for example.

At a more junior level, however, museum publishing offers plenty of opportunities to learn on the job. Illustrated books are labour intensive and complex to produce, and so publishing departments are often able to offer temporary positions relating to a specific project, helping with picture research or seeking permissions to reproduce content. These roles are occasionally paid positions, though often not – but an internship of this sort is a great introduction to the work of a museum.

A publishing job in this field is highly rewarding; working with interesting people you play an important part in delivering a lasting, visible manifestation of what the museum is all about. You are responsible for co-ordinating the input of a wide cast of contributors, from authors to designers and photographers to printers. Each project brings a new subject and a new approach. You will work with an exceptionally wide range of colleagues across the museum; as well as authors, you could be liaising with marketing, press, the shop, the photography studio, and more. Many museum publishers are deeply interested in the arts themselves: this is a vocational role.

As for the challenges, many come with the territory of complex project management. You will be reconciling conflicting objectives, managing egos, protecting sensitivities, challenging assumptions, running demanding schedules, and juggling several projects simultaneously. But if you mind passionately about what the museum is there to do, have a great eye for detail and people skills aplenty, then publishing may well be the job for you.

Retail

For many visitors, a trip to the shop is now an essential part of the visit to a museum or gallery. Whether it's a few postcards on a desk at the entrance or a huge emporium full of glossy art books and sparkling reproductions, any self-respecting visitor attraction is expected to provide some sort of retail offer. The aim, of course, is to create revenue for the museum while at the same time adding to the overall visitor experience.

Over the past 10 years, museums have recognised this and worked hard to respond. The difficulty was that it turned out to be a lot harder than it looked. For smaller museums, with limited resources, responsibility for running the shop was often devolved to general front of house staff or volunteers. Staff originally hired to work in the shop itself were expected to take on the buying, the stock control and the cash flow. In contrast, some larger institutions went completely the other way, recruiting high street retailers and consultants with little understanding of the context or shopping behaviours in which they were being asked to work. Neither solution really worked.

Of course, there were exceptions, and the best museum shops (as typified for many years by the Metropolitan Museum in New York) have always shown that it doesn't need to be like this. More recently, museum retailing has grown significantly in profile and reputation, combining more professional retail practices with an increased understanding of its distinct market. In the UK, training provided by organisations such as ACE (Association for Cultural Enterprises) and Heritage 365 have done much to improve disciplines and professional understanding – although this training is only open to those already working in the industry.

Different museums run their trading in different ways, but there are broadly three disciplines involved: Buying and Product Development, Merchandising, and Operations. A big institution will have departments for each, while in a smaller gallery, a single person may have to take on the whole process.

Buying and product development are popular areas to work in. To the uninitiated, the work sounds delightful: buyers and product developers spend time sourcing merchandise to sell in the shop and/ or searching the collections for inspiration. The reality is rather more complex. To buy professionally, your selection will be guided by detailed sales analysis and merchandising data. Much of your time will be spent negotiating the details of price, packaging, labelling and shipping. You will spend a lot of time saying no, and having to turn down hopeful designers and suppliers. You will be juggling your ambitions for the brand with the relentless need to drive sales and profit.

There is no formal training available as such, and those positions that do arise are frustratingly few and far between; successful candidates tend to be interns from elsewhere in the museum or enterprise company. There is not much overlap with the wider retail industry, where salary levels tend to be rather higher, career development more structured and buying specialisations more focused. This may change soon with the increase in niche retailing.

Merchandising is the function by which sales are planned and phased and stock is bought. As a merchandiser, you will be involved in forecasting how much is going to sell, of what, where, and when. Merchandisers work with buyers and suppliers to ensure that the right stock is being bought in the right quantities; their expertise is essential in terms of financial planning. The disciplines of merchandising need to be learnt, and recruitment to specialist positions comes directly from the retail industry, although more junior positions can learn on the job.

The third retail function is **Operations**. Also called Trading, or Selling, or simply Shop Floor, this is the front line: the shop as it is experienced by the museum visitor. Traditionally, many people working in museum trading started their careers on the shop floor, working as sales assistants before moving into office-based roles. This isn't as common as it once was: it's increasingly recognised that the skills needed to work on the sales floor are as specialist as any other, and retail managers are unlikely to employ people simply looking for a springboard into other positions – these CVs are the first to be turned down.

The reality is that working in a museum shop is a career choice in itself and one that suits many. There are growing numbers of senior sales staff who enjoy the working environment of a gallery and the sense that their work is contributing to something important.

It's also work that suits creative individuals with other interests. It fits well with the increasing 'portfolio' trend in employment, providing an interesting and flexible source of income to artists, jewellers and students. Customers have high expectations of museum shop personnel: they recognise the calibre of people who work there, and turn to them as a source of information and reference for the galleries and displays as a whole. Smart museums recognise this, and it's good practice to combine training and customer care principles across all front of house staff, including café and shop staff.

Image licensing and picture libraries

Generally known as the 'picture library', this is the department which looks after the photographic images that form a central part of most museum archives. The picture library usually supplies both internal and external customers, providing images for use in press, publishing and exhibition displays as well as for licensed commercial use. It's a business distinguished by large numbers of low-revenue enquiries and, like any archive, requires a great deal of housekeeping activity in scanning, filing, annotating and key-wording. This is good news for anyone interested in a museum career; working in the picture library or archive can be a great way of learning about a collection, and also a good source of opportunities for internships or temporary work.

The culture of museum trading

A career in museum trading is not for everybody. For anyone used to the business fundamentals of high street trading or commercial publishing, the juggling of wider objectives can be hugely frustrating. The trading year is dominated by programming and marketing beyond your control; there will be little understanding of your commercial deadlines; the infrastructure, IT and building layouts will conspire against you; indeed, your very mandate may seem secondary or even irrelevant to many of your museum colleagues. If you enjoy the catered certainty of a large corporate company – or the rewards and profit-related bonuses that go with it, then this is not the career for you.

On the other hand, you may find huge inspiration in working alongside people with completely different expertise to your own. You may enjoy the sense that your work is directly contributing to something worthwhile, a cause you truly believe in, not just the pockets of shareholders. You may get a kick out of walking past beautiful and remarkable objects every day, a salutary reminder that there's more to life than your job. And that has to be the best sort of job there is!

How to get in

Museum trading can be frustratingly hard to get into. Different places work in very different ways and there is no single business model to help chart a career path. At a junior level, it still holds true that voluntary work and internships are excellent ways of learning more about the way a business works and the collections it promotes. Working in museum trading is a profession in itself and is rarely a way into a job in another museum department: using it as a stepping stone won't wash.

At a more senior level, recruitment tends to be from the wider industry, i.e. publishers from publishing, merchandisers and shop managers from retail. Museum enterprises often advertise in trade magazines and in the *Guardian*, and it is worth keeping up to date with all museum websites, where positions are often advertised first. Reviewing such websites is also an excellent way of seeing the sorts of roles that come up and the types of experience required. Finally, don't be afraid to write in to a specific department to find out more about opportunities.

Case Studies

The shop floor: Interview with Farhanah and Ana, who work in the shop at the V&A

'We really like working here. The customers are pleasant and we love the things we sell; very stylish and not available everywhere else. Lots of people come here to buy presents and often ask us to help them make a selection, which always feels pleasant. Although we are working in retail, it feels special – the customers have usually enjoyed visiting the gallery, like using the shop before they go and leave in a good mood. We get to know the regulars very well; those we have helped in the past come and say hello – or let us know how the present we helped them choose was received. It's such a romantic place too – on Friday nights when we stay open late, the building and gardens are lit, there is music playing, and there is a fantastic atmosphere. It's lovely to watch couples wandering around and enjoying themselves – it's a very magical time. The shop staff are a great team too – a very friendly bunch – and our uniforms are smart. We wear black trousers and black t-shirts with a sparkly pink tie printed on the front. Now we sell a version of them to customers too – proof that they are really attractive.

'As shop staff we are a good team. We are fairly separate from the rest of the organisation – sometimes we only realise we are serving other museum staff when they show us their ID in order to claim a discount. Occasionally we will ask which department they work in, but there is not time for much more conversation than that. We have never heard of someone leaving the shop in order to work for a different department within the museum – this is a special form of retail, not an opportunity to work in the wider gallery world. It's funny that in my country (Spain) working in a gallery or museum shop is seen as something of really high prestige, but in the UK it is less so – people are always interested to hear that I work in the V&A, but it's up to me to tell them that the shop is a really special place too. If they come and visit, they can see what I mean.'

Publishing: Andrew Hansen, Managing Director, Prestel Publishing Ltd

'…what immediately springs to my mind is that, far from being a delightful and wonderful career within the museum world, publications can be considered the dishonourable, tainted end of an otherwise holy, high-minded world of pure art. Publications usually come under business development and the same people who must ensure the commercial success of the exhibition catalogues are often in charge of retail outlets, picture libraries and all that mucky end of the stick. These business or, heaven forbid, sales people, are often looked down on by the academics in their ivory towers, who don't like to dirty their hands with the sordid goal of having to make a profit.

'The publisher in such a situation is out on their own, whereas the exhibition curators, board of directors, trustees and especially the artists themselves may simply want to have an enormous book packed with text, expensive bought-in pictures from other institutions, outrageously expensive designers and production extras, huge print-runs to ensure maximum availability and then to sell this package at an unrealistic list price tantamount to giving it away. One priority to think about, therefore, might be to measure the print-run to run out on the very last day of the show. Some institutions even hold back trade orders in order to ensure continued supply to their own outlet. Travelling exhibitions can help immensely with the sale of foreign editions or even physical stock to participating institutions or commercial publishing partners overseas. Sometimes a museum may seek publishing partners like

Prestel, in order to maximise revenue from the trade sales, or go it alone and just use the various publishers' distribution services to maintain margins. To weigh up the pros and cons of each approach, the publications manager needs to have a sound financial background.

'Publishers in the museum and gallery world need to keep a level head in order to balance the potentially conflicting requirements of the institution and its curators, who may have an academic or proselytising agenda and the cold reality of trying to make ends meet. Curators may present completely unfeasible ideas (I have been presented with some quite risible and ludicrous ones in my time, but could not possibly name them here), which make no commercial sense or have no sales potential in the real world. Some first-hand experience with an independent publisher beforehand, therefore, can be of immense benefit to the aspiring museum publisher.

'So, it is by no means all wonderful in art book publishing, nor does it necessarily behove the publications manager to be yet another art historian – there are probably enough of those already in the mix. However, if you love art and love books and love the challenge of turning a possibly dry, dusty old tome on a recondite subject matter into a gloriously attractive and bestselling book that will appear to your great glory in bookshop windows and on front-of-house tables up and down the country at the height of the buzz, which you have created, surrounding your exhibition, then there can be no finer nor more rewarding profession.'

Catering: Helen Ruthven, former owner of the company which ran the cafés in three Edinburgh galleries 1984–2007

'I opened the first café at the Gallery of Modern Art in Edinburgh in 1984. This was a quite revolutionary innovation and the members of the management team at the gallery who wanted us (by no means all of them) really had to fight to get the idea accepted. Opinion was divided; some felt a café would bring in more visitors, others that we were wasting valuable space that could accommodate more art. It was at about the same time that Elizabeth Esteve-Coll, the newly appointed director of the V&A, caused huge controversy by allowing the advertising of the London museum as a 'lovely café with quite a nice museum attached'.

Now things have changed – exhibitions have to make money, or justify their initial estimates, and footfall is part of this. I know – having watched traffic in the foyer of the Scottish Portrait Gallery – that people sometimes come into the gallery to use the cafe and head straight out again if it is closed – but of course I also realise that a popular exhibition means we are busier in the café and takings rise (of which a proportion returns to the gallery).

'I think it is important to offer people a quality experience in the café and not just the opening of another branch of an international chain: local staff offering a local product – which is valued by the clientele for that very reason. I also feel that as a public institution, a gallery's café or restaurant should offer food which is accessible to all budgets, and it was always my aim to do this – without compromising the quality of the food available. In my opinion, a destination restaurant with prices to match is not appropriate to the gallery setting.

'We did sometimes get people wanting to work in the café in order to start a career in museums, but I always used to tell them that once the door is shut on the kitchen you could be in an airport or a hotel; the work is the same. Having said that, you do get a privileged view of what goes on within museums and, for staff who take an intelligent interest in their surroundings, it may qualify as useful work experience for building up their CV. And going through the famous doors can bring a thrill, as can the response of those who hear where you work – working in a gallery brings kudos. We have had resting actors as well as artists come and work for us, and those who stick at it enjoy being part of a strong team. The customers can occasionally be difficult and last-minute panics happen (arriving to find that the oven is not working, or suddenly finding there is a power cut before the food is ready) and it is the team effort and overcoming these issues together that brings job satisfaction.

'Cafés in museums and galleries are becoming more important as they create revenue, and publicly funded organisations have to show that they are responsible stewards of funds. What was once regarded as vulgar commerce is now seen as valuable because it yields a profit and is integral to the customer's overall experience of the venue visited. As time went on I ended up running cafés in three of Edinburgh's galleries. I have now sold my business but still feel proud of what we achieved – and value the experience gained. I saw a fascinating world from the inside.'

Chapter 9
Galleries that sell work

One of the most common misunderstandings about public museums and galleries is that they can offer advice to the public on the value of items. Staff deal constantly with those who, often having trekked long distances with bulky items in tow, have been told that the specific information they sought is not on offer: provenance yes, commercial value no.

There are, however, institutions that make a connection between an item and the price others will pay for it, and working for one of these can offer an interesting career within the wider world of museums and galleries. These institutions range from the commercial galleries that cluster in smart locations, to online selling through the Internet, from agencies that interpret historical documents and offer them for sale to art society exhibitions.

Why doesn't the maker or owner just arrange to sell it themselves?

Commercial galleries and other sellers act as intermediaries, representing the work of artists, makers or original owners and explaining it to potential buyers, in the same way as the sommelier in an upmarket restaurant will interpret the wine list, and advise on the best purchase based on an understanding of what the client's tastes are and what else they already have (or to extend the food analogy, what they will shortly have in front of them).

While the former British reluctance to summon up much enthusiasm for selling is being overcome on a daily basis through websites such as eBay, it's very hard to sell something in which you have a strong personal stake – as anyone who has tried to sell a car or their home may appreciate. An awareness of the value you place on something – whether it's based on how long you have lived there, or how long it has taken you to create it – can make it difficult to listen to someone valuing it purely as an investment, or who seems more interested in securing a discount than in the object in question. Hence, the art world has long relied on intermediaries to do the selling.

This is seldom a hard sell. Although a desire to own a work of art can become peculiarly intense, the potential customer is not purchasing a life essential such as food or heat and they do not *have* to buy. They may, in any case, be actively considering other possible uses for their funds (perhaps jewellery, items of furniture, garden or kitchen renewal, bespoke tailoring or other individual, commissioned items). All such purchasers are likely to be influenced by fashion, the media, and what their peers or influencers (and notably their spouses) are either currently buying or consider a good use of their money.

Selling items, whether historical objects, old masters or work by modern artists, involves making items accessible and attractive to a range of potential customers, who may have a variety of different buying criteria. Some may be buying as an investment, others seeking to purchase a present, either of their own or on behalf of someone else. Some may be seeking an display of conspicuous consumption, whether individual or corporate ('look at what we can afford'), others to fill space, or the pleasure of ownership. The skilled staff member will explore the reasons for considering purchase, spot the appropriate buying signals and deliver the information most likely to be of interest (and this may include saying almost nothing).

Of particular relevance to decisions to purchase are likely to be:

- **The unique nature of what is on sale**. If the artist is long dead, and the work rare, then obviously the opportunity to purchase is not repeatable. Even if the exhibition is of the current work of an artist at the beginning of their career, each item will probably be different. Purchase allows the customer to buy and/or own what no one else has.

- **Your own tastes and preferences**. These are highly relevant in helping you put together a collection of items for sale that makes a coherent offering that other people find attractive (and hopefully return to) and in explaining what is on offer to those who seek confirmation that they are buying something worthwhile. Every gallery owner I spoke to said that it was essential to offer work in which they personally believed and could justify as a good use of the money being spent, but there are grey areas: work you do not like but others do; commercial opportunities which seem to you distasteful and/or short term[1] and customers who see the negotiation of a discount as more important than obtaining the work. A degree of pragmatism will be demanded if the gallery is to stay in business with its reputation maintained.
- **The associated ambience you offer**. This may have a substantial effect on the willingness of your market to buy. It is usually achieved through private viewings (which offer the opportunity for a group of people to view the collection before others do, usually with a drink in their hands) or a privileged opportunity to discuss a particular object alone with its retailer, as a consultation before items are made available to other potential buyers ('I'm offering you first refusal').
- **Your ability to describe what you are selling**. This could be during a one-to-one conversation, through accompanying documentation, a brochure or pamphlet, on a website or via viral marketing mechanisms. Some of what is prepared may never get read, rather stored and held for the future, but its very existence confirms a value in purchase. For example, firms that retail historical documents provide highly specific supporting information detailing how the item fits within the wider historical narrative (e.g. it is signed by someone who was about to take part in a battle/lose his life/be discredited/ennobled) and this story will form a large part of the item's appeal to the buyer. Similarly, gallery owners

---

1 For example, prison art by notorious criminals has a ready market, which has nothing to do with the artistic merit or originality of what is on offer.

who can explain a particular work in the context of the artist's personal life or world events endow the work with an additional significance that can often make purchase more attractive.

Interview with Jess Wilder, co-owner of the Portal Gallery, Great Cavendish Street, London W1 (www.portal-gallery.com)

'I left the University of East Anglia with an BA in Art History in 1975. In those days such a degree was a relatively unusual commodity and, like many of my contemporaries, I fancied working in the world of commercial galleries. We were warned against getting our hopes up too high, but today there are at least dozen of us still so employed.

'I wrote to all the galleries and arts centres on the Arts Council list and offered to work for them in a very lowly capacity – I had no notions of sweeping in, flexing my degree, and was quite happy to make the tea. Out of the blue a man who ran a gallery in Canterbury contacted me. He could not offer me a job himself (he had six children he could employ, one of whom now runs his business) but he offered to accompany me to visit galleries in London; to use his contacts on my behalf.

'This was a gesture of extraordinary kindness – we were unknown to each other then, and there was no ulterior motive – although he has since become a very good friend. We met in London and together walked up and down Bond Street; he walking into the galleries, greeting his friends, and asking whether they had need of my services ('This is Jess…'). The twelfth gallery we visited was the Portal, and it just so happened that Kerry, the assistant of the two founders, had just been summoned back to Australia to look after her sick mother. They asked me if I could type, and I said yes, in the sure knowledge that by the time they next saw me I would be able to. My mother borrowed a typewriter from her place of work, and within two weeks I could do so. I was offered a month as a trial and so my life in galleries began.

'After a couple of years I decided I needed a change and went off and did the same sort of pavement crawl in Paris – and again found a job, although this time for about four times what I was earning in London (working in a gallery has never been well paid in the UK). The gallery needed someone who could speak English, and I found myself representing the organisation at a number of art fairs and exhibitions. My confidence grew.

'It was then that I got another call from the Portal. Kerry wanted to go off travelling with her partner and I was offered the chance to come back. I did so and pretty soon was in overall charge. The two owners (Eric Lister and Lionel Levy) were wanting less day-to-day management, and so it fell to me. And when Eric died he left me his share of the business – at the age of 35 I had half share in a prestigious gallery and Lionel, who been my boss, was now by business partner.

'Having reached this world through such a generous and unprovoked act of patronage, I do try to reciprocate. For those who are looking to gain work experience in a commercial gallery, I think that a personal call from someone who has done their research on the kind of thing we sell (figurative work, finely finished with a high level of detail, and "quirky" always appeals) is always better received than an e-mail, which you are aware has been much used as part of a wider campaign. You need to see how people are going to be to work with on a daily basis and experience their interpersonal skills first hand.

'We must not be squeamish about the fact that galleries sell: we engage with people and encourage them to spend often quite large amounts of money. But the art of selling is very much one of listening rather than talking, and sensitivity to the occasion is needed at all times. Sometimes the customer wants a complete description, at other times a few hints, at others silence and the chance to look in peace. Anecdotes about the artist or the period are often appreciated, as are interesting facts – most buyers like to know more about the person who produced the work, for they are going to live with the artist's view of the world for a long time! The most important thing is that just as each individual work of art is unique, so is each customer, and one must never use a "one size fits all" approach. I would expect those working with me to be good communicators, effective judges of character, alert to buying signals from visitors, and able to handle negotiations.

'Artists can be difficult people. They have strong egos and can be selfish and single-minded, but our job is to depersonalise any difficulties and represent them as professionally as possible. To find an artist who is commercially astute and can sell themselves is rare, and this would not influence my decision on whether or not to represent them – their work has to be the most important thing.

'Galleries are often perceived as posh and full of nicely spoken young ladies and, while manners are certainly vitally important, I hope we offer a warm and welcoming environment. It is important that anyone who works here has a rapport with the work we represent – otherwise they could not do the job. Sadly, all staff working in an environment that houses expensive goods have to be alert to the possibilities of fraud and theft, but we think we have our antennae well tuned – and of course effective security processes in place.

'Above all, we try to be accessible and friendly. We want to build relations with our customers, for them to feel confident that what we sell offers value for money and will be a long-term source of pleasure. If people suggest a discount I like to remind them that they surely want us to still be here to visit in future, and this idea is often well received. In this age of standardisation it's important to be able to buy something unique and special. As Michael Palin kindly said in his speech at our recent 50th birthday party, we continue to offer "an oasis of insanity in an ever more programmed world".'

Interview with Brian Eakin, Director, Eakin Gallery, Lisburn Road, Belfast (www.eakingallery.co.uk)

'I started the gallery 20 years ago; I had no professional qualifications in art, but a deep passion for it. I had been working with my father in his jewellery business in Portadown and I introduced the sale of art through the showroom – just as I later tried to showcase jewellery in the art gallery – but neither combination worked particularly well. So when my father retired, and I had to make a choice of what kind of retailer to be, I opened the gallery and decided to concentrate on art. I am lucky that I have found what I love doing also makes a reasonable business proposition.

'We sell only Irish art, or art by people who have a strong connection to here – they may have been born somewhere else and now live in Ireland, or went from here to somewhere else, but the affiliation still stands. People in Ireland like to buy from people whom they can both meet and have a connection with, and often they continue to buy from us even if they move away. We do get a few tourists popping in during the summer, but mostly it's the connection they are looking for rather than just a picture – something that reminds them of home, their ancestry or more immediate family.

'Buying art is a highly personal thing, and making a choice means expressing yourself. So it's important to stock a range of artists, not just the things I would particularly choose to hang on my own walls – although I see the appeal of every single painting we stock. People want something to connect to: a holiday, their children, a place they loved from the past (hence images of the Mourne Mountains always sell well). Younger people may choose something more abstract, but I do sometimes wonder about how artists who want to sell their work are being taught in art schools, because if you want to sell you have to produce something that others will want to buy. Of course every artist has their own individual style, and not all artists want to sell their work – and would rather produce something completely individualistic. But people liking what you produce sufficiently to want to own it is an important form of acceptance for an artist, and I know that during launch events artists whose work is being shown are often both extremely nervous and desperate for others to buy.

'Buying art is also a long-term decision: pictures are one thing that go into a house that tend not to come out again. You may reorganise what is on the walls to highlight your changing taste or most recent acquisition, but most people have fond feelings about how and when they bought a particular picture and would not part with it altogether. Buying something new can feel almost like a drug, something you are desperate to have, but it's also something that will continue to give pleasure as well as hopefully rise in value. I always advise people to choose what they like and want to live with rather than something they think will rise in value. But the bottom line is you get both the investment and the pleasure of living with it, so it's a good way to use your money.

'The reasons for buying can be varied. I would say only about five per cent of our regular buyers are serious art collectors, who are consciously building a collection. Sometimes they are looking for a present, sometimes to fill space in a new house. We do get a few people buying on behalf of others, as well as design agencies and hotels, although in recent times the credit crunch has meant there are fewer of them around. Others are choosing presents for their husband or wife, perhaps a significant birthday or anniversary. Most come in uncertain what they want, but sure that "I'll know it when I see it".

'The process of buying a picture is interesting. About half of those who want to buy do so, and take it away immediately, the other half say they will think about it and of these about half come back – but once customers have decided they want something, there tends to be an intensity to the process. Most will ring and pay for it over the phone and then come in and collect it in person. We don't hold pictures without payment (it's not fair on the artist, us or another customer who might want to buy what one customer has liked but not enough to make an immediate decision) so there is always the chance that it will be gone when they get in touch again. Those who buy long distance over the phone (and we sell a lot to England this way) usually want a conversation about what it is actually like, and I will stand with the catalogue next to the original to give a precise description of the colours and how they relate to the image in the catalogue. For those who want to buy a picture, but for someone else, we offer gift vouchers and it can be lovely helping a couple new to art choose something with which to furnish their first home.

'Our main promotional expense is the catalogue for each exhibition. We use high-quality photography and paper and send them out to our mailing list of around 4,500 people – usually six times a year. I know a lot of galleries cross people off the list if they have not bought anything for a couple of years, but I think it's good to remain in touch. Often people come in and say they have received a catalogue addressed to someone else who used to live at their address, and are curious, and of course new occasions to buy a picture crop up over a lifetime – weddings, 21st birthdays, anniversaries and so on. To be honest, it does not cost that much more to print 4,500 copies than 2,000 (although the postage is pro rata). We do get a subsidy for our costs from our link with Rosemount Estate (wines from Australia), who have sponsored our launches for about ten years now, but in return they get their name in front of our audience, and fine wine and fine painting probably appeal to the same market.

'The art market is closely tied to the economy and when things are going well we sell well – at its height we sometimes had people sleeping out in the street to be first in line to buy work by particular artists. Things have calmed down a bit now, and there is more time to consider and choose. For every new exhibition, we make the work available from receipt of the catalogue; people start buying immediately as many do not want to risk losing a work by an artist they have admired for a while – and the supply is not constant. On the day of the launch itself there is excitement in the air, and disappointment from those who have come for a specific item and found it is already sold. Some artists will oblige and paint something similar on commission, but of course they can never (and would probably never want to) recreate the image entirely; other artists simply refuse and see each work as different and non-replicable. We work with whatever viewpoint they have and help them through the process. We pay them as soon as we are paid, so we have a good relationship with them. We are inundated with artists seeking representation and get several applications every week – but probably only take on about two or three new artists a year.'

Interview with Sarah Ryan, founder of New Blood Art, an online gallery (www.newbloodart.com)

'I did a fine art degree, then took a PGCE to train as a teacher and taught art for seven years. I started New Blood Art in 2004. We sell work online by new and emerging artists.

'The idea behind it came from personal experience. Like many art students, I spent my time making work, supporting my studies through paid employment; in my case folding clothes in *Gap* and working in bars. I became increasingly aware that I was one of many other students busy creating, and that there were potential customers who might like to buy the work, but that making the link in order to sell it to them was difficult. It's hard for a new artist to be taken on by a commercial gallery because your work does not sell at sufficient prices to make the gallery's cut worthwhile – and the costs of running a physical gallery are very high. So all this art, that people might like to own, from artists who would like to sell, was just remaining in storage under art students' beds.

'I went to teach in Botswana for two years and returned in 2000 to find a changed world: the Internet had arrived, everyone was moving online – and this created the opportunity for my idea to take shape; the mechanism for linking artists and buyers now existed.

'We run an online art service, taking the work of new and emerging artists to potential purchasers; the prices are affordable because the artists are at the beginning of their careers and potential purchasers are offered privileged access – they don't have to go looking for it, and would in any case be unlikely to find it through commercial galleries. I find artists by visiting art colleges and talking to their tutors, attending degree shows and through word of mouth – artists now often come to us and say that friends of theirs have been happily represented by us and they would like the opportunity to show their work through us too. I like to review work by seeing digital photographs along with information on size and medium – as the work is to be promoted via a website it is important that it reproduces well in this format. I tend to make this the first contact with an artist rather than a personal meeting, which can be awkward if the work is not suitable for selling this way or you do not wish to represent them.

'We have a database of about 1,000 people to whom we promote. Buying something without physically seeing it at first hand can feel like a leap of faith, but most find that the experience positive, and over 60 per cent of those on our database are repeat purchasers. I often get to know them well through e-mails – and if I understand someone's specific taste I may try to alert them to new work by an artist they have bought from in the past, or work by a new artist I think might also appeal to them. People quite often ring to have their online selection confirmed ("what does it look like in the flesh?"; "is it nice?") and we get a lot of feedback afterwards from buyers who tell us they are happy with their purchase. Our customers tend to approve of our support for nascent artists, and of course they are getting access to affordable art in an easy way. We offer the option for people to return a picture (within 14 days) if they do not like it, but this has happened only a handful of times in five years of business – more usual feedback is that the item looks so much better than it did on the website. Interior designers and other clients who regularly need new work are a valuable source of income to us.

'We provide a forum for artists to speak to each other and are very conscious of our own role in supporting artists. I do not take on work I do not believe in; I firmly feel that we are making available affordable art that people want to own, and that represents good value for money. The artist gets 65 per cent of the selling price, and this can represent a substantial income to many at a vulnerable point in their career. Working as an artist can be lonely, and I know from personal experience how difficult it can be to sell your own work – I find it much easier to sell other people's and can pass on my genuine enthusiasm. The art teacher in me wants to nurture the artist, and having us believe in them and want to represent their work, can be a considerable support to their morale and motivation – many stay with us over the longer term, even when physical galleries start to sell their work. We also offer work experience to those keen to enter this world, and of course this equips them to go off and apply for other jobs in related galleries.'

Case Study: Selling on behalf of other artists

Interview with Jo Beale, Founder of The Jo Beale Gallery, Peggy's Cove, Nova Scotia (www.jobealegallery.net)

'The area around Peggy's Cove in Nova Scotia has always attracted artists, and many have made work here, but because there was no gallery to sell it through they tended to take it home and it got dispersed via a variety of different galleries and private sales.

'I have lived here for many years, working as an artist, and six years ago the opportunity came up to buy this house, which used to be the post office. Most of the properties here belong to the same fishing families that have owned them for generations, so the opportunity to buy one was significant. It is light and airy and makes a good space for displaying work. I take work from a variety of artists and the work is wide-ranging, from mounted photographic prints and limited edition prints, through watercolours and drawings to much larger oils. The prices are correspondingly varied. Some of our visitors have never been in an art gallery before, so it is important to have some work at lower prices and in more accessible (usually figurative) formats. Some customers want to take them away immediately, but we have now shipped all over the world (I thought this would be more difficult than it turned out to be).

'Best of all, we have a steady influx of visitors who are charmed by the place and delighted to take home a high-quality gift to remind them in future of their trip. As for selling my own work, I tend to concentrate on the art provided by other artists, all of which I feel strongly about and hence enjoy selling. Most artists find it difficult to sell their own work and I am no exception. The gallery occupies me for most of the summer (it is important for me to be here to talk about the work on display) but it gives me an income for the rest of the year that allows me to produce my own work during the winter.'

Case Study: Selling artwork in bad times

Interview with Susan Jones, researcher and writer on contemporary visual arts matters and Director of Programmes, a-n The Artists Information Company (www.a-n.co.uk)

'For artists and galleries who see selling as an important part of their work, it's vital to understand both why people collect art and the prevailing environment[2]. However good the work and however much advice the artist/gallery takes on marketing, client and business development, whether artists can make a living from selling art work is debatable – and even more so in a period of economic recession.

'So why do people collect art? For some it's for enjoyment or entertainment and a chance to be part of the art world. For others it's a business proposition.

'How society views the practice is changing. Thirty years ago the contemporary visual arts were largely regarded with disdain by the British public; opportunities to buy work were scarce and there were few private collectors. In recent years, it's become fashionable to be seen around contemporary art and among artists, and to become an art collector. London art fairs *Frieze* and *Zoo* have

---

2 Often referred to in marketing theory as PEST (political, economic, social and technological).

contributed to this change. Also influential in spreading the art-buying habit has been the Arts Council's 'Own Art'[3] scheme which offers interest-free credit on sales from selected galleries.

'But, in difficult economic times, artists and art lovers have had to find new and imaginative ways of tempting potential buyers to part with their money, and some interesting initiatives are emerging. Various examples follow:

'Set up five years ago, The Collective[4] grew out of a desire to enjoy art at home rather than considering it as something to invest in. The first group in London came together as friends who enjoyed contemporary art and, as they say on their website: "We enjoyed looking at art and talking about what we'd seen. And we were keen to live with art on a full-time basis. We came up with the idea of pooling our resources to buy work and then share it through presentation in our own homes."

'If the press is to be believed, online galleries such as New Blood Art[5], set up by artist Sarah Ryan have been weathering the recession quite nicely. A number of painters have seen the value of their work double in recent years, this being a major factor in setting higher prices for their new pieces. The gallery takes 35 per cent commission on sales – lower than the average commercial gallery – meaning a better financial deal for her artists, and quicker sales.

---

3 www.artscouncil.org.uk/ownart/index.html. A scheme designed to make it easy and affordable to buy contemporary works of art and craft, including paintings, photography, sculpture, glassware and furniture, and at the same time to widen the collector base. Buyers can borrow from £100 to £2,000 (which can be put towards items of greater value) and pay back the loan in 10 monthly instalments – interest free. The scheme is available through a network of over 250 participating venues throughout the UK and in the first five years of its operation, over a quarter of the sales were to first-time art buyers. A similar scheme (Collectorplan) has been operating in around 70 galleries in Wales for over 20 years – see the Arts Council of Wales website for a full list: www.collectorplan.org.uk

4 www.the-collective.info

5 www.newbloodart.com

'Some artists may see their careers flourish through exposure at Newcastle's Biscuit Factory – which they claim on their website is "the original art store". Britain's biggest commercial gallery comprising 35,000 square feet with two floors of exhibition spaces and two floors of artists' studios, it sells art and craft in a space that is relaxed and fun, with "Own Art" interest-free credit available. Bestsellers on the gallery's website are generally small framed work or craft objects priced at the £200 mark.

'Cutting out the middle-person can have its attraction for artists, who then don't need to be spotted by a curator or gallerist before they get to show. Often organised collectively by the artists, open studio events[6] have been promoted as a user-friendly way for the interested public to make contact with artists, engage them in conversation, to see demonstrations of art and craft techniques and hopefully then buy or commission. For the artists concerned, the overhead costs are relatively low – usually a membership fee to the group behind the venture and contributions to signage and promotions. Like fine art graduation shows at universities, they also offer a route for arts officers and curators to research interesting artists and see a range of new work. The success of open studio ventures however is generally counted in audience rather than sales figures.

'Described on BBC's *Imagine*[7] by Alan Yentob as "An ingenious way of bringing art to the people", the *Empty Shops Network* has moved fast up the recession-busting agenda. Instigated by the artist-led Revolutionary Arts Group (RAG)[8], it's part of a timely and strategic movement designed not to pretty-up down-trodden urban centres but to create a genuine route for artists' self-determined projects.

'By February 2009, about 10 per cent of the UK's shops were empty, with over 1,000 high street businesses closing every week,

6 www.openstudiosnetwork.co.uk

7 28 July 2009

8 http://artistsandmakers.com/staticpages/index.php/emptyshops

and the situation looked set to worsen. RAG's Dan Thompson says on their website: "Landlords letting artists, arts organisations and community groups use their empty spaces see the property looking great and kept in good order, and their business getting some great publicity. Users benefit from low-cost space on short and easy-to-manage leases, meaning they can take a bigger risk on bolder, more innovative and experimental projects and maybe even get a good business kick-started." Seizing the spirit of the time, the government put £3 million and Arts Council England £500,000 into developing such initiatives for 2009/10.

'At the Bigger Picture Gallery, Crystal Palace[9] artists can apply to use the space for nominal sums "for anything you want as long as it is art-based". Landlords and property owners are invited to register their interest or discuss the possible use of empty space to: "help your business and customers enjoy a rotating display of creative work, while you provide a showcase for local artist". Similarly in Colchester, Slack Space's[10] aim is "to fill the slack spaces in town with colour, art and laughter and to help keep our social, cultural and economic life warm in the chill of the recession."

'The Pretty Vacant[11] project in West Bromwich continues the theme, with co-organiser Gemma Hadley, a new graduate, reporting on her blog on www.a-n.co.uk/artists_talking on 20 August 2009: "In our wisdom (and lack of funds), we thought that it was a marvellous idea to set up this show in five days. This includes converting a neglected retail unit into something that vaguely resembles an exhibition space…Our shows are the perfect place to buy affordable and original art works, while supporting young artists in their early careers".[12] Financing for the project came

---

9 www.biggerpicturegallery.co.uk

10 www.iheartslackspace.blogspot.com

11 www.prettyvacant.org

12 www.iheartslackspace.blogspot.com

through a local fund to support entrepreneurship, awarded after a "Dragon's Den" style interview.

'Such grassroots projects along with the more democratic nature of Web-based art galleries are contributing to a shift in the way art is viewed, appreciated and acquired, suggesting a new type of sustainability and business model within contemporary visual arts, designed to last beyond the recession and into the next decade.'

Chapter 10
The educational role of a museum or gallery today

By Rachel Moss, Young People's Programmes Manager at the National Portrait Gallery

'Education, education, education' was Tony Blair's mantra as New Labour set out its priorities for the general election in 1997.

At the time I had just made the decision to leave my job as a primary school teacher to start a Master's degree in Museum Studies at the University of Leicester, with a specialist option in education. On joining the museums and galleries sector I discovered a new mission: to place 'education at the core of the museum'. Ten years on, has this mission been achieved and what is the educational role of a museum or gallery today?

Setting the context

Museum education began within the mid-19th century context of philanthropy and self-improvement, when public museums 'were an expression of enlightenment which produced an enthusiasm for equality of opportunity for learning...that collections which had hitherto been reserved for the pleasure and instruction of a few people should be made accessible to everybody.'[1]

Recorded school visits to museums in Britain began in 1984/5 with the opening of Haslemere Educational Museum. The first schools

---

1 Hudson, K. (1975) cited in George Hein, *Learning in the Museum – Museum Meanings*. London and New York: Routledge, 1998, p. 3.

museum service was set up between 1901 and 1914, at Leeds Museum. This was followed by the introduction of a special teacher to work with children in 1902, at the Manchester Museum. However, it was not until 1931, nearly 30 years later, that the first full-time education post was created – Schools Museum Officer at Leicester Museum.[2]

Jumping to the end of the 20th century, as I began my Master's degree in 1997 the newly appointed Labour government commissioned *A Common Wealth* by David Anderson,[3] Director of Learning at the Victoria and Albert Museum. This key report on museums and galleries in the UK, revised two years later in 1999, highlighted that education needed more resources and a raised profile within the museum and gallery sector, lobbying for additional funding. Around the same time, 1998, the Museums Association agreed a definition of a museum that began 'museums enable people to explore collections for inspiration, learning and enjoyment...',[4] which remains the same today. Education in museums and galleries was starting to become a key agenda.

A Common Wealth stated that 'provision for museum and gallery education is a patchwork', with half the museums and galleries surveyed making no specific education provision and only one in five having a member of staff specialising in education.[5] Since then this has increased greatly, but still depends on the size and type of a museum or gallery and how each one is funded. Some smaller institutions may still have only two or three staff as a whole. I have worked in two nationals (Tate Modern and the National Portrait Gallery), a corporate (the Bass Museum), two independents (the Serpentine Gallery and Mid-Pennine Arts) and a number of local authority museums. Within these organisations my role has been as a freelance

---

2 Carter, Graham. 'Editorial', *Journal of Education in Museums,* no. 1 September 1980, p. 5.

3 Anderson, David. *A Common Wealth: Museums in the Learning Age.* London: Department for Culture, Media and Sport, 1997.

4 Museums Association: www.museumsassociation.org

5 Anderson (1997) p. 3.

educator, as the sole education staff member, part of a small education team of three and now in a larger department of 13 (eight full-time and five part-time staff), shortly due to expand. Usually the number of education staff is supplemented by freelancers, including artists and historians.

Within museums and galleries, education starts with object-based learning, in a context different to that of the classroom. It is now acknowledged that people learn in a wide variety of ways and so museums and galleries respond to this by providing a range of educational or interpretative tools to meet multiple learning styles or intelligences.[6] Visitors may have the option to read a wall-mounted text panel or hand-held exhibition guide, take part in a discussion, follow a trail around the building, create their own artwork in a workshop, listen to an audio guide, handle objects, or explore other interactive gallery-based displays. Some of these activities are self-directed, whereas others promote group interaction depending on the preference for the intrapersonal or the interpersonal.

What is a museum or gallery educator's role?

Peter Clarke, who taught the specialist option in Education on the Museum Studies Master's when I studied at the University of Leicester, once asked the group what we expected mainly to be doing in our chosen profession. All of the responses were along the lines of 'inspiring people' or 'making museums accessible to all.' He surprised us by saying that the reality was that we would mainly be moving tables and washing up paintbrushes. Looking back I find this to be partly true, with my job ranging from tasks like these, to writing detailed strategic documents and funding reports.

The job of museum or gallery educator varies greatly each day as I take on the role of facilitator, manager, administrator, troubleshooter and broker; the latter between artists and visiting groups, and sometimes also external partners. I have found it of great benefit to have a

---

6 Gardner, Howard. *Frames Of Mind: The Theory Of Multiple Intelligences.* New York: Basic Books, 1993.

teaching background, although not all person specifications for museum or gallery education jobs will require this. I still work directly with an audience group to inform my work, although I am now much more office based. On the whole I employ freelance artists to deliver the education programme. This is a popular area of work, but difficult in terms of gaining regular employment within one institution. I prefer to have the financial security of a full-time job.

The museum or gallery educator role would suit someone who loves communicating with people and enjoys seeing the way that people respond to and develop during workshops, projects or events. This brings its own rewards and is why I am passionate about my job. It is not done for great financial gain, as it is often less well paid than teaching, or for great recognition, like that which a curator might get for putting on an exhibition. The job involves interacting with a wide range of people both externally and internally, the latter within the education department and also cross-departmentally with, for example, curatorial, visitor services, marketing, press and fundraising staff.

For anyone who is interested in moving into a career in museum or gallery education it is useful to have some experience, usually voluntary, as well as relevant qualifications. Many larger museums and galleries run competitive internships within their education departments. Alternatively, approaching a smaller institution could lead more easily to a work placement as these might benefit more from having extra staff. Qualifications include a Postgraduate Certificate in Education (PGCE), a Master's degree or diploma in Museum Studies, or even a course specialising in museum or gallery education. For example, the Institute of Education in London runs a Master's degree in Museums and Galleries in Education, as well as offering shorter courses in both Museum Learning and Learning in Galleries: Engaging with Visual Culture.

There are two key membership organisations that provide training, networking, resources, publications, advocacy and support for those working in museum and gallery education. These are GEM[7]

---

7   GEM: www.gem.org.uk

(the Group for Education in Museums) and engage[8] (the National Association for Gallery Education). GEM is most relevant for people working in museums, and engage for those within galleries. As a sector we are good at sharing experiences and offering opportunities for Continuing Professional Development (CPD). I am currently one of three London representatives for engage who offer advice and run seminars three times a year for members in the area.

Before being allowed to work with children, young people or vulnerable adults, everyone needs to be checked via the Criminal Records Bureau (CRB)[9] to verify their suitability for this kind of role. A new vetting and barring scheme is currently being proposed by the Independent Safeguarding Authority (ISA)[10] with the aim that checks will become portable rather than specific to working in one museum or gallery. In relation to CRB checks, each institution should have a policy on the protection of children, young people and vulnerable adults, as well as having a general education policy and an educational mission statement, underpinning the educational work taking place.

The value of an education programme to a museum or gallery

Audience development is an important issue for museums and galleries but is not solely the responsibility of education departments. Marketing teams often do visitor surveys and curators may respond to findings by putting on an exhibition aimed at a specific group. However, when it comes to targeting non-visitors, educators play a major part. When attracting new audiences, it is also important to remember the needs of existing visitors.

Originally museums and galleries focused on formal education for primary and secondary schools, but this has now widened to include

---

8 engage: www.engage.org

9 Criminal Records Bureau: www.crb.gov.uk

10 Independent Safeguarding Authority: www.isa-gov.org.uk

informal education provision for groups such as families or community groups. It is important that institutions attract visitors in their early years, as children are the future; at the same time there is an expanding ageing population. Inter-generational groups may even consist of a small child, a teenager, a parent and a grandparent, each with specific needs, learning styles and interests. These can be catered for by providing a wide variety of education programmes and types of interpretation.

My jobs have ranged from working with 'everyone' – nurseries, schools, colleges, community groups, families, teachers, adults, elderly people, physical and learning disability groups, people with visual impairments, mental health groups, refugees and homeless people, and even dog walkers – to specialising in one audience group. At the National Portrait Gallery I was recently recruited into a new role, Young People's Programmes Manager, focusing on 14 to 21 year-olds outside of school hours, to attract non-visitors to the gallery and therefore fill an audience gap.

By carrying out evaluation, museums and galleries can gain a much better understanding about different types of audiences, their needs and interests. Evaluation is integral to informing future developments, often taking place as consultation before an exhibition or programme of activity is initiated (front-end), as well as during (formative) and after it has concluded (summative). Visitors are sometimes invited to form one-off or more long-term focus groups acting as advisers to a museum or gallery. At the National Portrait Gallery I run a Youth Forum, which meets monthly on a Thursday evening. This is beneficial to the gallery as it provides ongoing feedback on the Young People's Programme, as well as wider areas identified by other gallery staff. At the same time, it is a peer-led programme where the members decide what they want to do, gain experience for their CVs and meet other young people with similar interests. So far, Youth Forum members have chosen images for the covers of leaflets, instigated an online writing competition, created a young people's guide to an exhibition, written captions for a project-related display, recorded an audio describing their favourite portrait, and carried out a branding exercise over the space of a year, culminating in their own logo. They are now planning a launch event to attract more young people to the gallery, including recruiting new members to the Youth Forum.

As well as audience development, a key reason that museums and galleries provide education programmes is to meet government strategies. For example, the report Every Child Matters[11] provides an approach for all organisations involved with services for children to ensure the wellbeing of young people up to age 19. In addition, the recently announced Cultural Offer is an exciting commitment from the Department for Children, Schools and Families (DCSF) and the Department for Culture, Media and Sport (DCMS) to 'ensure that all children and young people, no matter where they live or what their background, have the chance to engage in at least five hours of high quality culture a week in and out of school.'[12] There will also be a specific focus on youth leading up to the 2012 London Olympics.

Additional government funding is sometimes available to address strategies like the above, or activities resulting from these may appeal to trusts and foundations who regularly support education work. Businesses with philanthropic or social responsibility funding may choose to sponsor a high-profile exhibition while also supporting a programme of related workshops and events. Even applications to fund the acquisition of a specific artwork can be backed up by highlighting existing and potential educational programmes inspired by the work. In an unstable economic climate, museums and galleries will need to obtain funding from a variety of sources, and education can prove to be an attractive tool.

The value of an education programme to participants

Museums and galleries are focused on providing access to real artworks or objects, with educational activities taking the objects as a

---

11 Every Child Matters: www.everychildmatters.gov.uk
12 Cultural Offer: http://www.culture.gov.uk/images/publications/CreativeBritain-chapter1.pdf

starting point and bringing them to life through narratives, questioning and discussion. This could involve the exploration of issues relevant to participants, such as reminiscence with elderly groups, or increased knowledge and understanding in a specialist subject, for example the history of brewing. Workshops may include creative activities, such as taking photographic portraits, while at the same time developing technical skills, for instance on how to use different types of cameras and experimenting with lighting. Where possible, museums and galleries provide these educational activities for free, especially when aimed at children and non-visiting groups.

Museum and gallery educators often employ practising artists to lead workshops. Artists referenced in the National Curriculum for art are usually famous icons from the past, such as Van Gogh and Monet. Meeting someone who makes a living as an artist or a photographer can be very inspiring in terms of opening up career options. There is also likely to be greater opportunities for experimentation and risk-taking outside of the classroom, and the emphasis is more often on process than product.

With hard-to-reach groups, such as disaffected youth, educational activities can motivate, build confidence, raise self-esteem, promote teamwork, and in doing so develop key social and life skills. By working with groups like this over a period of time, the long-term aim is to empower the participants to become independent visitors and develop a sense of ownership. At the National Portrait Gallery, progression routes have been identified so that young people may start by participating in outreach sessions taking place in an environment they are already familiar with, such as their local youth centre, before visiting the institution as part of a group. Later they may feel confident enough to attend a half-day workshop on their own, next taking part in a three-day project and, if more committed still, they might then choose to join the Youth Forum to work with the gallery on a regular basis.

Young people who are 'not in education, employment or training' (NEET) need supportive venues outside of mainstream education to refocus their future aspirations. Museums and galleries can work in partnership with organisations such as Pupil Referral Units (PRUs) and Youth Offending Teams (YOTs) to inspire young people to gain alternative qualifications or accreditation. This could include the Arts Award[13], ranging in level from bronze to gold, where museum or gallery educators can receive training to become arts award advisers and their institution then becomes arts award centre. Another option is specifically devised qualifications through the Assessment and Qualifications Alliance (AQA) Unit Award Scheme,[14] giving students recognition of their success in a short unit of work. Within formal education, the new Diploma in Creative and Media[15] aimed at 14 to 19 year olds is currently being piloted in museums and galleries as a new type of accreditation, and Creative Apprenticeships[16] are being launched from September 2008. Having the opportunity to gain work experience in a museum or gallery can help with making important career decisions as well as enhancing CVs.

Other visitors to a museum or gallery who are not participating directly in educational activities can both enjoy and be inspired by seeing showcased work resulting from education programmes. This could be interpretative, for example audio guides recorded by ex-brewery employees in their own words at the Bass Museum, or through looking at displays of work resulting from projects – such as after-school courses involving primary pupils at Tate Modern – or even performances within the museum context, like youth dance bringing the historical gallery spaces alive at the National Portrait Gallery.

What's in a name?

Throughout my career, although I have carried out similar museum or gallery education roles, my job title has varied. Originally I was

---

13 Arts award: www.artsaward.org.uk

14 Assessment and Qualifications Alliance Unit Award Scheme: web.aqa.org.uk/qual/uas.php

15 Diploma in Creative and Media: www.skillset.org/qualifications/diploma

16 Creative Apprenticeships: http://www.ccskills.org.uk/Qualifications/Creative Apprenticeships/tabid/82/Default.aspx

Education Officer or Education Co-ordinator, working with a wide range of visitors. When my job has focused on a specific audience group, this has featured in my title, for example Assistant Curator: Schools Programmes (Tate Modern), or Young People's Programmes Manager (National Portrait Gallery). Interestingly at Tate Modern the word 'curator' was included with the aim of creating equal status between exhibitions and education staff. I have also seen the names of education departments change over the years, and I have worked in both 'Interpretation and Education' and 'Learning and Access' teams. Recently both Tate Modern and the National Portrait Gallery have renamed their education departments 'Learning'. Alternative department names include 'Learning and Participation' (Southbank Centre) and 'Interaction' (Artangel).

In line with this, the narrow definition of an education role in museums and galleries – the path that I have so far followed – has developed to include posts that involve working outside the institution, such as outreach work or within the realm of Public Art, often blurring the line between education and curatorship. One such example is the Community Projects Curator role at Art on the Underground. Since 2000 this organisation has been working with artists, sometimes in partnership with a museum or gallery, to create and present new artworks to enhance the journeys for people using the London Underground system. So while institutions still aim to attract audiences through their doors, art is also being taken out into the 'real world' and being placed in an everyday context.

The future

In the 10 or so years I have worked in museums and galleries, the emphasis has shifted from 'education' to 'learning'. There has also been a move from the mission of locating 'education at the core of the museum' to learning becoming available museum or gallery-wide. I believe there will always be a place for education or learning departments but that the responsibility for learning needs to become spread throughout each museum or gallery.

In a world full of developing technologies, learning also needs to go beyond the walls of the institution. Virtual or e-learning has started to become a big growth area within the museum and gallery sector. Tate has even defined Tate Online as their fifth gallery. We have come a long way since public museums were first set up in the mid-19th century. Who knows where we will be in another 150 years?

Recommended reading

Taylor, Barbara (ed.), *Inspiring Learning in Galleries*. London: Engage, 2006.

Hooper-Greenhill, Eileen (ed.), *The Educational Role of the Museum: Second Edition – Leicester Readers in Museum Studies*. London and New York: Routledge, 1999.

Hooper-Greenhill, Eileen et al, *Inspiration, Identity, Learning: The Value of Museums*. London: Department for Culture, Media and Sport, 2004.

Moffat, Hazel and Vicky Woollard (eds.), *Museum and Gallery Education: A Manual of Good Practice – Professional Museum and Heritage Series*. Lanham: AltaMira Press, 2000.

Case Study

Interview with Pooja Raj Kalyan, member of the Young People's Programme Youth Forum at the National Gallery

'My family have never been interested in art, but I got very involved in the subject at school. I enjoyed some really good teaching there and would hang out in the art department a lot. I was part of the 'gifted and talented' scheme within our school and one of my teachers suggested I apply for the Young Graduates in Museums and Galleries (YGMG) scheme, which offered a two-week 'back-stage' tour of a range of galleries and museums, giving the chance to see inside them and how they work, followed by a two-week place-ment at a venue of your choice. The scheme was very competitive, but I was accepted and then chose to work in the National Portrait Gallery, which is how I met Rachel Moss, the Young People's

Programmes Manager. I became part of her Youth Forum, a group of people aged between 14 and 21 who encourage visitors of the same age to come in and enjoy what is free for all to share. We have a meeting once a month and, although we do not have a budget of our own, we have access to funds to support the ideas we come up with – if they are approved by the gallery staff we work with.

'Some of the events we put on have been such fun to work on and I have really enjoyed taking part. Anyone who is in the gallery at the time can join in, and we try to encourage as many young people as we can to come in specially. One event I particularly remember was when 15 portraits were selected and young people were offered the opportunity to choose one and be dressed and made up to match. It was fascinating and really made people look at the details of the costume and how the individual is presented on the canvas.

'After a few months I had the opportunity to apply to be a "visitor services assistant". The gallery takes on about 12 at a time, every now and again, and the number of people applying is huge – most of them already have BAs in Art History or a similar expertise. I am proud to say I was the youngest person ever appointed to this role – I was still at school at the time – and am continuing now that I'm in my first year at the London College of Fashion, studying broadcast journalism. The commitment is 12 hours a week, which combines well with my studies and it is a paid role. I wear a uniform of a red shirt and am assigned to various galleries in turn to answer questions from the public and help them locate things they want to find (sometimes a specific portrait, sometimes the bathroom). I really enjoy the work and love answering their questions. You get moved quite regularly and so don't get bored with any single room. Until I worked here, my inclination would always be for modern art, so I have been surprised at how much I love the older pictures – my favourite is the portrait of Barbara Palmer (née Villiers), Duchess of Cleveland (and mistress of Charles II) with her son, Charles Fitzroy, presented as Madonna and Child by Sir Peter Lely.

'I love talking about the gallery and encouraging others to come. My family was not that interested in art but have become much more so, although my brother says I talk about it too much at home. I have also made many new friends, those for whom an interest in art is much more an accepted part of life (such as my new friends at university) and this has made me see that I am not so unusual. I think my self-confidence has grown substantially through the project. There are few people from other ethnic backgrounds working in museums and galleries, and I am proud to be one of them.

'In the future I may decide to work in this world, but I also want to work for a big brand, such as Tate or perhaps Chanel. The gallery feels different now, and sometimes it is hard to look at the images on the wall when I am busy planning events or thinking about how to write a leaflet to encourage others to come in through my work on the Youth Forum. That's why it's so lovely to be in the gallery answering questions and just looking yourself when things are really quiet. My favourite time of all is Friday evenings when music is being played and you can wander around looking and listening at the same time.'

Part 3:
Preparing to find a job

Chapter 11
The advantages of a Master's degree when seeking a career in museums and galleries

By Ann V. Gunn, Lecturer in Museum and Gallery Studies at the University of St Andrews

In 1987, when the Museums and Galleries Commission published a report on *Museum Professional Training and Career Structure*, between 30 and 50 postgraduate students a year completed a Master's degree in Museum Studies at the universities of Leicester and Manchester.[1] Two decades later, figures gathered by the Museums Association (MA) showed that there were 529 students enrolled on 13 courses recognised by the MA.[2] This 10-fold increase reflects a number of factors, including the growing professionalisation of museum work, the greater number of museums and galleries and the wider availability of postgraduate courses. And it does not include the many other courses in, for instance, heritage management, tourism, art and curatorship, or arts management, which have also developed in recent years.

While this increase in student numbers inevitably leads to greater competition for the available jobs, it also demonstrates that there is a wide demand for postgraduate training.

---

1 Museums and Galleries Commission. *Museum Professional Training and Career Structure: Report by a Working Party 1987.* London, 1987, p. 30.

2 Davis, Maurice. *The Tomorrow People: Entry to the museum workforce.* London, 2007. www.museumsassociation.org

---

What do you get from a Master's programme that you can't get from other museum training?

First of all, you will get what you get out of any postgraduate work – a chance to extend your learning beyond the undergraduate level, the opportunity to begin to specialise, to work in depth on a topic or field of study, to advance your knowledge and to develop your expertise. A Master's degree can be a step on the way to further academic work and a doctorate.

A Master's degree can sometimes provide a vocational component to your training, complementing or enhancing academic knowledge gained in a first degree and introducing you to a particular area of professional practice. It is often also an essential professional qualification. For mature or mid-career students, a Master's degree might provide an academic break, and chance to rethink and change direction. It can be an opportunity to re-skill or enhance existing skills – for example people in business management might study for an MBA in order to broaden their knowledge, put their day-to-day work into a theoretical framework and increase their promotion prospects.

Whatever your academic area, a Master's programme will provide you with intellectual training. You will have to develop research skills to explore your subject; read, assimilate and apply the theoretical background; acquire a body of knowledge; collect and analyse data; solve problems; evaluate and think critically, analytically, and reflectively; organise your thoughts, communicate them effectively and write articulately. You will have to manage your time and your research project and learn to work independently.

A Master's degree in Museum and Gallery Studies will be both theoretical and practical, academic and vocational. Museums require people with practical abilities as well as intellectual skills, so almost all courses have a very strong vocational flavour, and include practical and applied elements and work placements based in museums and galleries. Assignments for assessment of the taught course will rarely be confined to academic essays, but will involve evaluation exercises, report writing and other formats. Teaching may involve group work, seminars, handling sessions and demonstrations, visits to museums and exhibitions, talks from visiting professionals, student presentations, discussions and debates, as well as formal lectures.

Project work and placements

An important element of most museum and gallery studies courses is practical project work. This will teach project management skills, such as how to define aims and objectives, identify the skills and resources required, manage time effectively and how to work with others. Projects may be undertaken by an individual or as part of a group so students will need to be both motivated self-starters and also good team players. Students may then be required to write project reports not only describing what they did, but also reflecting on what they learned.

A very valuable part of many museum studies courses is a placement in a museum. This gives students the opportunity to work alongside and learn from professionals in a wide variety of museum work, to see how theory underpins best practice and to get hands-on experience. Placements can also help students decide if museum work in general, and one branch of it in particular, is really what they want to do.

Diploma

In the UK, many students take a diploma after finishing the taught element of a postgraduate course, rather than continuing on to research and write a dissertation. This has been regarded as a perfectly acceptable qualification, especially for those who are going into areas of museum work which do not require research skills. However, the intellectual training required for research is also needed for museum staff undertaking market research, visitor studies or exhibition evaluation so progression to the Master's degree is now more common.

Dissertation

For most Master's degrees, a dissertation is written after the taught element of the course. This gives students the opportunity to carry out some original research, developing research questions and thinking about research methodology as well as undertaking some in-depth reading and developing critical and analytical thinking skills. The topic could be chosen strategically to enhance employability or it could be an opportunity to expand an area of academic interest or extend specialist interests. For anyone wishing to become a subject specialist curator, the dissertation could be tailored to an aspect of that subject or could be based on a particular collection. Because museums and their collections are so varied there is a rich and virtually endless vein of material to be mined for object-based research projects. Students looking to have careers in other areas of museum work can find plenty of scope for original research topics in museum ethics, collections management, audience development, visitor studies, exhibition evaluation, learning theory, interpretation, and so on.

Curriculum

Each museum and gallery studies course is different with its own unique emphasis, but on the whole they follow similar broad outlines. Most incorporate the main features of the International Council of Museum's (ICOM) International Committee for Training of Personnel (ICTOP) syllabus (1981) and *Curricula Guidelines for Professional Development* (2008).[3] These guidelines identify five areas where particular 'competencies' are needed: general skills such as problem-solving or good communication skills; museology – understanding museums and their purposes; the management skills needed to run museums

---

3 http://ictop.alfahosting.org/images/pdf/icom_basic_syllabus_1971_1981.pdf
ICTOP *Curricula Guidelines For Professional Development*, revised ed., February, 2008. http://ictop.alfahosting.org/images/pdf/ictop%20curricula%20guidelines.revdocument081.pdf. See also The Museum Career Development Tree: http://museumstudies.si.edu/ICOM-ICTOP/index.htm

efficiently; public programming; and collections and information management.

ICTOP recommends that museum training programmes should consider the reasons for, and functions of museums; how collections develop and how they are used, researched and cared for; what kind of services and programmes are provided for the public; how to provide the greatest possible access to museum collections while also preserving them; and what skills are needed to run all of a museum's different activities. Therefore most courses will cover the theoretical framework and the social and political context within which museums operate, the history and development of museums and galleries; the different definitions, types and purposes of museums; collections, their development and management; interpretation; audiences and their varied needs and a wide range of management topics from financial planning to personnel.

The American Association of Museums (AAM) Committee on Museum Professional Training (COMPT) has issued standards and best practice guidelines. While these look at a whole range of training programmes, you can use them to assess the content and delivery of degree courses you may be applying for.[4] The guidelines cover four areas: programme goals; content; instructors and instructional approaches and responsibilities. COMPT has also carried out research to find out what the museum community felt was required from the training provided by museum studies courses for entry-level positions. Based on feedback from museum professionals, the study came up with a list of topics for a core curriculum which include: museum departments and professions; museum ethics; laws and regulations; museums as educational institutions; collections care and conservation; museum history; museum finance; governance and organisation and museums and technology.[5]

---

4 http://www.compt-aam.org/resources/standardsguidelines.html

5 Reynolds, Terry R. *Training for Entry-Level Museum Professionals. A Report prepared for the Committee on Museum Professional Training, American Association of Museums.* Washington, 2000. www.compt-aam.org/images/Reynolds_Survey.doc

---

How do you find out about courses?

In the UK, museum and gallery studies courses advertise in the MA's *Museums Year Book,* in the monthly *Museums Journal* and on the MA website. There are currently over thirty courses offering postgraduate courses in museums, galleries, conservation or heritage studies. A number of courses were until recently known as 'recognised courses'. These courses met certain standards set by the now-defunct Cultural Heritage National Training Organisation (CHNTO) and these validated courses were recognised by the MA as approved training for Route C for the Associateship of the Museums Association (AMA). They are listed on the MA website in the Professional Development section.[6] CHNTO ceased to exist in 2002 so the MA was unable to add to this list any of the courses set up since that date. The Sector Skills Council now responsible for museums and galleries (Creative and Cultural Skills) has discontinued the process of course valida-

---

6 http://www.museumsassociation.org

The recognised courses were:

University of Birmingham, Ironbridge Institute (MA in Heritage Management)

Bournemouth University (MA in Museums and Collections Management)

University of East Anglia (MA in Museology /Museum Studies)

University of Essex (MA in Gallery Studies)

University of Greenwich (MA in Museum Management; MA in Heritage Management)

University of Leicester (MA in Museum Studies; MA in Art Gallery Studies, MGeol in Geology, Museums and Earth Heritage)

City University London (MA Museum and Gallery Management)

University College London, Institute of Archaeology (MA in Museum Studies)

University of Manchester (MA in Art Gallery & Museum Studies)

University of Newcastle, International Centre for Cultural Heritage Studies (ICCHS) (MA in Museum Studies; MA in Heritage Education and Interpretation; MA in Art Museum and Gallery Studies)

Nottingham Trent University (MA in Heritage Management)

University of Southampton Winchester Campus (MA Museum and Galleries: Collection Management pathway; MA Museum and Galleries: Culture, Collections and Communications pathway; MA Museum and Galleries: Access and Learning pathway)

University of St Andrews (M.Litt. in Museum and Gallery Studies; M.Phil in Museum and Gallery Studies/National Trust for Scotland Studies)

---

tion. At the time of writing the MA has just re-launched the AMA and no formal qualifications are now required to register for this.

Among the Master's degrees offered by the recognised courses are: Heritage Management; Museums and Collections Management; Museology; Museum Studies; Gallery Studies; Museum Management, Geology, Museums and Earth Heritage; Heritage Education and Interpretation; Museum and Gallery Studies and National Trust for Scotland Studies. The degree titles reflect the different emphasis of each course – for instance Heritage Management or Collections Management. The larger departments offer a choice of modules for those who wish to specialise in, for example, art galleries rather than museums. In addition some courses favour a particular subject specialism. For instance, the Birmingham University course at Ironbridge would suit someone with an interest in industrial heritage whereas the University College London course is more suited to those with experience in archaeology. On the other hand, although the University of St Andrews course is based in the School of Art History, students are welcomed from all academic backgrounds and interests. Prospective students for any of these, or the many more recently established courses, should do thorough homework to make sure the chosen programme meets their needs and interests.

It is also very easy now to find courses on the Internet. A number of websites have worldwide listings of courses, including The Smithsonian Center for Education and Museum Studies (SCEMS) Training Program Web Sites Directory and the Global Museum site.[7] The latter lists 23 courses in the UK including courses specialising in, for instance, Maritime Heritage, Conservation, and Critical Museology. In the US nearly 50 courses are listed and in Canada, eight institutions offer courses including the well-established programmes at the Universities of Victoria and Toronto. Nine courses are listed in Australia and New Zealand, and 32 in Europe.

---

7 http://museumstudies.si.edu/TrainDirect.htm
www.globalmuseum.org

Museum studies courses in the US are also listed on the website of the Association of College and University Museums and Art Galleries (ACUMG).[8] This compilation also includes undergraduate courses and single modules. The 2009 ACUMG conference addressed the topic of museum studies and the round-table discussions can be found on their website.[9] One participant recorded 33 undergraduate programmes and 56 graduate programmes.

Many course providers also run part-time and distance learning versions, which would suit students who are already working and do not want to take a year out. Some of these allow part-time students to study a module with the full-time students; some require attendance at a number of separately run residential schools, or a single summer school. Students considering this type of course must ensure they have access to a computer and the Internet.

How do you get on a course?

Most courses are heavily oversubscribed for a limited number of places. A good undergraduate degree is a pre-requisite for any Master's programme. While it seems that the majority of applicants have studied a humanities subject, the subject of your undergraduate degree is rarely a deciding factor for acceptance on a course.[10] Museums and galleries are multi- and inter-disciplinary institutions which need people interested in the arts, sciences, IT, management, marketing, material culture, education, publishing, tourism, events management, business, public relations and so on.

To give yourself a competitive edge it is essential to demonstrate your enthusiasm, interest and commitment. Many applicants have undertaken voluntary work in a museum during summer vacations for example, and this also gives you the opportunity to decide if this really is what you want to do. It is also important to target the course

---

8 www.acumg.org/studies

9 www.acumg.org/conference09.html

10 Davis, op cit, Appendix 1, p. 6. The most common subjects were history, archae-ology, art history and classics.

---

most likely to meet your interests, so you must do your homework about the different courses; look at the website, visit, and talk to others who have done the course. The Museum Discussion List, Museum-L, frequently features requests for recommendations for museum studies courses from prospective students, particularly in the US, and the archive of discussion threads might also contain some useful information.[11]

In the UK the Museums Association has been at the forefront of efforts to bring greater diversity into the museum and gallery workforce through their *Diversify* scheme. This has brought museums and course providers together and through the provision of bursaries, has allowed students from minority ethnic backgrounds to gain experience and a post graduate qualification. The latest round of grants in 2009 was targeted at a wider field of under-represented groups, including those from low-income backgrounds, and deaf and disabled people. Information about the scheme can be found on the Museums Association website.

Interviews

Many museum studies courses interview applicants and this is also a good opportunity for you to decide if this is the course and the university for you. As well as seeing the facilities available you might have the chance to meet the staff and talk to current students about the course. Use an interview to ask questions about opportunities to further your particular interests, and also to find out about student destinations and the employment records of graduates from the course.

Career prospects

It is important to be realistic about career prospects in the museum sector. It is a highly competitive market and not everyone will

---

11 www.finalchapter.com/museum-l-faq
   http://home.ease.lsoft.com/archives/museum-l.html

---

succeed in getting their ideal job. There is also considerable debate about whether a postgraduate museum studies course is essential for museum work, with conflicting messages coming from employers. On the one hand, job criteria often specify a postgraduate qualification, while on the other, applicants are often told they are over-qualified and have not acquired the desired practical or managerial skills on their course. There are other ways to begin a career in museums, such as traineeships, apprenticeships, or coming in from another sector such as education or marketing. Therefore it is important for you to decide that the Master's degree is the route for you.

In addition to the benefits outlined above, until recently a postgraduate museum studies qualification, along with two-year continuous professional development (CPD) was one route for eligibility for the Museums Association AMA. The MA expected the qualification to demonstrate a broad understanding of museum work and museum principles. Whether or not a postgraduate qualification remains as one possible criterion for the AMA, knowledge of the sector beyond your own workplace is likely to be required. The broad view and theoretical underpinning delivered by a postgraduate course is very useful as you begin a career in the museum sector, and is not something you can acquire from work experience. The research, organisational and communication skills acquired from writing a dissertation, the ability to absorb and evaluate information and to think critically and reflectively will never be wasted as they are skills which are transferable to most areas of museum work.

Case Studies

The following three case studies feature graduates from the University of St Andrews' Museum and Gallery Studies course. They have been chosen to illustrate the variety of backgrounds from which students come and career paths they follow, show something of the range of topics that can be researched for a dissertation and to demonstrate some of the benefits of a Master's degree.

Interview with John Burnie, volunteer in an independent industrial museum

John took the two-year part-time MLitt in Museum and Gallery Studies at the University of St Andrews. His dissertation looked at the development of quality assessment schemes in museums, such as Registration and Accreditation. This gave an historical and theoretical context to the actual work going on at his museum.

'As a volunteer in a mainly volunteer-run museum, there were two main reasons for my seeking a qualification in museum studies. The first was that Accreditation required my institution to have a qualified museum professional available to it, and the second was that as a self-taught museum volunteer (a process that consisted largely of learning from mistakes), I needed a more rounded view of the body of knowledge that a museum person requires. In addition, there was the interesting, if slightly scary prospect of going back to university after a decade or two in industry.

'The course was accessible to me because it was available on a part-time basis, over two years, through just a few concentrated weeks of teaching at St Andrews, with assignments and project work to do at my own pace in between. My organisation was able to get a grant to cover part of the cost of the fees. It was good to meet other students sharing the same professional interests and excellent to add knowledge to my existing museum experience.

'This was a very practical course, and the project work was planned between me and my tutor to be both instructive and of useful benefit to my museum. As a result, while I use my new knowledge usually without thinking how I came by it, I still use several of the assignment outcomes in my daily work, and think of sunny days in St Andrews!'

Interview with Jessica Burdge, Curator, Museums Collection, University of St Andrews

After her undergraduate degree, Jessica took the full-time one-year MLitt Museum and Gallery Studies course. Her dissertation topic was Curating Architecture at the Victoria and Albert Museum.

'With an undergraduate joint honours degree in art history and English and some time working in a library as well as a little experience in cataloguing on a SCRAN[12] project, I felt that an MLitt in Museum and Gallery Studies would offer the professional preparation required to embark on a career in the museum sector. It provided me with a greater level of practical experience through work placements and exhibition projects, as well as theoretical understanding, discussing topical issues and ethical questions. It increased my familiarity with a wide range of sector organisations, and current issues and initiatives, in a way that continuing to volunteer or getting an entry-level job would not have done. I have now worked in a few different types of museums and related organisations (heritage organisation, independent museum, government body/museum membership organisation, university), and the wide understanding gained from my museum studies course proved useful when working in these different environments.

'On graduating in November 2005 I worked initially for the National Trust for Scotland as a property assistant/guide, and also carried out some research on properties on a voluntary basis. In January 2006 I started a new job with the Scottish Museums Council (now Museums Galleries Scotland), working on a Collection Level Descriptions project, creating a database of CLDs for member museums and galleries across Scotland. Later that year I moved to a position in an independent museum, as assistant curator (maternity cover) with the Scottish Fisheries Museum, and almost a year after that moved to my current position as collections curator in the Museum Collections Unit of the University of St Andrews (starting as maternity cover, now on a permanent contract).

'While my first few positions perhaps did not justify a postgraduate qualification in terms of salary (although this was often a desired specification and was certainly applicable to the work), by 2007, only

---

12 SCRAN is an online education resource containing digital images from Scottish museum, galleries, archives etc. www.scran.ac.uk

two years after graduating, I had gained a position which could justly ask for a postgraduate qualification, both in terms of the level and responsibility of the position and the remuneration. I certainly feel I would not have achieved that first 'foot in the door', to gain the experience which has allowed me to develop my career in this way, without the MLitt in Museum and Gallery Studies. While no course can give you the same experience as I have gained over the years by working in the sector, it did give me the confidence that I had the skills and knowledge to apply for entry-level museum jobs.

'Achieving an MLitt entailed writing a dissertation in addition to completing the taught course which led to the postgraduate diploma. Personally, I enjoyed this opportunity to look more closely at a particular aspect of museum work and to carry out more academic-style study. While I don't think that this additional part of the course had a significant influence on gaining my early employment, it has definitely helped in my current position in an academic institution. Indeed, with the recent emphasis in the sector on collections research, having this basis of research skills that I developed through the MLitt would be of benefit in whatever type of museum I might be working in.'

Interview with Susan Lewandowski, Assistant Curator, Musical Instruments Collections, Department of World Cultures, National Museums Scotland

Susan was an overseas student from the US and was already working in the museum sector. She undertook the full-time Museum and Gallery Studies MLitt course. Her dissertation looked at the history, development and use of print rooms in a variety of Scottish museums. As research is recognised as a core function and responsibility of national museums, research skills are important for curatorial posts.

'My career was stalled. After several years' working contracts in various types of museum jobs – from finance and development to collections management – I realised I needed an advanced degree in museum studies to take advantage of a wider range of opportunities and push my career to the next level. I had worked hard to build a good reputation within my community, but when applying for jobs outside the area, particularly at national museums, my application wouldn't pass the first round of cuts despite all my experience. I didn't have the basic qualification – a museum studies degree.

'When choosing a course, I looked for a programme that would provide me with new challenges, something beyond what I had already learned on the job. I was too familiar with the course at my local university – I had worked with many of the tutors and trained a few of their interns. I looked beyond my comfort zone – internationally. I wistfully dreamed of working with the extensive older collections outside the US. The programme at St Andrews, with its good reputation, very limited class size, and practical focus fitted my criteria.

'Even though returning to student life was difficult after a long time in the work force, it allowed me to explore unfamiliar areas of museum work. I enjoyed the camaraderie and support fostered by the small class size. St Andrews' strong network throughout Scotland gave me the opportunity to meet and work with museum professionals at both small museums and the large nationals. I gained a clear understanding of the organisation of various heritage institutions in Britain, quite different from what I was familiar with in the US. These new experiences and wider perspective were essential in helping me realise my goal of working at a Scottish national museum. Research is essential to my position here on the Royal Museum Project at NMS. While the official job duties of an assistant curator do not include research, in reality, everyone here undertakes research. A curatorial position requires the ability to gather and disseminate information quickly and the research component of the MLitt is very important in developing these skills.'

Chapter 12
Finding work experience

With so many people pursuing relatively few jobs in museums and galleries, how do you make your application stand out? The way to do this is by showing that your application is based on a realistic understanding of the world you want to enter, and that you have relevant and first-hand experience to offer. Both of these can be achieved by having work experience on your CV. It does not have to be work experience in the kind of institution you aspire to work in long term – you may in any case refine or sharpen your ambitions in the process. What matters is having some.

How to go about finding work experience

Firstly, don't be shy. Organisations are familiar with the concept that those wanting to join this world need to get some first-hand experience on their CV before getting any further. They will probably also be sympathetic, remembering that they were also once in this position.

In theory, any potential organisation or institution where you might end up working could provide work experience, and there are also related options (marketing, fundraising, catering) that you could pursue. But before we start thinking about how to find some, let's be clear about who benefits – you are more likely to be successful in finding a placement if you are aware of what the host organisation will get out of you as well as how much you want a placement.

The benefits of work experience to you

- You get a space on the inside of an organisation; for as long as you are there you are *part of them*. If you handle the opportunity well, this could be extended into a reference, and you will meet colleagues and maybe even a mentor you can keep in touch with in future.

- You gain first-hand experience of the world you want to join, a view on how things work – and the ability to both put this on your CV and have something to talk about during interviews (very common).
- You may be allocated a project of your own to look after, which allows you to make a difference – and can be highlighted to particular effect on your CV.

What you have to offer in return

- you will work for nothing (and all budgets are under pressure);
- you supply extra help – they are overworked and could do with some assistance;
- you are a quick learner and they won't have to spend ages explaining how things work;
- you fit their ethic and will both speak and behave appropriately – you can be trusted to represent them;
- you are pleasant company.

Never forget that even though you are offering your services for nothing, the setting up of placements is not an unalloyed pleasure. Time has to be taken to explain the role, the context and the rules and this has to be redone every time a new placement starts. The designated manager (who has probably not volunteered for this) has to keep in touch with interns, monitor progress and check that they are carrying out the role as they want it carried out – and at the same time manage their own workload. They bear the risk of having to redo what a placement student has done badly, and must now be completed having been started. They will not want the placement student to be nipping in to fill them in on their progress or happiness quota, or check details on an hourly basis, however welcome they may have made you feel on your first morning and told you to 'just ask if you need to know anything'. Having reviewed the placement reports of our students from Kingston going out into the workplace, the most frequent aspect to draw positive comments was that they were self-sustaining and self-motivated, willing and helpful. In summary, they got on with what they were asked to do – and were quick.

How will you support yourself?

Most placements are unpaid, although you may sometimes get travelling expenses. Ethical objections may arise. In addition to exploiting a willing potential workforce, you may quite reasonably argue that the ability to take on an unpaid placement means that the profession is limiting the demographic breadth of its potential intake to those who can afford to work for nothing.

In fact, unpaid placements are becoming a regular occurrence in many professions; an informal test on how committed individuals are to seeking to enter the world they claim they want to join. However you decide to proceed, if you want a placement you will have to find some means of supporting yourself while you undertake it; maybe to increase your student loan or live at home. Alternatively, can you fit a placement around your working hours, maybe two days a week on your placement and the other three in paid employment?

How to find work experience

Before going any further, you need to update your CV (see Chapter 13), as the first response to any request for work experience is to ask to see this document. You can adapt it as you progress, but a basic CV will be needed.

As to where to send your CV when seeking a work placement, think carefully about any contacts you have. Your first reaction may be 'none at all', but if you discuss this with your parents or university lecturers you may find there are people you could get in touch with. Perhaps there's a guest lecturer who has visited your university in the past, or do you know any former students who are now working in significant positions or any family contacts who could perhaps pass your application on to the most appropriate person? Thinking about your contacts is, in any case, not a one-off exercise, but rather an ongoing process. Record names and contact details and keep them somewhere you can find them again (not just on your phone, unless your method of backing up the information held there is particularly rigorous). Drawing others into helping you is not the one-way street it may seem. Most people like to be helpful, and being able to give a helping hand to someone who is in the position they were in 15 years ago may both give them a sense of progression themselves, or the feelgood factor that comes with providing support (if you want first-hand experience of this, go and give blood, and see how you feel afterwards).

Once you have trawled your own contacts or those that have been recommended to you, make a list of organisations you would like to work for, starting with those most geographically accessible. Then do some research. Find out about the organisations you plan to contact – by visiting them if possible, looking at their websites, and searching your memory for instances and anecdotes that you could mention at an interview, or in your covering letter (one of my own earliest memories is of seeing the blue whale in the Natural History Museum, and it has fuelled a lifelong desire to see a live one; at the time of writing a group of paleontologists has come up with a new theory on dinosaurs and challenged the angle at which the Diplodocus really held their head, saying it was more likely to have been upright – like the Brachiosaurus – than traditionally assumed).

Once you are ready, ring up or send an e-mail to find out the name of the person who handles work experience in the organisations you have selected, and ask if you can have speak to them. Be brave – it really is a good idea to call rather than just send in a CV first – because that is what everyone else does.

State your academic stage – so if you are a final-year undergraduate, or a postgraduate, say so (so they don't get you confused with 16 year olds seeking work experience) and that you would really like to come and work for them. They will probably ask you to send in a CV, and if you have spoken to them already it means you can include a letter referring to your conversation and getting their name right. (If you get passed on to the HR department when you ring, it's not a brush off but rather you have moved one stage further inside the organisation).

Then address a letter directly to the person you have spoken to, enclosing two copies of your CV. Mention that you are doing this so they have an additional copy to pass on to a colleague. Make the accompanying letter personal to the organisation you are applying to (or the individual if you know them); make a link between your seeking work experience and knowing something about them and what they do. If there is a sense of urgency in the voice of the person you have spoken to, by all means send your CV by e-mail – but follow up with a printed version, because that means you will be included in the pile of other applications. If you only send an e-mail, you leave the choice (and associated cost) of whether to print it out to them, and they may not.

Be available for work for as long a period as you can. Some organisations have a rigid policy of two weeks per placement but last-minute no-shows are not unusual, and if you are already there, and the placement student scheduled for the following week fails to appear, you may get an extension.

In addition to writing speculatively to organisations, look out for forthcoming special or short-term exhibitions that might be put on by museums and galleries. These tend to play a key role in attracting people into museums and so often have accompanying short-term staffing needs. In general it will be the collections department that deals with the loan of items, but the exhibitions department that deals with temporary displays and the associated staffing requirements. The education department may also take on short-term staff to help with a temporary exhibition so it may be worth asking them too.

How to accept an offer

Sometimes the offer of a placement will be made through an e-mail or a phone call, but more commonly it is followed up by a letter confirming the timing of your placement, where you should report to and any house rules about hours of work and health and safety. This is excellent news, and now you have a foot in the door. While swiftly returning the form you are required to sign and date – speed is important to ensure the opportunity comes to you and not the next person on the list – it's a good idea to get in touch and ask if you can go in and see them. You really want to find out what you will be doing, who you will be reporting to (and if possible meet them) and to try to let them know you are capable, willing and very keen. The 'willing' part is particularly important – no one supervising a placement student wants to feel an obligation to have to negotiate over menial tasks that will be part of your work.

'A willingness to be involved in all aspects of running a museum is helpful. Sitting on reception may not sound exciting, but it does give first-hand insight into who is visiting and when, what they come in to do, how long they stay and what they think of the merchandise available for purchase. And it's also you who tends to get the first-hand feedback on whether or not they have enjoyed the experience!'

PETA COOK, CURATOR, KINGSTON MUSEUM

At the end of the week before you start, send an e-mail confirming that you are looking forward to joining them.

How to behave on a placement

Once there, make yourself useful – without excessive limelight-seeking. The everyday tasks can teach you as much about how an organisation is run as the most senior ones and it is important for everyone to understand the grassroots systems and ethics on which the organisation is based. Don't be grand; just because you have a degree, or even two, does not mean you should look down on those who do not. Here are some further tips:

- Treat it as a job. Be punctual, courteous, stick to office etiquette and style of communication in replying to e-mails. Look like you are part of the furniture – 'the shiny new addition to the team that they didn't even realise they needed'.[1]
- Don't get drawn into feeling resentful about not being paid. This is a means to an end and you understood how work experience was organised before you applied. Even if it occurs to you that you are doing the same work as the person who has a paid job and they are coasting while relying on unpaid you, don't even think of voicing this to anyone else within the organisation – or frankly at all.
- Remember that your hosts are seeing you in the context of who was there before so don't be tempted to criticise those you are working with or the tasks you have been asked to do. They know each other better than they know you.
- Do what you get asked to do really well; make suggestions after you have been there a while (not in the first few days) and then feed them to your line manager to show that you understand how the hierarchy works. They are looking for a team player, not the next director.
- Try to find out who is who and to meet the key people – the people working for them as well as those in the key roles; they too will become significant. Write down their names and check the spellings. You never know when you will run into them, so be prepared to say something pithy and not too long – the museum director you meet in the lift will probably not be expecting a PowerPoint presentation on where he is going wrong.
- Be enthusiastic (but not excessively so). Smile. You will get noticed for it.
- Mark your departure in an appropriate fashion. Take in a box of home-made biscuits (home-made because it shows care has been taken) rather than funding a booze-up in the pub. Write notes of appreciation to those who have helped you, and ask discreetly if you can keep in touch.

---

1 Sarah Townsend, work placement student in publishing.

And afterwards

Remain in contact with former work colleagues, without stalking them. Remember that once you have moved on, the next placement student will have moved in, and although, to you, the shared time was unforgettable, you are in fact one of many. Write and say thank you – and I do mean write. Take trouble over what you send. Remember that advertising for staff takes time and effort, and so if an HR manager remembers a placement student who was particularly helpful, and the opportunity for some additional paid hours occurs at short notice, you may get offered the role – because your availability and the fact that you have already been tried out and found satisfactory, gives you the edge.

Case Studies: Work experience

Interview with David Falkner, Director of the Stanley Picker Gallery in Kingston

'Each year we put up notices in the faculty asking for volunteers to get involved. This has now evolved into a regular pattern. About 20–30 initial volunteer students usually beds down into a group of around 10 who are truly committed. We try to ensure they have as varied an experience of the gallery as possible, and get involved in all aspects – from helping with the educational work, invigilating[2] and front of house, to pouring wine at receptions and sending the 'mailout' for new installations. I try to impress on them all that communication is of vital importance, whatever part of the job they are involved with, thus recipients of the mailshot can be made to feel welcome by the way the invitations are worded, and this careful attention to detail needs to be maintained in everything we do. I try to encourage them to engage as fully as possible in all aspects of the venue – as running a gallery involves a huge number of different aspects, from the mundane (is there any graffiti on

2 Or sitting with an exhibition

our signage, is the entrance porch clear of litter?) to the specific (how do we write programme notes to get the audience to appreciate what is being shown – and encourage them to value the experience and tell others?).

'When I receive speculative applications from people seeking work experience, I appreciate it if they have thought about why they want to come to us and what they think they will both get out of the experience and offer us. We have one year-long placement which is paid, and this can be adapted to the skills being offered by the applicants.

'Given that we only have two members of core staff, there are so many ways in which volunteers can help – with marketing, publicity, database management and administration. Those who have found out about the gallery and thought about how what they can offer us is relevant to the skills and aptitudes we need, stand a much better chance of being taken on. The package they send in to advertise themselves does make a difference. Our role is to communicate the gallery and its value to the wider community, and so if they are unable to communicate their value to me, I would be concerned at how good they would be at expressing our mission to the outside world.'

Interview with Peta Cook, Curator, Kingston Museum

'As regards work experience, I am always sympathetic to those seeking it because it was my route into the profession. I try to make it a structured use of both their and our time, defining projects within the museum that need thinking about and so being able to match the skills of the volunteer with the things we need doing. My current list includes a collections audit of the museum store (including cataloguing and photographing what is held in boxes); involvement in collection resource development (work on subject or period specific boxes such as The Tudors, Victorians and World War II); exhibition development in connection with the exhibition to tie in with the 500th anniversary of the accession of Henry VIII to the throne, and work on learning links for the Muybridge Retrospective that is planned with the Corcoran Gallery in Washington, to celebrate the work of the pioneering moving image photographer Eadweard Muybridge who lived in Kingston. Which learning links are developed – whether for adults or as part of the school curriculum – is flexible. There is also the opportunity to work in partnership with the Tate's learning team in London).

'We tend to get two kinds of application for work experience. Firstly from graduates, often with a degree in history and sometimes with a postgraduate qualification in museum studies, enclosing a CV and requesting that we 'keep them on file' should a vacancy occur. I try to write back saying that the route into this world is usually via work experience and to send them information on the projects I have available at the moment, but given that we don't have any official vacancies for paid employment, their speculative letter in search of it is unlikely to be progressed.

'The second sort of application comes from students, either pre-, post- or during a Master's course in museumship, this time seeking work experience. Again I send them the list of projects and make a sustained attempt to match the skills of those who reply to actual projects. Managing volunteers (we have over 40) takes a lot of time and effort, and I have instituted formal induction and training procedures, and try to spot specific requests. Applicants are always keen to stress their academic credentials, whether acquired or prospective, but the one thing I look out for is practical experience; the physical handling of objects in a museum and an appreciation of a museum's ethics. One of the most important principles is that while we will attempt to help the public understand their treasures if they bring them in to show them to us, we can never offer advice on their monetary value. So if you have worked in a museum before, or spent time in one observing, be sure to let me know you understand this.

'When you make an application to a museum, do ensure you cover all the questions I may think of as I read what you send – so if your postal address is far away, make it clear that you have already thought through how you will get to work and where you will stay. We get many more applications than we are able to satisfy, so the fewer doubts you raise in my mind, the better. Do find out about us before you apply – it always shows when someone has taken the trouble to do so.'

Interview with Mary Bee, Portal Gallery, London

'I wanted to go to art school and my father would not let me, so I always had a passion for art and wanted to work with it. Mind you, when Jonathan took me on to work in his gallery full of sculpture,[3] I knew nothing at all, so the learning curve was pretty steep.

'Given my start in the business, I always look for aptitude and personality when taking on staff, rather than formal qualifications. You are taking on someone with whom you will be spending an awful lot of time, so it's important that they are lively, bright and take the initiative.

'Artists are better served by an intermediary explaining their work than by doing it themselves, but it's a question of matching the right level of information to each individual customer. Staff need to be intelligent and articulate, of course, but also to be engaged by the work themselves – you have to be moved by the work in order to move it on.

'We have employed the children of friends and relatives, and also many students from the Royal Academy of Art, which was just around the corner from where we used to be. We receive many letters and e-mails from those looking for work in galleries, and some we hang on to, should an opportunity arise.

'We reply to everyone who writes to us, and it's hard to say why I hang on to some CVs but not others. Some people just display an

---

3 The Jonathan Poole Gallery.

empathy or a quirkiness in their covering letter or make themselves sound appealing in a way that is both tangible yet hard to define. I am looking for a willing attitude and enthusiasm, and sometimes this comes over in what they send in, sometimes not.'

What to do if you still can't find any work experience, or in between placements

Look out for related activities that could support work experience or replace it if it is particularly difficult to secure. For example:

- Produce a family archive of history or photographs.
- Catalogue and reorganise the books at your family home into a library, for example, separating them into reference and fiction and considering how to look after rare, fragile, the most frequently used and the titles that you decide you want to have on display; consider how to reconcile different family views on how this process might be managed, and whose should prevail.
- Join a relevant local society – perhaps a history or archaeology society – both in your home town and at university. As most such organisations are seeking to widen their network, they might be particularly keen on younger members, and if you find yourself on the committee it makes another useful addition to your CV and even perhaps the source of a reference. The Geography Society in the town where I grew up included a range of geography professors who lived in the town and, through their personal connections, they always managed to obtain a very high standard of speaker.
- Does your university department or hall of residence have an archive or boxes of historic stuff that no one has got around to sorting out? Could you write something for the student newspaper about its history or about famous previous residents?

Part 4:
How to get your job

Chapter 13
How to create an eye-catching CV

If you look in the careers section of any bookshop you will see that the world is not short of books on how to prepare an effective CV. So rather than giving you line by line guidance on what to say in yours, I am going to give you a few suggestions to bear in mind.

The CV is a representational document; it should take your name, qualifications, skills and aptitudes to the door of your potential employer and create a sufficiently strong impression that they decide to interview you. So it supports your personal application rather than replacing it; it needs to provide enough information to convey the breadth of what you have to offer, which can be supported and expanded upon at an interview. While it should remain recognisably a CV, it is a document that represents an individual and so also needs to convey your personality, which is why I am not advocating a 'one size fits all' approach.

Bear in mind that your CV will probably not be read in the order it is written, and not even all of it may be considered: most usually CVs are placed in a pile until all applications have been received, and then they are worked through, with the 'possibles' placed in one pile and the 'nos' in another. Your place of education and the qualifications you emerged with will be noted, along with any relevant work experience, but then there may be a quick skip through the other information presented. Your name and contact details will be considered (how far would you have to travel for interview; would you be likely to relocate if offered the job?). There are ways of guiding the reader's attention, maybe by providing subheadings or the effective use of space that draws attention to the most important parts of the application (key aptitudes or referees).

One section that always gets looked at is the applicant's interests, not because these are a key reason for appointing someone, but because they convey something of the personality of the applicant: most organisations are looking for team players and someone who will both fit in and make their own individual contribution. Above all, remember that when you are seeking employment in a museum or gallery, your CV will be read by people of discernment, but it also has to make it through the earlier, administrative stages of recruitment to check that you are suitably qualified for the job. So while it must be legible, your key achievements and aptitudes need to stand out and it should also convey a sense of someone who has thought about how to present information and for whom presentation is important. Fulfilling both objectives at the same time is harder than it sounds.

Some specific guidance

Above all, your CV should be a flexible document. You can keep a standard outline on your computer, but tweak it according to the role you are applying for. For example, the headings under which you feature information (personal details, paid employment, work experience, education) are fairly standard, but think carefully about what order to put them in and which should receive the most emphasis.

Content of a CV

1. **Concentrate on what you can offer potential employers rather than what you want from them.**

Think through your career to date (both at university and in the workplace) and present it in terms of what you have learnt that might be useful to a future potential employer rather than what you have specifically done. Thus if you have spent time writing a leaflet and then standing in the street handing it out to passers-by to encourage them to come into the museum, think about the wider implications of what you were doing:

- Working on a campaign to widen participation and increase attendance, including the development and distribution of a flyer.

2. Include non-work experience.

Most people have more of this than they realise at first, so have you:

- Been on a committee and got involved in any project to change people's minds?
- Been involved with local (or national press), say as part of a campaign?
- Played a representational role (on the school council, in the local area?)
- Raised money for charity?
- Won awards at school or university?
- Set up a new society or organised something that others attended? Even if the event was for a family occasion, or a surprise party for a friend, this can reveal your organisational skills.

Anything that shows that you can both organise, implement and work with others is a useful addition to your CV.

3. Don't add anything you don't want to be asked about

For example work experience that did not go too well, embarrassing middle names, specific interests such as morris dancing or train spotting.

4. Present your interests.

This is a key area of the CV in which to strike an empathetic chord with your potential interviewers, so think carefully about what you select and make them specific rather than general. So rather than listing 'reading', say what books/authors you like:

'Trollopes: Fanny, Anthony and Joanna'

The same goes for travel: 'Umbria' is more interesting than 'Italy'. If you like the architecture of a specific period, say which building draws you most:

'1930s architecture, with a particular passion for the de la Warr Pavilion'

Never, ever be tempted to include something that you cannot justify at an interview, just to look interesting: if you say you love white water rafting and then come up against an expert at white water rafting but can't name any stretches of water you have personally navigated, you will look pretty foolish.

5.   Offer referees in support of your application.
Two is usual, and if applying for a job straight from university it would be unusual if one were not your tutor, and a second perhaps someone from a work placement. Do ensure you have kept them up to date on your activities since leaving their institution. From experience, it's frustrating to receive requests for references from students you last remember from four years ago, or perhaps do not remember at all (given that you have a different class each year).

Presentation of a CV

1.   Make sure it is grammatically correct.
You are contacting a market that is specific and detail orientated, and spelling and other grammatical mistakes will jump out at the reader. In particular, check that all your key/bullet points are formatted in the same way, so for example:

- two years' work experience in my local museum;
- I regularly helped out with outreach events on public holidays.

would be more logically presented as:

- two years' work experience in my local museum;
- tegular assistance with outreach events on public holidays.

Bear in mind that a CV that is packed with 'I's can cast doubt on your value as a team player.

2.   Print it out on good quality paper without making it look such good quality that it seems inflexible. CVs that are bound in expensive folders may look impressive initially but are not easily adapted to fit specific job applications. They also risk looking showy and raising the issue of how good you are as part of a team (key question).

3.   Make best use of the space

It should be obvious that it is a CV, so consider putting your name at the top of the document, rather than 'Curriculum Vitae' – and then a top tip is to put your name and contact details at the bottom of the page, so people have to flick through what you say in order to find this.[1]

4.   Offer your contact details

Include the telephone number on which you prefer to be contacted. If you have a flatmate with a questionable telephone manner – such as the 'hilarious' habit of answering the phone and pretending to be someone else, or who is lax about taking messages – give your mobile number. Say if there are any specific times of the day when you cannot accept calls ('mobile, before 9.30 or after 5.30, please leave a message in between these times'), and remember to keep it charged and to check regularly for messages. Think too about establishing a sensible sounding e-mail address: bambamlovespebbles@hotmail.co.uk may amuse your friends but is less intriguing to a potential employer.

Before you start your job hunt, think carefully about the image you are presenting of yourself on Facebook and other social networking sites – employers increasingly look here for guidance on what kind of job potential employees might make of representing *them* to the wider world.

5.   Consider what typeface to use

It should be something that is legible, but conveys the essential you. So do you want to use serif (as in **Times New Roman** with the twiddly bits on the edges of the letters or **New Baskerville** which is the typeface used in this book) or sans serif (for example, the typeface **Tahoma**). If you are able to, try to find out which typeface the organisation you

---

1   With thanks to Janice Pickard, Careers Consultant at Kingston University for this idea.

are applying to uses and do likewise. Be warned, typefaces date very quickly, and an application submitted in **Comic Sans** or a handwriting face will attract negative attention.

6. Include plenty of space
It is space in a document that draws the eye in, not text, so make sure your document has eye-catching space at regular intervals rather than covering every part with text. Use a ragged right-hand margin rather than justifying your text.

7. Don't make it too long – two pages is plenty.

There is no need to include the following:

- Your date of birth
- Your marital status or number of dependents
- Your salary expectations
- Your photograph
- Too much detail of how wonderful you are – keep it succinct. This is a document to reassure a potential employer, not to give pleasure to your parents.

What to send with your CV

All job applicants need a basic CV that can be adapted to the specific job you are applying for. Some organisations have their own application form, in which case you will have to adapt the information you have to the questions they ask.

When responding to a specific advertisement, send an accompanying letter outlining your particular desire and aptitude for the post being advertised. It should be addressed to the individual named in the advertisement (and triple check to ensure you spell their name correctly – it's easy to make a mistake) and make reference to what they have asked for in the job outline. Be sure to edit the name and address to make sure it's addressed to the institution you are applying for, rather than sending it to the same organisation you drafted the original letter for (again, so easily done). Better still, start from scratch each time – the result will be fresher and more immediate, and ironically probably take you less time than adapting a previous version.

About three paragraphs is usually enough, perhaps one saying you are applying, a second saying why you are particularly attracted to this post, and a third outlining your specific qualifications. You should conclude by saying you are available for interview.

Have you ever wondered why each direct marketing package, selling anything from conservatories and double-glazing to new credit cards, always includes a letter? It's because studies of how these items are opened, read and responded to (and these studies do take place) routinely report that the one item in the package that always gets read is the accompanying letter. The same goes for job applications. A CV may appear standardised, but it is in the letter that you make your specific individual pitch – and it is worth taking time and trouble to get it right.

- double check that you have got the addressee's details right – nothing is more obvious to the recipient (and less obvious to the sender);
- ensure the layout is interesting and tempting to read (three paragraphs of different lengths is more eye catching than three that are exactly the same size);
- mention any personal link you have with the organisation you are applying to in the opening paragraph – visits as a child; inspiring items held; attendance at a lecture given by a key member of staff;
- the letter should match your CV – same typeface and paper quality – so as to make an attractive whole;
- do not justify the text, it looks blockish and uninviting (rather, leave the right-hand margin ragged);
- sign your letter with an ink pen not a blotchy ballpoint.

If they say that they do not acknowledge applications, consider enclosing a stamped-addressed postcard (with an image you have chosen to represent you) to be returned to you.

Paperclip your letter to your CV (and postcard if you are including one) and then place it in an appropriately sized envelope. Do not spoil the look of your package by over-folding and hence squashing the contents – consider how they will come out at the other end. Along the same lines, if you are sending just three sheets of paper, they may bear up to the ravages of the postal system, and hence arrive in better shape, if you make a single fold in the middle and put them in a C5 envelope – single sheets in a C4 envelope may arrive looking particularly battered.

Handwrite the envelope (using your good quality pen), making sure it is legible, correctly spelt and conventionally laid out. Visit a Post Office, have it weighed and ensure you add the right postage (larger envelopes now cost more than smaller ones). The last thing you want is for your material not to arrive because you have paid insufficient postage – which would mean the recipient had the choice of either choosing to pay the difference or deciding not to bother. Show your attention to detail by getting this right. If it is an option, choose attractive stamps and stick them on straight.

Last semester I taught a module on preparation for a career in marketing and communications at Kingston University. It was interesting that many of the MA students saw applying for a job as a numbers game: you send off 500 applications and out of these you may get X number of interviews and X number of job offers; and the more difficult the economic conditions, the more you have to widen your starting point. It's one strategy but, as the course progressed, speaker after speaker confirmed the value of taking time and trouble – to make your applications count by making them specific.

Applying for a job in the world of museums and galleries is *more* difficult than in some professions in that the number of applicants vastly outweighs the number of jobs on offer. It's a much better strategy to make every single application count – or as one potential employer said of a poorly drafted application: 'If you don't care, why should I?'

Chapter 14

How to put together a job application for an advertised post

The first task is to find a job advertisement to reply to. Some are advertised through general websites (see Appendix for details), others will appear within the staff requirements for an umbrella organisation, thus the advertisement used as a case study in this chapter, for an Assistant Keeper for Aberdeen Art Gallery and Museum appeared on the Aberdeen City job page on the website along with advertisements for a Housing Assistant, a Senior Cook and a Driver/Handyperson.

Enlist others to help you in your search. If you are studying for an MA in Museum Studies or Curatorship, your lecturers may well try to circulate information on openings that reach them, but of course these will then be made available to the entire cohort, including some of last year's students who are not yet employed. Many people find their parents and wider family a useful job-searching resource, and they can often pick up references in local papers which may be worth pursuing (if you wish to return to your home area). Flexibility is important:

> 'In logistic terms, a career in this world does require you to be mobile, and to fit your friendship and family patterns to that mobility – and I mean internationally, not just within the UK. Jobs are rare and need to be moved to, whether in the UK or overseas.'
>
> DAVID FALKNER, DIRECTOR, STANLEY PICKER GALLERY, KINGSTON

Once you have found a job to apply for, note the date by which you must apply, read the person specification carefully and note the process by which to progress your application (if you send in a CV and a covering letter and they have asked you to contact them for an application pack, then you have shown that you are not particularly detail-orientated).

Before you even think about completing the application form, or sending in your own application, you must devote careful attention to the role for which you are applying. Remember that time and effort is put into drafting job descriptions and advertisements, so respond with similar care. Some employers now use computer programs to do a first sift of applications; these programs look for a match between the verbs used in the job advertisement and the verbs used in the applicant's response – in other words has the applicant based their application on the information provided about what the organisation is looking for? A useful tip is to follow the advice commonly given to those preparing for oral examinations in foreign languages at school – listen out for the verb and deliver it back, with an example attached.

For an example of this process in practice, here's an advertisement that appeared on the website www.museumjobs.co.uk

Organisation:	National Media Museum
Salary:	£13,343 p.a.
Type:	Full-Time Position
	Contract: 12 months fixed term
Location:	Bradford, England
Closing Date:	Thursday, April 23rd, 2009
Job Ref No:	

Job Description:
Job Title: Collections Access Assistant
Salary: 13,343 per annum
Full time, 36 hours per week
12 months fixed term
Closing date: 23rd April 2009

Award winning, visionary and truly unique, The National Media Museum embraces photography, film, television, radio and new media, including the Web. Part of the NMSI family of museums, it aims to engage, inspire and educate through comprehensive collections, innovative education programmes and a powerful yet sensitive approach to contemporary issues.

Insight is the Collections and Research Centre of the National Media Museum. Joining the Collections team, you will research, identify and repatriate archived material to facilitate and encourage public access. Specifically, your work will focus on the Zoltan Glass project.

Glass was a Hungarian photographer who specialised in documenting the pre-war German car industry and also undertook glamour and advertising photography. The Museum holds over 12,000 images of his, some of which are currently being catalogued, digitised and sequenced.

Required Skills:
Demonstrable experience in collections care/management and access gained within a museum/heritage environment is essential. Keen to learn, you will be able to understand and engage with the Zoltan Glass project, as well as embracing the broader access and outreach philosophy of the Museum. An up-to-date knowledge of cataloguing and documentation best practice is also important – ideally supported by a natural, ongoing interest in photography and other media.

Application Instructions:
To apply, please write with full CV and covering letter to: The HR Department, National Media Museum, Bradford BD1 1NQ or email: recruitment@nationalmediamuseum.org.uk

We regret that we can only respond to successful applicants.

Here is the job advertisement again, this time with some helpful notes on what to consider before you think about responding.

Job Description:
Job Title: Collections Access Assistant[1]
Salary: 13,343 per annum
Full time, 36 hours per week
12 months fixed term[2]
Closing date: 23rd April 2009

Award winning, visionary and truly unique,[3] The National Media Museum embraces photography, film, television, radio and new media, including the web. Part of the NMSI family of museums,[4] it aims to engage, inspire and educate[5] through comprehensive collections,[6] innovative education programmes[7] and a powerful yet sensitive approach to contemporary issues.[8]

---

1   You would probably be working for the Collections Access Manager, who may look after several different collections.

2   This is a job that offers only a year's contract. It may get extended, but it may not, and whereas it may be a good starting point on your career, and a useful addition to your CV, but you will have ensure you are accessible if you are selected for the role, and so move to an accessible location.

3   These three words are probably part of their overall ethos/mission statement and will have been drafted with care. Have a think about the implications. Where else could you get access to the sort of resources they hold? The British Film Institute and various television stations and newspapers might have some, but this museum offers the history of all media under one roof. Try to find out something about the collection's history, when it was set up and what it tries to do. Visit if possible.

4   Google this. What is NMSI? What other collections belong to 'the family'?

5   Three key verbs, and probably part of the organisational plan which will have taken time to draft. Your response should pay attention to these clear priorities and you should think about how you can engage audiences, inspire them and educate them to understand more about the collection.

6   What do they have available and how much more is in the archive?

7   With what age groups? For adults or children or both? Is there a regular programme of talks about the collection given to groups and organisations in the area who ask for one?

8   Can you think of any case histories, where media reporting played a part in the story? The death and subsequent reporting of the reputation of Diana, Princess of Wales is an obvious example

---

Insight[9] is the Collections and Research Centre of the National Media Museum. Joining the Collections team, you will research, identify and repatriate[10] archived material to facilitate and encourage public access.[11] Specifically, your work will focus on the Zoltan[12] Glass project.

Glass was a Hungarian photographer who specialised in documenting the pre-war German car industry and also undertook glamour and advertising photography. The Museum holds over 12,000 images of his, some of which are currently being catalogued, digitised and sequenced.[13]

Required Skills:[14]
Demonstrable experience in collections care/management and access gained within a museum/heritage environment is essential.[15] Keen to learn,[16] you will be able to understand and engage with the Zoltan Glass project,[17] as well as embracing the broader access and outreach philosophy of the Museum.[18] An up-to-date knowledge of cataloguing and documentation best practice is also

---

9 The specific job being advertised is with the Insight Team, so be clear about what it does.

10 This could be worth a question at interview. In this context, what does repatriate mean? Does it mean giving stuff back to donors or encouraging the gift of materials to the museum that support the archives they hold?

11 The role requires the incumbent to promote understanding and encourage people to use the collection.

12 Google him and find out more.

13 How far have they got with this?

14 These are the things you must have for this role. Go through this list particularly carefully.

15 Probably gained through work experience.

16 Willing and not assuming that you know it all already.

17 How did the Glass collection end up here? A good question to ask at interview.

18 The job is two-fold, they want you to both work on the Zoltan project but also be part of the team, getting involved with other initiatives/their wider ethos.

important[19] – ideally supported by a natural, ongoing interest in photography and other media.[20]

Application Instructions:

To apply, please write with full CV and covering letter[21] to: The HR Department, National Media Museum, Bradford BD1 1NQ or email:

recruitment@nationalmediamuseum.org.uk

We regret that we can only respond to successful applicants.

Case Study: Job Application

The following advertisements, for Applied Art Keeper and Assistant Keeper, appeared on the Aberdeen City Council website in May 2007. The footnotes in this section provide a detailed analysis of the job advertisement and the skills and competencies sought by Aberdeen City Council.

---

19 Most job specifications divide the skills they are looking for into 'essential' and 'desirable'. 'Knowledge of cataloguing and documentation' are the latter rather than the former, but a candidate who can offer both 'essential' and 'desirable' has an advantage. Try to think of an example of your experience for each of the areas suggested, and confirm that you are eager to learn/gain more experience.

20 If you know little about photography, but still want to apply for the role, buy yourself some photography magazines, find a friend whose hobby this is, try to find some relevant exhibitions to attend, and start learning. You should not present yourself as an expert, and if you try to bluff you will get found out, but arriving at an interview for this role with no understanding of photography would seriously affect your chances of getting the job. The same goes for your interest in the media. Think about this before you apply.

21 This is a most important part of the application process and it should make a link between your CV, which will probably have been compiled for general job applications, to this specific role and your particular desire to fill it. See Chapter 13 for more advice on how to write an effective letter to support a job application.

We are looking for two committed,[22] versatile[23] and energetic[24] museum professionals to join the Applied Art team[25] at Aberdeen Art Gallery and Museums.[26] The museum service holds an exceptional Applied Art collection[27] ranging from ceramics and glass to fashion and textiles and our outstanding metalwork, jewellery and craft holdings[28] are the result of our innovative and bold approach to contemporary collecting.[29]

Keeper, Applied Art

Working with the Art Gallery and Museums Manager[30] you'll develop the collection,[31] manage our 16th century town house – Provost Skene's House,[32] and lead the team. You'll bring a record of curatorial practice, exhibition development and project management[33] and be committed to making our collection

---

22 They will need to be convinced that you truly want this job and see your career in this sector.

23 The job description will relate to the role envisaged but they will want you to be flexible, willing to muck in and not stick to strict demarcation zones – see Chapters 1 and 2.

24 Self-starting, with lots of get up and go.

25 Implies this already exists, but note they are advertising for both Keeper and Assistant Keeper at the same time. Are these new roles or is there a ready-made team in this area? If you are planning on phoning Christine Rew, this would be a good question to ask.

26 Find out about them. Where are they? Is it one art gallery and several museums and if so which ones are they?

27 Find out more. Not just about what is held, but how it is regarded. If you are enrolled on a museums course, can your lecturers give you anything to read on the collection and its significance?

28 Find out about them all.

29 What do they mean? Purchasing, or persuading people to give?

30 Whilst this is a senior role it is important to imply both that you enjoy being part of a team and respond to direction.

31 How? What ambitions are there for this and is there an associated budget?

32 Look it up and find out more.

33 These are the job essentials and you will need examples of how you have achieved all three; what you have done and the difference you made.

fully accessible to visitors.[34] Experience of working in a museum environment is essential, as is having knowledge of at least one of the subject areas covered by the collections.[35]

Assistant Keeper, Applied Art

Assisting the Keeper,[36] you'll play a key role in making our collections accessible through exhibitions and displays,[37] lectures[38] and the Web.[39] You'll have good collections management and documentation skills[40] combined with specialist knowledge of at least one area of the collections.[41]

To find out more about these posts call Christine Rew, Art Gallery and Museums Manager, on 01224 523672. The closing date for the above vacancies is Monday 11th June 2007.

---

34 See Chapter 2. Ease of access and promoting wider usage, both by groups who know of the organisation and those who don't.

35 Find out what they are, so you can make your expertise clear.

36 You need to show that whilst you have initiative and drive, you are happy to be part of a team and enjoy working with others; in the process subtly making it clear that you are not someone who prefers to operate on their own/does not like being told what to do.

37 It sounds as if it will be your responsibility to suggest which special exhibitions are put on, and if approved do the organising.

38 You could be required to give talks for a variety of organisations and societies from local history groups to the WI; many programme managers for such groups are looking for spaces to fill. You must match what you deliver to the audience you address, always bearing in mind that your aim is to encourage wider engagement with the Aberdeen Art Gallery and Museums – to prompt others to value what is available.

39 You must be interested in website development and access to the collection through this route. You may or may not be required to do the updating (although state in your application if this is an area of expertise or previous experience), but you must be interested in how this route to market is used.

40 Proof of this needed, state the experience you have and then give concrete examples of how this worked in practice.

41 Find out what they are and try to match your experience.

Following the principle outlined above, rather than just reaching for the phone and trying to talk to Christine Rew (who would be your eventual boss if you were to be successful), find out more about the organisation and what is required. You may eventually decide you do want to ring for more information, and it looks keen if you do, but the call should only be made once you have done your basic research, with a ready list of sensible questions you want to ask.

This advertisement was spotted by Kate Gillespie, who at the time was studying for an MLitt in Museum and Gallery Studies at the University of St Andrews. She applied on 11 May 2007, well before the closing date of 11 June, and found out at the end of June that she had an interview. The interview took place on 11 July and she was informed the next day that she had the job.

Kate applied online, but the following are extracts from her CV which gave the potential for linking what they were looking for and what she could offer.

EDUCATION

Higher
The University of St Andrews: September 2006 – August 2007.
M.Litt with Distinction in the Dissertation in Museum and Gallery Studies.[42]

The University of St. Andrews: September 2002 – June 2006.
2:1 MA Honours Degree in Art History[43]
Honours modules passed include: The 'New Style' in Eastern Europe; Venetian Art in the Age of Reform; Titian and His Age; Rubens & Rembrandt: Parallel Works; Aspects of Surrealism; and The Renaissance Court of Urbino.
Year long Dissertation 'Problems Concerning Titian's *Venus and Musician Series*'.

---

[42] Studying for a relevant higher degree, i.e. showing commitment to seeking employment in museums and galleries.

[43] Relevant degree. Strong university reputation in this field.

Other subjects studied at University include: Psychology, Philosophy, Social Anthropology, Classics and Medieval History.[44]

PREVIOUS EMPLOYMENT

Part time waitress/shop assistant. September 2004 – August 2006. The Coffee House, St. Andrews.

Job entailed product preparation, customer service, window display, cash handling and training new members of staff.[45]

Welcome Host. Summers of 2002 & 2003. Scottish Borders Enterprise.

Role comprised liaising with the Scottish Borders Tourist Board, assisting visitors to the Scottish Borders with any enquiries they may have had and conducting tours for groups of French visitors.[46]

Campsite Courier. Summer 2004. Ian Mearns Holidays, France.

Responsibilities included the general running, representation of the company and dealing with the families from all over Europe on three different campsites based in Normandy, Ile de France & Picardy.[47]

Summer Internships with Scottish Borders Council Museum & Gallery Services. Summers 2005 and 2006. Details below.

WORK EXPERIENCE

Classroom Assistant. June 2001 – 2002. Hawick High School

Assisted teachers in second year Art and French classes. Supervised pupils' work. Helped children (ages 13-15) with any problems they had for example grammar, spelling, reading and practical work.[48]

---

44 Broad education.

45 Shows an ability to work with the public, but the useful mentioning of handling money and training others implies a maturity and a willingness to take responsibility.

46 A PR role showing that she can represent an organisation and at the same time give practical advice.

47 Implies flexibility and familiarity with other languages and a willingness to use them. Implication that she is good at thinking on her feet and problem solving.

48 Has experience of working with children, useful for museum education programmes.

Summer Placement with Scottish Borders Council Museum & Gallery Services. June – August 2005 and 2006.

Shadowed the Visual Arts Officer for the summers of 2005 and 2006. Assisted with exhibition preparation and gallery management in four galleries across the Scottish Borders. Duties included researching, cataloguing, exhibition design and installation, couriering, press office and reprographics work.[49]

August 2006 worked on local Archaeological Society Anniversary exhibition. Activities included exhibition design, preparation and installation, educational work and reprographics.[50]

Art Education Research Project. September 2006 – April 2007.

In conjunction with the five Schools of Art in Scotland; Glasgow School of Art, Edinburgh College of Art, The Royal Scottish Academy, Duncan of Jordanstone College of Art and Gray's School of Art conducted an audit on their collections to highlight the strengths and weaknesses of each institution. Liaised with curators, archivists, librarians and conservators, while gaining experience in collections management and preventative conservation.[51]

Interview and selection

'It takes a long time to make an effective application for a job, but what is often not appreciated is how much time it takes for the employers to draft a person specification, write an accompanying advertisement, sift through the applications, make a shortlist, inter-

---

49 Lots of relevant experience backed by having had the gumption to seek the role and sustain it over two summers (means it must have gone well).

50 Again, relevant experience gained through volunteering. Implies commitment.

51 A university-based project of work offering further relevant experience. In the process, she demonstrates an ability to liaise with other institutions, and work in cross-organisational teams, from which may be deduced tact and diplomacy.

---

view those selected for the final stage of the process and then make an appointment.

'In this case the person specification and job advertisement were drafted by Christine Rew, who would be the eventual line manager, but were checked by me, as Aberdeen City Council is the ultimate employer. The interview panel was to consist of three people: Christine as Art Gallery and Museums Manager, me as Service Manager, Culture and Leisure for Aberdeen City Council (museums come under my remit as do arts, libraries, development and education and sports) and a third 'external' member; usually either an academic from one of the two universities in Aberdeen or another colleague from a different part of the council.

'The advertisement drew about 40 responses and then the three interviewers each went through the applications, along with Christine Rew's person specification and a list of the (a) essential and (b) desirable personal attributes sought. We looked for a full match in the former, and as much as possible in the latter, and each drew up a list of those we should interview. We then compared notes and made our final selection for the shortlist. We would generally try to interview no more than six to eight people, and if we were unable to reduce the list down to this number would assume our advertisement had not been drafted with sufficient precision.

'Kate's application was certainly strong, but within an impressive field. Although young she had amassed a lot of work experience and clearly shown her commitment to a future spent working in museums and galleries. What I do remember about her interview was her enthusiasm and the trouble she had taken to find out about both the collection and those she would be working with if she got the job. For example, Christine Rew is an expert in applied art and has written extensively on it, and Kate showed that she was familiar with both the collection and Christine's research. This impressed us all and her appointment was a unanimous decision.'

Neil Bruce, Service Manager, Culture and Leisure, Aberdeen City Council

Kate Gillespie's current role

Interview with Kate Gillespie, Assistant Keeper (Applied Art), Aberdeen Art Gallery and Museums

'At school I had always loved art but thought there were no jobs available in this field, so I made a sensible choice and went to the University of St Andrews intending to study psychology. But Scottish universities require students to take a variety of subjects before specialising, and after two years sampling other options (philosophy, anthropology, as well as psychology and history of art) I found the latter was by far my preferred choice and continued with a single honours history of art degree.

'Having made my choice, I started thinking about employment and wrote to my local authority offering myself for voluntary work during the summer vacation. I heard back from the local Visual Arts Officer for the Scottish Borders and ended up shadowing her for about three months during the summer before my final year as she established a temporary exhibition programme for five local galleries. The work was unpaid, although some costs were reimbursed. I lived at home and financed myself through the proceeds of the part-time jobs I had had while a student – waitressing in a cafe and working in a bar. I had very little spare cash but I did feel I was making an investment in my future – I could suddenly see career options opening up. I just loved the work – in fact so much so that I went back the following year to work for her again, and she was my referee for all subsequent job applications.

'I got a 2.1 in history of art. After graduating, I enrolled on the MA in Museum and Gallery Studies at St Andrews – a year-long course running from September to May for the PG Diploma, or until September if you decide to present a dissertation and emerge with a Master's degree.

'The course covered all manner of things, from curating temporary exhibitions to researching and developing the university's permanent collection, and from devising educational programmes to writing marketing materials. We were also given a lot of advice on applying for jobs (preparing an appropriate CV and on what to say in accompanying letters) and how to perform in interviews (what to find out about beforehand, with the offer of practice interviews if needed).

'We were encouraged to apply for a variety of jobs rather than to be picky and hold out for a specific role and my applications included roles in education, audience development, curatorship and so on. I saw my current job advertised in May and applied immediately, and found out I had been successful in July. The gallery manager and I then negotiated when I would start as she was keen that my dissertation would be finished by the time I began – opportunities to complete it would be limited with a full-time job. I do think that students are often completely unprepared for what hard work it is starting a full-time job after the rather laid back life of a student.

'My job is varied and no two days are the same. It is my responsibility to curate the Applied Arts and Craft collection. Our craft collection is particularly strong and I suggest ongoing and temporary exhibitions from the permanent collection. There are certain fixtures in our calendar – the Aberdeen Artists' Society Exhibition every spring and the BP Portrait Award Exhibition, which comes to us after it has been on display at the National Portrait Gallery. We try to have a family-orientated exhibition in the summer and this year it is to be the illustrations of children's book illustrator Lauren Child.

'Developing the collection is another of my responsibilities. The purchasing budget is very limited, but when we are offered things to buy we can sometimes make a case for acquisition through the Friends of Aberdeen Art Gallery and Museums, and this is how we were able to buy an arts and crafts necklace designed by Ann MacBeth, a key addition to our collection. I attend art fairs and take part in competitions that might bring additional funds and attention to the gallery. For example, I have just been on a trip to New York, for contemporary craft curators in Scotland, and in May

I am taking part in the 'Collect' craft fair in London. To coincide with this, the Art Fund has invited galleries with a strong collection of crafts to bid for the purchase of an item for their collection. Ten bids have been accepted and five will be chosen – if ours is successful, that means we will gain a new item of specific relevance to our collection, at no cost to us.[52]

'I have sought to develop links with the Fine Arts curators within the gallery, and exhibitions we have put on so far have offered a more joined up approach than had previously been the case.

'I spend time cataloguing what we have, preparing audience information for new exhibitions and educational events, and giving talks to relevant groups in the area. We have a series of lunchtime lectures and I take part in these too. On occasion I help with the packing and transporting of works of art to galleries we are lending to; providing a personal courier service.

'A part of the job that is seldom considered is the answering of queries from the general public, which takes a lot of my time. The questions come in a variety of formats, from letters and e-mails to people arriving at the front door with an item in a black bin liner. Some want to know something of the item's provenance, but often they are seeking information on its value – which is the one thing we are not allowed to advise them on. We have to refer them to relevant dealers (without recommending anyone specifically). Often people have seen items featured on television programmes about antiques and realise they own something similar – and so want to have this confirmed.

'Similarly, members of the public frequently offer items to the gallery as gifts, but given that our storage facilities are limited and our ability to catalogue our existing collection is under severe pressure, we have to be careful about selecting those we are able to accept. Often members of the public have no concept that other

---

52 The bid was successful and an 18ct gold and enamel neckpiece by Jacqueline Ryan was added to the collection.

people might be offering items too, and diplomatic handling is required. Taking additional material into the gallery should be done in the context of the collection as a whole, and expand both understanding and appreciation – there is little point in adding items that no one has time to research and will never be seen again.

'Another part of my job is to manage the volunteers who work in the gallery; some help with routine cataloguing and checking, and other tasks that full-time staff do not have time for.

'When people are giving their time for nothing it is important that they feel valued, but it is equally important that we provide training in gallery practice and care, and that we encourage them to appreciate our priorities and the significance of the collection.

'It's a fascinating world and I feel privileged to be part of it.'

Chapter 15
How to give an effective interview

An interview is a chance for an organisation to see whether you match up to the CV you have sent in: to estimate how you might do the job they have advertised and how you might fit in with their team. Most employers are looking for people who can not only do the job required but also who will be harmonious work colleagues and fit into the wider environment. An interview offers the chance to assess both of these. So if your job application has been drafted by someone else, or after substantial input from others, this will show during the interview.

The key to an effective interview is preparation. It is essential that you:

- understand the organisation you have applied to work for;
- have a clear grasp of what they are looking for;
- are able to demonstrate that the skills and competencies you offer are the solution to their recruitment needs.

You must be able to demonstrate all the above succinctly – because the interview may last no longer than half an hour, sometimes less.

1. Understand the organisation you have applied to work for

You will have already carried out a lot of research to get to this point, so now is the time to both revisit the information you acquired, and think about the organisation again. If possible, visit it in person and have a look around; if distance prevents you from doing this, try to get as much information as possible online (lots of museums and galleries now offer virtual tours through their websites). Do a Google search on the organisation; see what is said about them on Wikipedia; follow up references to key management changes (has there been a new director or significant purchase in the last few years?) and talk to anyone you know who has been involved with them. Also, find out what is topical both in the local area (the website of their local paper may tell you much) and in the national and international world of museums and galleries (as I write there are initiatives to match the launch of the film *Night in the museum* with night-time openings of a number of British institutions).

2. Have a clear grasp of what they are looking for

Go back through the job advertisement you responded to and think about the key verbs used, what they said about themselves and what this is likely to imply about the organisation as a whole. Now do the same for what they say about the desirable skills and attributes of the person they want to employ. Summarise these thoughts into two lists, which might look something like the following:

How they see themselves
- a very significant organisation in the region;
- part of the local cultural scene;
- javing an increasingly national and international reputation;
- as a centre of learning and knowledge;
- accessible, friendly and encouraging to those who are not familiar with museums.

What they are looking for
- someone who shares their priorities;
- organising abilities, both for self and others;
- an ability to communicate with all sectors of society, including those unfamiliar with museums;
- tact and diplomacy.

3. What you are able to offer

Refer to the lists you made, firstly of how they see themselves and secondly of what they are looking for. Now read a copy of what you sent in response; the document that presumably made them consider that you are a possible good match for what they are looking for (because they have asked you for an interview).

As you read through these documents, think clearly about how your job experience and personal qualities match up. Do you have a genuine interest in what they do? For each of their priorities and stated requirements, try to think of some practical examples from your past that illustrate your suitability and commitment. So if they describe themselves as outward looking and seeking to engage with new audiences, think about how you can prove you are too. Have you any experience of organising publicity; trying to engage people in things they at first assumed were boring (through organising an event or a reading that challenged assumptions or giving a talk to a group that helped to change minds)?

The practicalities of being interviewed – before you get there

- The offer of an interview will probably come by phone, so once you have made a job application, make sure you carry your diary, some notepaper and something to write with around with you at all times. If you have a large bag, check that these items are accessible quickly!

- If the offer of an interview comes by post or by e-mail, as well as noting the time and date in your diary, be sure to confirm the arrangements back to the sender. If you don't, they may assume you are no longer interested in the position and give the slot to someone else. And do this in the style with which you wish your application to be considered – so in appropriate business language, not just 'great thanx'.

- Double check the location (institutions are often spread over several sites) and how to get in (interviews may be held on the days that galleries are closed so gaining access can be difficult). Write down specific names and extension numbers you have to contact in order to get inside. If you have only been given the details of the person interviewing you, ask for an additional administrative contact name and number for the day (those in the interviewing room will be tied up seeing the person before you and have their phones switched off). Do this in case of problems on the day so you can let them know what is happening. Make sure you have this information to hand (load the numbers into your mobile phone right now).

- Work out how to get there on time; there is nothing more stress-inducing for you, and irritating for the potential employer, than being late – and one late interview makes everyone else late too. Allow time for train delays, heavy traffic on the roads, difficulty in finding somewhere to park. If driving is the only possibility and the institution is in a city centre, ask if they have parking available on site – many have a 'visitors' spot available on a first come, first served basis.
- Dress appropriately. The general guidance is that you should think laterally rather than making an automatic decision to wear a suit. A job in a gallery or museum tends to be a creative role, so try to express your personality in the way you dress – not in an outlandish way, but to show you are an individual and have taste and discernment. Ensure your hands and nails are clean, that your hair is freshly washed and that you smell pleasant. If you are brave enough, ask your friends to tell you whether there are aspects of your appearance that mar the overall impression. For example, do you wear too much make-up, or is your habit of shaking your head to slip your floppy fringe sideways inclined to annoy? Are there any particular words that you use too often? Don't forget that you never get a second chance to make a first impression.
- Develop a firm handshake. Practise until this is good – most interviews will start with a handshake and the proffering of a limp lettuce leaf does not get things off to a good start.
- Take along something to write with and on – you may want to make notes during the interview – such as the names of those who are interviewing you. Writing things down (without doing so excessively; this is an interview not a lecture) also fixes them in

your mind – and from their point of view looks as if you are taking things seriously.

- Remember that anything you put on your CV or in your accompanying letter will be seen as fair game for questions, so take some time to think through all you have listed and what you might get asked. Why did you spend two weeks on one placement and two months on another? Take a particularly close look at your specified interests; if you have listed reading remember the last few books you have read. Similarly, given the kind of job you are applying for, be ready to say which collections you have visited recently and what you thought of them, in insightful rather than judgemental terms.

Practice interviews

If possible, do a practice interview with friends or colleagues – get them to ask you all the questions that are tricky to answer. There are books available on how to answer tough interview questions – the problem is that your interviewers may have read them too. A better way of preparing for an interview is to think through your own real responses to difficult questions, ones which put your competencies in the best possible light but also reveal your individuality. Consider the following:

- What do you have to offer?
- Why should we employ you?
- What use did you make of your time at university?

If you are doing an MA in some aspect of curating or museum studies, you will find your tutors are probably willing to help you practise for an interview (it's in their interests that their graduates find jobs and so recommend the course to others).

Dealing with tricky questions

Some interviewers use a controversial statement to see how interviewees respond under pressure – and how good they are at thinking on their feet. To spot potential areas that might arise, think about the opinions you hold about this world and then invert them, so for example:

'Isn't your MA in museumship just a finishing school?'

'Why on earth should museums be funded from the public purse when such a small sector the population visit them regularly?'

Make a positive link between what you can offer and what they are looking for. Don't tell them things they don't need to know or that will make your application less attractive to them. Stress the positive – university as an opportunity to study what you were really interested in rather than three years of late nights and no responsibility; your first work placement as a valuable chance to see a museum from the inside rather than feel exploited because everyone gave you dogs-body jobs. Don't complain about previous employers, whether the individual line manager or the organisation as a whole. It's never a good idea; this world is small and there's a good chance your inter-viewers may know those you are complaining about. Instead, say what you learned in the process – and why you really want to work for those interviewing you *now*.

How to behave during an interview

- Be mindful that the interview may start before you are aware of it – lots of firms include other staff in the process, and someone who is disdainful towards the receptionist, or who at a pre-inter-view briefing with all the candidates shows no interest in talking to anyone other than the senior management doing the actual interviewing, may get no further. Someone will probably take you from the waiting area to the place where you are to be interviewed and may chat to you on the way, to try to put you at your ease. Follow their lead, answering the questions you get asked.
- The interviewers will probably start by introducing themselves and shaking hands. They will probably expect you to be a little nervous, so may start by asking you something banal, about your journey there or whether you have been to the location before.

Answering gives you the chance to hear your own voice in this very strange situation – trebly so if you have never been interviewed before. Get used to it! It's an artificial situation but one in which you have to play a role, and make it clear to the interviewers that they should choose you. You are probably best placed to do this if you appear confident (without being arrogant), competent (without being over-bossy) and articulate (without being over-opinionated).

- Build rapport; listen to the tone of voice they use when asking you questions and try to respond in a similar vein. Think back to your foreign language oral examinations at school and how you had to listen out for the verb being used, and respond in kind.

- Talk from memory. Even though you made sheaves of notes in your preparation for the interview, and you really want the interviewers to know how seriously you have taken this opportunity, leave the notes in your bag. If you must have something to refer to, make a one- or two-word cue of the three most important things they need to know about you and put this somewhere discreet – perhaps on the cover of the notebook you are carrying. But whatever you bring in and refer to will get noticed – and many people can read upside down.

- Try to make eye contact with everyone during your time in the room, not just the person asking the question. It's standard practice for the interviewers to discuss beforehand what they should ask and then divide up the questions between them, so assume your answers are interesting to them all.

- Listen to the question in full before you answer. If the questioner is particularly long-winded (not all interviewers are particularly good at interviewing!) then try to paraphrase what they want to know before you reply – without sounding as if you are trying to correct them. Listening to the question in full gives you time to think. If you don't understand, ask them to explain in more detail or say 'that's interesting – can I just clarify what you are asking?' – and try to summarise. If you don't know where to start, are unclear what they are looking for, or fear getting it completely wrong in a highly political situation, consider a theoretical response, outlining various opinions. For example, if asked: 'Where do you stand on the issue of charging for admission?', and you know this is being hotly contested between the gallery and the local council, but not which side of the fence those interviewing you are sitting upon, you could say: 'Opinion is quite divided. Some people feel that charging deters, others that it makes people value what they are visiting in the same way that they expect to pay for any form of entertainment' and then quote some experience you have had in an institution where you have been doing a placement or read of in the professional or general press. Follow the politician's hierarchy when providing examples and move from personal, to local to national (about which they will know vastly more than you), so:

'I remember as a teenager, visiting Paris for the first time, being surprised to see that in other countries you are charged for admission.'

'In Kingston we have found that making a standard charge for school parties, to cover the costs of arranging a guide, has had no detrimental effect on school bookings.'

'It's all part of a much bigger issue to do with how heritage is valued and funded.'

- Once you have answered a question to the best of your ability, remain quiet rather than rambling on. This shows you understand the value of concision.
- Some interviews now require you to make a short presentation on your skills or aptitudes and the key thing here is to check how long you have been allowed for your contribution. Bear in mind that repeating out loud what is displayed on a PowerPoint slide may quickly become very tedious and it is usually better to have just a few words on screen to use as prompts and to remind those listening to you where you have got to. I have seen interviewees set up presentations in the interview room – attaching notes and string to the walls

and so on – and if this is your intention be sure that you have sufficient time to do this effectively and have practised it beforehand.
You also need to find out about the space you are occupying – how
big, how small, how much string you will need and if you are allowed
to use sticky substances on the walls. You don't want your nerves
being further augmented by last minute surprises.

- At some stage in the interview you will be asked if you have any
questions, so be sure to have a couple up your sleeve. They should
be points of information you want to have clarified, not aggres-
sive questions along the lines of 'Why on earth don't you…?' You
could ask about the interview process and what happens next, or
if the person interviewing you would be the person you report to
if you got the job. Another good tactic is to use the time for questions as an opportunity to highlight something you want them to
know you are interested in and that they have made only passing
reference to – but for which regretfully there is no time for further
discussion right now. Asking when they will let you know is a good
way to end as it implies that there may be other people after you
too/that you are particularly keen on this opportunity. Or you
could just remind them that you really do want this job (sounding
keen rather than desperate).

- When it is clear that your time is over, don't try to prolong it. You
have had your share of the spotlight. Shake hands again and
thank them for their time. Try to do so with sincerity.

What to do afterwards

- A note of thanks is always a good idea – well expressed, not over-
gushing, but sincere. Refer to something that interested you
particularly, or that you saw on your tour of the neighbourhood
afterwards – which shows you were looking around as someone
who might want to live there.

- Keep the pad, diary and pen handy in case they ring you for a
second interview. In which case you go through the whole process
again, with a different outfit/shirt/accessories and questions.

Chapter 16
How to handle a job offer – or respond to disappointment

When I was a student and busy applying for jobs, the difference between success and failure was measured in time and substance. Time, because a quick response was usually good news, and a delayed one bad. And the substance (or otherwise) of the package I subsequently received in the post was also significant: thick was good (because lots of supporting information had to be required, filled in and then returned), thin was bad (just a letter telling you no).

Nearly 30 years on, and despite the arrival of the Internet, mobile phones and other methods of near-instant communication, nothing much has changed. Museums and galleries still tend to operate a formal, polite system that informs in this way. They are measured, courteous and detail orientated.

I'm going to begin by taking a positive response to disappointment. Of course it can be devastating to be told that the job on which you had your heart set has gone to someone else, but in strategic terms, you were actively considered – just not successful. I have spent a lot of time working in direct marketing and people who used the response device to let you know they did not want to order (as opposed to not responding at all) were considered second only in importance to those who put in an order, because it showed that they had weighed up the options and decided against; they remain prospects for future custom. So if you were on the shortlist, but did not make the final selection, you did very well indeed, particularly given the number of people who apply for such vacancies. So chalk it up to experience; it's their loss and better luck next time.

How to respond to disappointment

There are two things you should definitely do, and one you could think about. The first is to review how the interview went and how it could have gone better. I don't mean in a dismissive 'I was rubbish' way, but by thinking carefully about what happened, the questions that were asked, what you said, and what might have gone better. Go through the process in some detail and write your answers down.

Although you may be tempted to come up with sweeping generalisations, or think you remember little, if you begin the process of analysing what went on, you will find you recall more than you think you do. You could either do this exercise on your own, or as an interview with a trusted friend asking you the questions. So:

- Timing and arrival. Did all go as planned? Were you flustered or calm?
- Did you meet any other candidates and how did this feel? Did you talk to those who were already there? Who took you to the interview room and how did this feel?
- When you were escorted into the interview room, what happened?
- Who was there and did you understand the role of each person?
- Did you arrive in a relaxed frame of mind; did they make you feel at your ease?
- Did they know who you were and seem interested in finding out about you?
- What did you wear and what were they wearing? Was there an empathy or did you feel awkward?
- What questions were asked and what was your response to each one?
- Did any of your responses seem to surprise them? Did anyone start writing or sit back in their chair after you had said something?
- Did they ask you if you had any questions and what did you come up with? Did they give answers that satisfied you?

- How did the interview conclude?
- How much eye contact did you have from them during the interview; did their facial expressions (or those of any particular individual) give anything away about what was going on? Did you give them enough eye contact?
- Overall, how do you think you came across to them? Try to see yourself from *their* point of view, based on your responses to these questions. Would you perhaps have seemed over-keen; *extremely* detail orientated – and so lacking an overall understanding of the sector or the requirements of this specific job; insufficiently informed about them?

Ask yourself too if the institution matched up to what you thought of it before you got there, from the image you gained from its reputation, publications and Web presence. Could you see yourself fitting in there? Did you really want to relocate there? Was the job what you really wanted to do, given that once you had accepted employment with them it would have been on your CV for ever – and having accepted it you were probably bound to give them at least two to three years (or there would be questions about that at the interview for the next job). Try to do this in a spirit of genuine enquiry rather than thinking that, as they did not want you, you certainly don't want them.

Once you have thought through these questions, the second thing you can do is to ask the organisation for some feedback. If this is a public organisation they may already have offered you someone to talk to, as part of best practice; but even if you do not get offered feedback you can still ring and ask for some. Don't ring them five minutes after receiving your letter – when you feel raw and crushed – but do take the opportunity to do so once you have thought through your answers to the above questions. You can gain some really interesting information in the process, information that will help you with your job search in future – and if you did not particularly want this job (and so are not emotionally vulnerable), feedback on how you came across can be particularly revealing. So, were you let down by your skill-set and understanding or was it what you said on the day?

Are there gaps in your experience or were you just outshone by a particularly outstanding candidate? Remember, you are ringing to hear what they have to tell you, not for you to tell them where you went wrong or to re-interview for the same post, so listen carefully. Have a pen and paper to hand before you make the call so you can note down the important points. This is really important and useful, because most of us have little idea of how we really come across to others.

The third thing you can do, *if you still want to work there*, is to write and express your disappointment and remind them that you remain someone who would like to work for them. And if this is carefully expressed, without sounding needy, stalking or over-argumentative (because they made the wrong decision in your opinion), it can end up being a letter they hang on to and keep. First appointments do not always work out; vacancies may occur in other departments, and if they feel a certain sense of obligation to you, because you got so near and were disappointed that you did not get the final position, you may be well placed for the future.

How to accept a job offer

Well done. You will have received a satisfyingly thick package through the post and need to make a quick decision about what to do. A few questions to ask yourself first:

- Is this a job you really want? It's not uncommon for people to apply for jobs that are on the edges of what they want to do rather than centre stage. So if you are waiting to hear back about another job you know you want more, then a call to that organisation, to ask when they can let you know, is appropriate. You could say that you have received a job offer from another organisation and need to know if they would like to employ you, because they are your first choice. Even if they cannot make a quick decision this should sharpen their awareness of your value.

- There isn't usually a difficulty in asking the organisation offering you a job for 24–48 hours to think it over. Again, this may sharpen their awareness of your value, as other people are clearly interested in you too.

- Is the salary what you were expecting? Most jobs with public organisations are accompanied by a sliding scale of options (between X and Y), so if you have measurable experience and can justify being further along the scale, it may be worth pushing a little. A response along the lines of 'I very much want this job but was hoping that the salary would be towards the higher end of the range specified' might go down well. It certainly shows you take yourself seriously, and now is the time to do it. If it is agreed, it becomes part of your annual salary on which percentage increases are calculated and based. Once you are established in a position it can be very difficult to renegotiate a salary, which is why in the early stages of their careers many museum and gallery staff move jobs relatively quickly, in order to improve their remuneration. Such conversations are better handled face to face, so if this is not possible be *very* careful about how you prepare for a phone call or draft an e-mail.

'I have never heard of anyone querying the salary, certainly not new graduates. I think we are so pleased and overwhelmed to actually have a job that we take whatever we get offered.'

RECENT APPOINTEE

- Read all the small print they send. Look at the hours of work (do these fit with your commute and would an earlier start be possible?), how long is the probationary period (does this match the professional standard?), what holidays are you entitled to and what start date do they suggest? Think now and query before you start, as once you have signed and returned that piece of paper it will be difficult to renegotiate – and by coming back to them again you will have made it clear you did not read all the paperwork the first time around. Are all of these acceptable? Is there anything you need to do or finish before you start (move house, buy a car, complete your dissertation, see your parents, visit Venice?) Do try to take at least a week off between one job and the next, just to clear your head.

- Return the required forms, within the dates specified, and with a polite note saying how much you are looking forward to joining them. Respond in the same format in which they made the job offer, matching the formality of the language they used and the style too (and even the typeface if you can work out what it is).

- If you do decide to accept, then stop job hunting now. It's not fair on others, and it is extremely mentally draining to carry on looking for a job when you have already agreed to take one. The world of galleries and museums is a small one and people talk, and so being caught out in duplicitous dealings could be extremely harmful to your long-term prospects. The current job offer could be removed.

- Let those who provided your references know that you have been successful and thank them for their support. If you have just emerged from a Master's degree in museum studies, again a note of thanks and information on what you are about to embark upon is a good thing to do, ditto to those who have given you work experience. Not only are you thereby building the network of people who like you and see you as 'one of theirs', you are generously confirming that you did not do this all on your own.

Chapter 17
Your first job and your future

This final chapter looks at how you might develop your career in future. Firstly we'll look at employment patterns and then move on to some useful hints for building a career. Given that this book may be read by many, with different talents, inclinations and objectives, the advice offered can only be generalised.

Employment patterns

A career in museums and galleries tends to offer a greater degree of freedom than in some other professions; it seems you are not locked into your initial role for ever. My own background is in publishing and in this profession it can be hard for someone with previous employment history in scientific or professional publishing to change to another subject area, or for an editor to become a marketer. In the world of museums and galleries, however, I found repeated instances of those who had moved around between academia, art publishing and the museum world with relative ease or, within individual institutions, between interpretation, curatorship, programme planning and education – some of them were interviewed for this book. Such moves are by no means automatic and in each instance an effective case would have to be made, but there is seemingly a wider acceptance of the value of diverse skills and experience and how they contribute to this world as a whole. Given the reduction in core funding, and the institutions' need to raise some of their own income in future, this trend has been boosted by trying to widen participation and involve more people in what our public institutions seek to offer:

> 'According to sculptor Sokari Douglas Camp, he (Neil MacGregor, Director of The British Museum) holds 8am meetings at the museum where you're likely to find yourself sitting next to an MP, a trustee or a TV presenter, all debating a series of objects that he has selected from the collection. "You come out feeling totally energised."'[1]

The level of pay has been covered already and it is not advantageous. Often the only way to progress a career is to move from one institution to another, gaining financial increments along the way. But in doing so the individual assumes the risk of not ending up where they want to be, and many will decide to stay put because of the congeniality of the working environment or the kudos of the collection and therefore find their salaries increase only at the rate of annual increments.

In general the directorate is predominantly male, with other employment patterns you might expect (more men than women working as curators, more women than men in education) but there are pockets of change, for example female directors of four important London institutions – the Whitechapel Gallery (Iwona Blaszczyk), the Camden Arts Centre (Julie Lomax), the Serpentine Gallery (Julia Peyton-Jones) and the Imperial War Museum (Di Lees).

In terms of career planning and working out where you will be in five or ten years' time, it's largely up to you. You will find there is little in the way of formal career analysis or guidance and, although there is an appraisal system and CPD[2] is held as a good idea, it will be up to you to ensure it happens and, given that the advantage is yours, perhaps on occasion to fund it yourself.

---

1 Quoted in interview of Neil MacGregor, Director of The British Museum by Liz Hoggard, *The Observer*, 26 March, 2006. http://www.guardian.co.uk/artanddesign/2006/mar/26/heritage.parthenon

2 Continuing Professional Development. Compulsory in some fields such as healthcare. It is noted as a principle objective to work towards in this field, but is largely up to you to arrange. Some funding available through professional associations such as The Museums Association – see the appendix for useful addresses.

> 'My last job funded CPD, or rather if you came up with something you wanted to do, they would consider paying for it, and as part of this I got to the Venice Biennale. I am going again later on this year, but this time I am paying. It is more important to be there and maintain my currency within this world than fight over who will pick up the bill. In the long run the beneficiary is me, as I build my career.'
>
> EDUCATOR WORKING FOR A GALLERY

Most organisations have a training department and, although there may be regular general staff training to make best use of the limited budget available, it can be hard to access the funds for training the individual.

What is essential for career progression in this world is networking, and there are many formal and informal means of getting to talk to colleagues in other institutions. For example, the directors of London galleries and museums meet at regular intervals and there is a similar grouping of the heads of learning. Relatively recently a forum of those running young people's programmes was established by three people – and the last meeting attracted over 20 attendees. This world is used to sharing information and being fairly open about plans, and so opportunities to meet are enjoyed.

My other generalisation is that this is a world where most people are employed rather than self-employed. Museums and galleries are, in general, willing to work with personal decisions to increase or reduce working hours. In part, this is perhaps not surprising, given that the opening hours usually extend further than the working day – juggling staffing cover means there is experience of flexibility. Many staff cut back on their hours to fit with personal circumstances such as planning a family and the desire to utilise their skills in a professional capacity (the 'portfolio career'). There is experience of both maternity and paternity leave.

There have been attempts by some to do their job on a freelance or consultancy basis, but they tend to stand out because they are unusual. For employees who want to cut down their hours, maybe to fit in with family commitments or a change in lifestyle, it can be easier to do this within the structure of an organisation, and to build up their hours at a later date, rather than to leave altogether and try to make a freelance employment path on their own:

> 'In logistic terms, a career in this world does require you to be mobile, and to fit your friendship and family patterns to that mobility – and I mean internationally, not just within the UK. Jobs are rare and need to be moved to, whether in the UK or overseas.
>
> 'Some people manage a career as a freelance – maybe offering short-term administrative assistance or a role as a temporary curator, but my sense is that first you perhaps have to have made a reputation within a series of fixed positions before others would hire you to work for them on a project basis. As freelances obviously only earn when they are working (not during holidays or fallow periods), this is difficult within our low-pay sector.'
>
> DAVID FALKNER, DIRECTOR, STANLEY PICKER GALLERY, KINGSTON

But self-employment is possible, as the following two case studies illustrate.

Case Studies: Self-employment

Interview with Jeremy Theophilus, self-employed museum consultant

'Whereas ten years ago there were relatively few opportunities for freelance work within the museums and galleries sector, today the number has increased. This may be due in part to the increasing professionalisation of the sector, with many would-be entrants taking a course in museum or gallery studies which leaves them equipped with a variety of transferable skills. These they can use within a variety of host organisations – so if they do not get a job in a museum or gallery (whether by inclination, because the right opportunity has not come up, or they were unsuccessful at interview), some move into arts marketing, arts administration or publishing, often on a freelance basis. And, of course, once a freelance path is established, others may choose this option too, either due to life circumstances (e.g. the decision to start a family or work for oneself, or take a part-time role instead of a full-time corporate career).

Why would an organisation choose to use a freelance rather than an in-house member of staff?

'The main reason is usually the ability to park a particular project with someone who has specific responsibility for its execution. In-house members of staff may have a variety of different priorities and perhaps conflicting line management expectations, and so being able to allocate a specific job to an external member of staff, with an associated budget and timeline, may be an effective way of managing resources. The budget for a freelance member of staff can also be written into the project specification when funding is sought, and so itemised separately from the organisational over-head.

'The downside can be that the wider dissemination of what is learnt in the process of managing the project, and the sense of involvement for the organisation as a whole needs to be carefully managed.

What particular skills does the freelance need?

- Sensitivity to the host organisation. The opportunity to work on a single project with an allocated budget and timeline may be one that in-house staff would appreciate too.
- Good communication skills. To establish at the outset what is required, how much involvement and over how long.
- Self-organisation. In particular an ability to relate time spent to funding sought. The freelance needs to be particularly sensitive to the allocation of their time and what they are earning and be able to make the case for further negotiation either of budget or allocation of responsibility in return.
- Self-motivation – it can be lonely, and the client seldom wants to know if you are having trouble meeting the brief.

- Good at juggling. One of the client's main reasons for putting a job out of house may be that they want someone's undivided attention on it – but of course the freelance usually has to manage a portfolio of work, while keeping a weather eye out for the next project.
- An aptitude and appreciation for the fluidity (or insecurity) of temporary work arrangements. Some people would like the security of a permanent position; others find that having once been brushed with the freelance paint it can be hard to find a full- or part-time position again, because they are seen as a little too independent or not understanding of corporate communications or politics.
- The confidence to network and explain your skills to others. In general, museums and galleries may be willing to pass on the names of those they have found useful in a freelance capacity, but be much less willing to give details of those who have helped with long-term vision for their organisation, thus the more senior you become the more discreet and indispensable you will have to be.

'My career has flipped back and forwards from being employed (running galleries and art centres) to working as an independent curator, writer and project manager, but I now feel I have found the right balance. I set up a partnership with a colleague and, although we are based in different places (he in Manchester, me in Suffolk), we meet regularly, at least once a week, and communicate online. We offer each other mutual support and encouragement – and as we have complementary skills and competencies, the work tends to be challenging and diverse.'

Further information:
www.afineline.co.uk
www.hat.mmu.ac.uk

Interview with Jo Graham, former full-time museum professional; now an independent consultant working across the cultural and heritage sectors

Jo runs Learning Unlimited, an independent consultancy working across the cultural and heritage sectors. Her experience includes strategic planning, exhibition development, audience development, community engagement and learning. She is probably best known for her work on family and Early Years audiences in museums (www.learning-unlimited.co.uk).

'Being a self-employed museum consultant was never something that I dreamed of. It was never the answer to that tiresome question you get asked from time to time: "Where would you like to be in five years' time?" Having been a consultant for nine years now, however, I find it difficult to think about doing anything else.

'So, if being a consultant wasn't my career destiny, how did I come to start my own business? I started out as a teacher, but I could never settle in any one school for very long. There always seemed to be something new I should try: a different year group or a different kind of school. Having taught for around six years, I began to think I was interested in learning but not so much in teaching, so I started to think about other jobs.

'I applied for a job as Learning Manager at the Science Museum in London and, to my surprise, got the job. Working at a large national museum was a fantastic development opportunity. I was able to get such varied experience from education management, to becoming Head of Interactives, then moved on to exhibition development and finally audience advocacy. So why leave that and take a risk in being self-employed?'

What are the advantages and disadvantages of working for yourself?
'Although undoubtedly there are benefits to being self-employed, there are plenty of disadvantages. Taking the step away from employment was largely a practical decision for me, because it offered me a way to balance my work and family commitments. I

had two pre-school children and a partner with a stressful job. Self-employment gave me a measure of control over how much, when and where I worked.

'On the positive side, my work seems to be infinitely varied. I am always trying new things and working with new people, so it never gets dull. The income is potentially good, although of course never guaranteed and not as good as it first appears when you factor in holidays, sick leave and having no pension. For me, the autonomy has been fantastic. On a training course long ago I did a team assessment and found that I like to be a "joiner": someone in the middle of the wheel, making connections and helping others achieve what they need to. Being a consultant has meant I can work right where my strengths are. The final advantage is the feedback. You only get work if you're good. It's as simple as that. So you don't need annual appraisals. You get instant feedback from every project you work on.

'On the minus side, the job turns out not to be totally flexible, unless you aren't relying on the income. I am the main breadwinner in my family, so I need to work full time and therefore have less choice about which projects I engage with. Of course I can give myself days off, but then if a project really needs you that day, you tend to feel you should work. The financial insecurity should be a downside, but I have been fortunate in the projects I've secured and the number of teams that have come back to me for more work. Tendering for new work is my least favourite part of the job. There was a time when it felt like I was going for interviews every month. As you gain experience, however, it seems that you do a lot less tendering. You are able to go for longer contracts and clients can invite you to tender, which is a little less scary. For some people working mostly on your own and having to rely completely on your own expertise might not appeal. You can feel very exposed. It is worrying when you look in the diary and there is nothing booked in when the project you're on is completed.

Top tips for maintaining a freelance career in museums and galleries

1. Get connected

Starting out, it was really useful to already have lots of contacts because it gives you a competitive edge and boosts your confidence.

2. Get a good-sized contract

My first contract was to write a set of activity books for teachers. It gave me enough guaranteed income for the first two months of self-employment and left me enough time to bid for other work.

3. Have a wide skills base

When I was first self-employed I did a lot of writing and evaluation work as well as strategic and exhibition work. It's good to have something in your "offer" that will always be in demand. For me that's probably evaluation.

4. Try to vary your work

I try to get a balance of face-to-face work with teams and work at home. I also mix writing, delivering training, advising and mentoring, with interpretation work, evaluation projects, exhibition development and strategic planning. It's surprising how often the skills and understanding developed in one project are useful for another.

5. Be disciplined with yourself

When you're working from home it is easy to be distracted. It feels odd to begin with, but being strict with yourself about having 'work hours' and keeping some kind of time sheet to track time spent on each project means you get more done.'

Eight sound pieces of advice for career planning (whether or not you intend to stay in the world of museums and galleries)

1. Collect (appropriate) qualifications

You may be weighing up the options about whether or not to do an MA or a PhD. If you have the inclination and the chance is there, take it. It is surprising how often having an extra few initials after your name makes a difference, particularly when a field is crowded. As a newly appointed medical consultant said to me recently:

'After finishing my three-year medical degree, I stayed on for an extra year, ending up with an honours rather than an ordinary BSc in medical sciences. Most people did the three-year degree and then moved straight on to the clinical part of their training. I only did the extra year because I wanted to stay at university until my girlfriend graduated, and I quite fancied being president of the union, but, ever since, that additional qualification has made a huge difference, giving me the edge in job applications, interviews and appointments. A decision that was taken relatively unthinkingly, and that involved only one extra year of study, has turned out to be very significant – simply because most people don't have an honours degree.'

2. Find a mentor

Find someone who wants to help you in future. This could be someone you work with or someone you admire; they don't have to offer you advice (indeed a mentor who just reels off solutions may be not particularly useful). Rather seek a wise listening board, who helps you come up with your own solutions. As to what is in it for them, most people like to be helpful, and helping others makes you realise the extent of your own seniority and grasp of your profession. A mentor may well enjoy encouraging someone younger than they are, and feel good in the process (the next time the opportunity arises, go along and give blood and see how walking away having done something selfless makes *you* feel positive).

If you do find a mentor, don't keep ringing up for advice – try to consolidate your thoughts and questions for discussion at an occasional opportunity to meet – limit sudden calls for genuine emergencies. Send the odd postcard or e-mail that fills them in briefly on what you have been doing, and don't worry if you don't hear back. When you do meet, do ensure that you listen – find out about their career and absorb all the anecdotes which can be very revealing, such as networking opportunities that led to hearing about a job opportunity or a specific project that turned out to be significant; guidance on the politics of how the profession works can be particularly instructive. And for whatever help or support you receive, even if it's just the chance to listen and meet, bear in mind that your mentor probably has endless other ways they could use their time, so remember to say thank you. And don't assume a mentor is only useful in the early stages of your career; objective and wise counsel is always valuable.

3. Build a network

Build a collection of colleagues, friends and other people you may be in touch with. Talk to them and be interested in what they have to say. Find out via this grapevine what is going on and acknowledge their input, particularly if you find out things you would not otherwise have known.

4. Make a plan

Prepare a plan based on where you want to be and what kind of person you think you are. Make it logical, taking into account your known strengths and weaknesses. Revisit it at regular intervals – most lives are not linear.

Along the same lines, consider your priorities and what you want from your job and your life. I remember being particularly struck by hearing journalist Katharine Whitehorn talking on Radio 4's *Desert Island Discs* about how much she hated boarding school, but how in the process it gave her a very clear idea of what happiness was, and that thenceforth she could always tell if she was happy or not. I regularly run workshops for people who want to write, and often the audience consists of those who are well paid and highly valued by their organisations (as evinced through their job titles and salaries) but feel deeply unfulfilled.

So as you progress, keep a sharp eye out for what motivates you, where and when you are happy. Do you thrive best in a large or a small organisation? Do you like working in a team? What gives you job satisfaction? Does belonging to the organisation matter to you?

How much does your job matter to you – is your job what allows you to live your life, or perhaps it IS your life? You don't have to change your job or circumstances to fit this dawning awareness all at once, but a feeling of moving towards what motivates you is a healthy direction.

5. Lead an interesting life

Do different things. Trying out new things always gives you a fresh perspective. Without going out on a limb and being seen as awkwardly different, become known as someone who has interesting ideas and is not bound by convention to dismiss or sneer at something that is not a natural part of their cultural inheritance. Be aware of popular trends, as these impact on the public's willingness (or not) to spend time in your institution and the values they place on leisure: by understanding trends, you can influence them. So visit new places and as well as spending time on the main attraction, visit the shop, the tea room or restaurant – and even the bathrooms.

Be willing to get involved with any experiments that are run within your organisation: new initiatives; working parties on issues that interest you, the management or both. Volunteer.

6. Think positively

When things don't work out as planned and you find yourself in a difficult place, it is tempting just to keep going, all the while comforting yourself with the fact that the workplace, or life in general, is unfair. Rather than just keep going, try stepping off the hamster wheel and thinking about what you are doing and what is to be gained by simply carrying on. People who work with addicts often concentrate on how to change behaviour: predicting a different outcome without changing any of the parameters that put you in that position in the first place, is unlikely to bring success. So rather than taking refuge in whinging, examine whether a difficult situation you face now has happened before (are you becoming a natural victim?) or if this is a new and tricky problem that you need to think about.

Try to develop a genuinely self-reflective attitude. The most perceptive people tend to be those who know what they don't know – or are aware of their limitations. This enables them to be both realistic about their own aspirations and genuinely appreciative of the skills and expertise of others.

7. Manage detail

Read the small print. Become known as someone who is careful with detail, and then people you deal with will take more care in what they send to you – and everyone's game will improve. Try to 'walk through' all plans before sharing them; think about the practicalities and how they might feel to outsiders. Consider too the 'what ifs?' – would what you have suggested still work? Try to spot pressure points in a plan – are there convergences of funding, responsibility or staffing that could result in crisis?

Consider the likely reactions to proposed plans and how you would respond to the most obvious criticisms (without sounding overly defensive). Try to do this by widening your game, quoting instances from the press, society's current leisure patterns (e.g. the rising number of restaurants offering breakfast; the growing number of bicycle sales) or visitor attendance patterns at other types of institution that confirm a trend you have spotted. Keep an eye out for surveys (and not just the ones related to your area of professional expertise) which isolate trends that are important to you too; consider surveying your own visitors and finding out what they think – this may throw up a completely new way of presenting value to your market. Look at a situation from different points of view other than your own.

Think what people might complain about (society is becoming increasingly litigious) and also what might attract them, and try to see a situation from a variety of viewpoints, taking into account other people's priorities, rather than just your own. As John Ruskin said in 1858:

'Perhaps some of my hearers may occasionally have heard it stated of me that I am rather apt to contradict myself. I hope that I am exceedingly apt

> to do so. I have never met with a question yet, of any importance, which did not need, for the right solution of it, at least one positive and one negative answer.'

For example, a new exhibition of objects from a 19th century house might make an important new collection available to the public, but remind your visitors of their grandparents' house. I asked a child who had been to the National Portrait Gallery in London what had impressed her most, and she said the fact that all the pictures in the gallery actually belonged to her (staff had discussed the meaning of a 'public collection' with the children). Things you take for granted may be news to others.

Bear in mind too that in terms of getting people to attend an event or a cultural institution, the easiest option for them is always no – and there may be many different sorts of no to each yes, so for example:

- the transport was difficult, I did not know how to get there;
- the opening times were not convenient (when is it open anyway?);
- Granny was staying and it would be too far for her to walk from the car park, and once inside there would be too many steps for her to manage;
- the children wouldn't like it;
- it's too cold at this time of year.

The more information you provide, catering for a variety of possible difficulties that the potential visitor might think of, the greater the chance of your sounding welcoming and inclusive – and those potential visitors may decide to come along.

8. Be proud of what you do

> 'Pride is like a perfume. When it is worn, it radiates a sense of self the world reacts to.'
>
> *STEVIE WONDER*, ESSENCE, *1975*

Do your job to the best of your ability and if you find you don't like it, try to find the positive – something that you have learnt in the process that you can take on to further equip you for your next role.

Understand what you have to offer the organisations you work for and where your value lies. Don't keep reminding your employers of this (tedious) but do have an appreciation of what you offer right now, which parts of you are not being used to the full and where you might go in future.

Postscript

To the prospective employee seeking a job in museums and galleries it may seem that Duell's maxim is true – they may wonder how they can add value within this mass of complexities, or make their own application to be part of it stand out.

Here are 10 ideas worth taking forward – most are under consideration already and each is certainly worth vastly longer deliberation than the single paragraph allocated, but they may be useful fodder when preparing for interviews.

What's still left to do in museums and galleries?

1.   Widen the demographic basis of those who are encouraged to visit. 'Museums cater for children up until the age of 12 and for adults from the age of 16, but for no one in between' (Joanna Moorhead).[1] 'Teenagers test the boundaries of socially acceptable behaviour and, as such, groups of youths can arouse the suspicions of museum staff through boisterous behaviour.'[2] Discuss.

2.   Use museum and gallery expertise internationally, e.g. on conservation and consultancy projects that spread international

---

1   *Museums Journal*, Issue 106, June 2006, p. 20

2   *Teenage Kicks: developing teenage audiences within museums*, Laura Paterson, Dissertation as part of an MLitt in Museum and Gallery Studies, University of St Andrews 2008

understanding. Examples include Neil MacGregor, Director of the British Museum, getting involved in the safeguarding of the contents of Iraqi museums, or putting on an exhibition at the British Museum featuring the 16th/17th century flowering of Iranian art which paralleled the Elizabethan renaissance in England of the same period. MacGregor firmly believes the museum should be a global resource: 'A collection that embraces the whole world allows you to consider the whole world,' he argues. 'The non-European world isn't "other" any more; it's part of us.'[3]

3.   Make the expertise housed within museums and galleries more available through mass communication channels. Perhaps curators could talk about the fascinating objects they look after on daytime television, or teachers might talk about why they organise school visits and what the children get out of it.

4.   Reinterpret existing understanding of your collection rather than just accept it. All research is influenced by the culture and time within which it was written. Challenging previous understandings may lead to interesting new ideas.

5.   Provide full access to collections online so that visitors can access these virtually, whenever they need a summary of what you hold or want to check a specific detail. Visitor numbers through the door will not necessarily fall – because access online often prompts a visit to see the collection 'in the flesh' – and in the process the collection's influence may increase.

6.   Make museums and galleries places that people want to visit by installing new attractions that are sympathetic to the organisation's functions and premises – or ones that are not sympathetic, but that draw in new audiences.

7.   Increase the role, voice and associated credit of the practitioner/ maker/artist by involving them in what is displayed; for example

---

3   Quoted in interview of MacGregor by Liz Hoggard, *The Observer*, 26 March 2006.
    http://www.guardian.co.uk/artanddesign/2006/mar/26/heritage.parthenon

through examination of the working practices of those who created what is stored and on display and their modern-day counterparts.

8.   Appeal to the audience's senses. For example, the Jorvik Viking Centre in York drew our sense of smell. What else could be harnessed? The same goes for different learning styles (written, auditory, practical). Now that we understand them, how could they be harnessed within museums and galleries?

9.   What is it worth? The most common misunderstanding among the public is that museums and galleries will try to establish the value of items owned by individuals. So rather than simply aiming to put the public right, should institutions consider adopting this role, perhaps on a 'drop-in clinic' basis? Along the same lines, how about some public lectures or tours on what individual items in a collection, or the value of the collection as a whole, are worth? Both ideas would be very newsworthy and could attract useful publicity.

10. 'Museums belong to everybody. They exist to serve the public and should enhance the quality of life for everyone, both today and in the future. They receive funding because of their positive social, cultural, educational and economic impact.'[4] We should work towards the widening understanding that museums and galleries are of use to all and so should receive stable and unquestioned funding.

---

4   Museums Association Code of Ethics

Afterword

In 1980 I very nearly embarked on a career in museums and galleries. I had a good degree in history and history of art from the University of St Andrews, a place on the Manchester Museums Course, a passion for enthusing about pictures to others, and two lots of work experience under my belt. But I was equally keen on books, reading and the associated pleasures, and hence swithered between museums and publishing. The latter eventually won.

But having decided against a career in museums and galleries, I have remained their passionate fan, attending exhibitions myself, ensuring our four children had access to them as a staple of their growing up, with my husband building an extensive collection of art and regularly using examples from this world when, later in my career, I morphed from publisher to provider of information about how to get published/get into publishing.

I have discovered that when working with authors, if you relate a story of what has happened to a fellow writer, most concentrate on wondering who the author is, and why they were singled out – and jealously often blocks the point being made. But use an example from the life of an artist or actor, and they can really absorb the issue. So Tilda Swinton lying in a glass box in the Serpentine Gallery[5] is an excellent example of what is intrinsically fascinating to the general public – and how writing that similarly engages, gets read. Museums and galleries also provide me with a means of explaining complicated ideas to students – Cornelia Parker's exploded garden shed, exhibited in Tate Modern[6], remains my favourite method of explaining how to deal with over-complicated text. I advise that they should, just as she did with the shed, (this time metaphorically) blow it up

---

5   *The Maybe*, Serpentine Gallery, 1995
6   *Cold, Dark Matter, An Exploded View*, Tate Modern, 1991

and see what substantial chunks are left, and use these as the 'big ideas' on which to base a new version – rather than seeking to tinker with it and produce a kind of school pupil's 'French translation' which, because it is managed word by word, usually makes less sense than the original. And the dynamism of starting again and adding energy usually takes far less time than the painstaking fiddling with an unsatisfactory existing version.

In 2007 I co-wrote a book on careers in publishing, and was subsequently approached by Lisa Carden, Commissioning Editor of A&C Black, about an idea she had for a similar book on museums and galleries – and could I recommend anyone to write it? I made a few enquiries, but pretty soon found the diversity of organisations and roles within this world was so wide that I felt an objective outsider might be able to do a good job – and so volunteered myself.

It has been a hugely enjoyable – albeit rather expensive – year. I have visited a wide range of different organisations, road tested their cafes whenever possible (with my staple fare of a pot of tea and a slice of carrot cake)[7] and patronised the associated shop. Both The Portal Gallery and The Eakin managed to sell me a picture in the process. I have met people I would have encountered on the Manchester Museums Course, had I taken up my place, and had privileged access to a wide number of fascinating people.

Many of these now need to be formally thanked. I would particularly like to thank Kate Gillespie, Ann Gunn, Rachel Moss, Sandy Nairne, Laura Paterson and Jo Prosser.

I would also like to thank: Terry Baverstock, Jo Beale, Mary Bee, Susannah Bowen, Gyles Brandreth, Neil Bruce, Jessica Burdge, John Barnie, Cortina Butler, Steve Carey, Gill Casson, Malcolm Chapman, Jane Cholmeley, Peta Cook, Louise Coysh, Gwenda Constant, Brenda Conway, Louise Coysh, Nicholas Crofts, Paul Dearn, Claire Dyson, Brian Eakin, Jo Elner, Lorna Ewan, David Falkner, Mike Fisher, Lydia Fisher-Norton, Ruth Gimlette, Jonathan Glasspool, Jo Graham,

---

7   Overall winner, The National Portrait Gallery café in London, with the Scottish Portrait Gallery in Edinburgh a close second.

Andrew Hansen, Philippa Heath, Jo Graham, Kathryn Hallet, Andrew Hansen, Jane Hudson, Peter Humfrey, Jocelyn James, Tracey Jerrard, Christopher Johnstone, Kate Knowles, Linda Lambert, Susan Lewandewski, Su Jones, Muriel King, Jayne Knight, Elliot Lamble, Catherine MacDermott, Joanna Moorhead, Claire Mulley, Paul Nesbit, Henry Noltie, Philippa Ouvry, Michael Palin, Colin Philpott, Sophia Plender, Poogia Raj Kalyan, David Rae, Christine Rew, Sandy Richardson, Helen Ruthven, Sarah Ryan, Graham and Edna Scott, Anne Sebba, Desmond Shawe-Taylor, Rosie Smith, Esther Solomon, Kris Stutchbury, Kirsten Suenson-Taylor, Helen Sunderland, Alice Tate-Harte, Jeremy Theophilus, Jane Thompson-Webb, Timothy Walker, Helen Ward, Jess Wilder and Louise Wirz.

Finally thanks to Lisa Carden, Ellen Grace and all the team at A&C Black, copyeditor Jan Bowmer, my agent Jenny Brown, and my family – who have been my accomplices on so many occasions.

Appendix: Useful organisations and contact details

American Association of Museums (AAM)
Focal point for professionals in museums and museum-related fields.
www.aam-us.org

The Art Fund
An independent charity that exists to save art for everyone to enjoy. For further information about working for a heritage charity, as outlined in Chapter 3, e-mail: **info@artfund.org**
Job information: **www.artfund.org/about/jobs.html**

Association for Cultural Enterprises (ACE)
The Association for Cultural Enterprises promotes commercial best practice in the UK's cultural and heritage sector by providing training and networking opportunities and facilitating the sharing of information and experience between its members.
www.acenterprises.org

Association for Heritage Interpretation (AHI)
The Association for Heritage Interpretation is a key forum for anyone interested in interpretation – the art of helping people explore and appreciate our world.
www.ahi.org.uk

Botanic Gardens Conservation International (BGCI)
The international networking organisation for botanic gardens has a wealth of information about botanic gardens and links to kindred

organisations. Its 'garden search' online database of botanic gardens and their facilities lists those with galleries and museums.
www.bgci.org

British Association of Paintings Conservators-Restorers (BAPCR)
The BAPCR was founded in 1943 as The Association of British Picture Restorers (ABPR), and is the professional organisation for conservator-restorers of paintings with over 400 members internationally
www.bapcr.org.uks

Collections Link
The national advisory service for Collections Management managed by the Collections Trust in partnership with the Institute of Conservation (ICON) and the National Preservation Office (NPO).
www.collectionslink.org.uk

engage
A membership organisation representing gallery, art and education professionals in the UK and in 15 countries worldwide. Engage promotes access to, and enjoyment and understanding of the visual arts through gallery education.
www.engage.org

English Heritage
Partly funded by the government, English Heritage works to conserve and promote the historic environment by providing public access to heritage sites and helping people to understand the past.
www.english-heritage.org.uk
Job information: **www.english-heritage.org.uk/server/show/nav.18150**

Group for Education in Museums (GEM)
Promotes the importance of learning through museums, galleries and other cultural organisations. UK based but with an international membership.
www.gem.org.uk/home.html
Job information: **www.gem.org.uk/jobads/jobads_menu.html**

ICON

A charity committed to the conservation of cultural heritage in the UK. Membership includes over 3,000 individuals and organisations from across the conservation community. Of particular value is the ICON Conservator Register (see 'Find a conservator' on their website), which allows free access to information on ICON members, by specialisation and region. ICON supports the principle of parity across the heritage professions when promoting the skills and value of conservators, curators, librarians, archivists, archaeologists and historic buildings specialists.

www.icon.org.uk/index.php

Institute for Archaeologists

The Institute for Archaeologists (IfA) advances the practice of archaeology and allied disciplines by promoting professional standards and ethics for conserving, managing, understanding and promoting enjoyment of heritage.

www.archaeologists.net

Job information:

www.archaeologists.net/modules/icontent/index.php?page=28n

International Council of Museums (ICOM)

International organisation of museum and museum professionals.

http://icom.museum

International Institute for Conservation of Historic and Artistic Works (IIC)

IIC membership is open to everyone with an interest in conserving the world's cultural heritage: to conservators and restorers, to conservation scientists, architects, educators and students and to collection managers, curators, art historians and other cultural heritage professionals.

www.iiconservation.org/index.php

International Licensing Industry Merchandisers' Association (LIMA)
Promotes the growth and expansion of licensing. LIMA sets standards of ethical and professional conduct, provides information and education on licensing, and is a valuable forum for networking.
www.licensing.org

Museums Association
The Museums Association represents both the people and institutions constituting Britain's museums and galleries, i.e. both employers and employees.
e-mail: **info@museumsassociation.org**
www.museumsassociation.org

Museums, Libraries and Archives London (MLA)
MLA London is the strategic development agency for museums, libraries and archives in the region.
www.mlalondon.org.uk

Museum Professionals Group
MPG is a membership organisation which reflects the interests and aspirations of people working in or for museums.
www.museumprofessionalsgroup.org

Museum Store Association
US organisation with the stated purpose of advancing the success of cultural commerce and of the professionals engaged in it.
www.museumdistrict.com
Job information: **www.museumdistrict.com/JSClass/jsearch.cfm**

National Association of Decorative and Fine Arts Associations (NADFAS)
An arts-based educational charity, with over 340 societies in the UK and mainland Europe, all subscribing to the basic aims of the advancement of arts education and the appreciation and preservation of artistic heritage.
www.nadfas.org.uk

National Heritage Training Group
Training and professional development for the heritage sector, in particular, the support of traditional building skills.
www.nhtg.org.uk

The National Trust
The National Trust is a charity that protects, and provides public access to, historic houses, gardens and ancient monuments – as well as many other sites such as reserves, archaeological remains, castles and villages.
www.nt.org
Job information: **www.ntjobs.org.uk**

Portable Antiquities Scheme
A voluntary scheme to record archaeological finds made by members of the public in England and Wales.
www.finds.org.uk

Royal Entomological Society
Plays a major role in disseminating information about insects and improving communication between entomologists.
www.royensoc.co.uk

Index